SNAPSHOT TRADING

SNAPSHOT TRADING

Selected Tactics for Short-Term Profits

DARYL GUPPY

Wrightbooks

First published 2002 by Wrightbooks
an imprint of John Wiley & Sons Australia, Ltd
42 McDougall Street, Milton, Qld 4064

Office also in Melbourne

Typeset in 11.5/13 pt Goudy

All charts created by MetaStock, GuppyTraders Essentials and MarketCast

© Daryl Guppy, 2002

Internet: <100035.406@compuserve.com>, <www.guppytraders.com>

Reprinted August 2004, June 2008

National Library of Australia Cataloguing-in-Publication data:

Guppy, Daryl, 1954–
Snapshot trading: selected tactics for short-term profits
Includes index
ISBN 0 701637 29 3
1. Day trading (Securities). 2. Stocks. I. Title.
332.64

Cover design by Rob Cowpe

Printed in Australia by McPherson's Printing Group
10 9 8 7 6 5 4 3

Disclaimer
The material in this publication is of the nature of general comment only, and neither purports nor intends to be advice. Readers should not act on the basis of any matter in this publication without considering (and if appropriate taking) professional advice with due regard to their own particular circumstances. The author and publisher expressly disclaim all and any liability to any person, whether a purchaser of this publication or not, in respect of anything and of the consequences of anything done or omitted to be done by any such person in reliance, whether in whole or partial, upon the whole or any part of the contents of this publication.

Also by **Daryl Guppy**:

Share Trading
Bear Trading
Trading Tactics
Chart Trading
Better Trading

Published by Wrightbooks, an imprint of John Wiley & Sons Australia, Ltd.

Market Trading Tactics
Better Stock Trading

Published by John Wiley & Sons Inc. Available for the international market.

Trading Asian Shares

Published by Butterworth-Heinemann.

Daryl Guppy is the editor of the Investors' International Bookshelf:

The Basics of Speculating by Gerald Krefetz
The Day Trader's Advantage by Howard Abel
Options – Trading Strategies That Work by William F. Eng
Trading Rules by William F. Eng

Published by Wrightbooks, an imprint of John Wiley & Sons Australia, Ltd.

Contents

Contents *(Cont'd)*

BEERSHEBA
AND BEYOND

Many years ago the government gave me the opportunity to drive M113 armoured personnel carriers. These were fast tactical vehicles and we trained in rapid deployment tactics. These tactics relied on the same speed and agility that had added the Australian Light Horse cavalry charge at Beersheba to the regimental colours. Successful short-term trading calls for the same speed and agility and in this book we examine the discipline, routines and some of the procedures necessary for survival in this dangerous field. We deploy our trades with speed and precision, and extract them at the first sign of overwhelming danger. These are cavalry trading tactics and should not be confused with a cavalier approach to risk and reward in this market timeframe.

A few traders apply these tactics every day, but most of us only belong to the cavalry part-time. We use these tactics in nervous, unstable and volatile markets. In essence these are defensive strategies designed to limit the time spent in the market. Speed offers protection and limits risk by reducing the time a trade is open. If we believe the market is nervous it makes more sense to snatch profits from short-term trades than to buy into a stock near the top of its uptrend, hoping it does not sink.

The tactical success of an armoured cavalry unit often depends on the tools it has at its disposal – an armoured personnel carrier, a platoon or company of troops and enough firepower to overcome the enemy. Similarly, success in short-term or day trading rests upon five elements:

1.   Reliable real-time data supply

2.   Effective end-of-day charting and analysis

3.   Straight through order processing

4.   A broker that offers effective stop loss and contingent buy order services

5.   Your full-time attention while every trade is open.

Please do not kid yourself. Day trading the market is no less dangerous than dropping troops out of the back door of an armoured personnel carrier while under fire. It requires total commitment, constant training, and courage borne of confidence in your skills. Anything less invites, in our case, a financial disaster.

The first day I was introduced to the standard infantry weapon on the rifle range, I was perplexed at the degree of caution shown by the weapons instructor. He took a lot of time – an inordinate amount of time it seemed to me – explaining the dangers. Gung-ho and pumped up, all the recruits just wanted to jump straight in. After all, the L1A1 SLR worked on much the same principle as the semi-automatic .22 calibre rifles, which many of us had used at home for shooting rabbits.

His concern was well placed. These were dangerous weapons and in the hands of inexperienced recruits they had the power to inflict widespread carnage and great personal damage. Treated with respect, and used with skill, the weapon was a tool that ensured a soldier's survival. The instructor's method was to make us fear him even if we didn't fear the weapon in our hands. This would give us time to survive and learn to use it effectively.

We cannot use this bullying approach in this book and yet the techniques discussed have the power to inflict substantial financial damage when applied carelessly. It may appear that we take a lot of time – an inordinate amount of time – in the first section examining the dangers of short-term and day trading. We hope it is time well spent and that if you take the time to start at Chapter 1 then you will be rewarded with a better understanding of how to more effectively use the instruments of trading success discussed in later chapters.

The gullible are easily separated from their money by a promise of quick and large profits, so in planning the structure of this book, we deliberately saved the discussion of our profitable and favourite intra-day trading techniques until last. These have reputations for glamour, but they are a collection of dangerous weapons – lethal at short range. They are sure to disappoint the aspiring day trader raised on a diet of media hype and looking for easy money. The returns appear to be small change and the work required for mastery is time consuming. There are no easy profits here.

We have grouped intra-day, overnight, and two to seven day trades under the banner of 'short-term trading'. Where we need to discuss specific techniques we specify which type of timeframe is best suited. This 'snapshot' trading is the focus of this book.

Snapshots are not pictures. This is not a photo opportunity. Tourists take pictures, but our objective as traders is to take *money*. This means that, like a marksman, we must wait until we can take the perfect snapshot at the market.

There is no room for sloppy pot shots because our trading survival depends on lethal accuracy. Our objective is to score a bullseye with every trade. We show you some of the techniques you need to become a skilled marksman. Reserve the camera snapshots for pictures of you as a winner with a grin.

'Position trading' includes trades designed to span weeks or months. Entry and exit decisions are always based on end-of-day data and designed for execution in the next day's market. The skills learned here form the basis of short-term trading success. We show how these skills are refined and applied to short-term trading.

'Investing approaches' use months or years as a timeframe for performance and decision making. The attitudes and assumptions used here do not apply to short-term trading.

This book brings together for the first time material published as individual short articles and trading notes in the Guppytraders.com weekly newsletter, *Shares* magazine and various websites over the past decade. We have also included new material and have tied the differing techniques together under a more structured approach. Many of the examples used in this book are drawn from trading notes written in real time and show the real-life application of specific techniques to exploit recurring short-term opportunities. Some of the examples are of personal trades and the notes reflect the anguish created when market reality collides with theory, particularly in relation to warrant trading.

We use the day traders' notations throughout the book, so stocks and derivatives are generally referred to only by their ASX three or four letter code. When we trade we type MSH into the order screen rather than Morning Star Holdings. Part of the day trader's lexicon is a good working knowledge of stock codes.

The approaches included in this book are a personal selection of day trading and short-term tactics we apply to Australian markets. It is not an exhaustive exploration. There are many different ways to trade this short-term timeframe, some more effective or less effective than the ones included here. We encourage readers to explore these avenues and we provide references to other resources in the text.

SHIFTING CASH

How effectively we shift money from the market into our bank accounts depends, to a significant extent, on leverage. It comes in two important forms. We explore the exact implications of this in later chapters but as an introduction we need a working definition.

The most commonly accepted form of leverage is instrument leverage using some type of derivative product. These products include warrants, options, futures contracts and some hybrid futures contracts based on options or stocks. The leverage comes from the multiplying effect created by the way a small amount of up-front money gives the trader the right to purchase something of potentially much larger value in the future. We might not be able to afford to buy many NAB shares at $30.00 each even though we are confident our analysis confirms a strong uptrend. Instead we buy the right to purchase many NAB shares for just a few dollars using the warrant market. If NAB shares rise we have the ability to 'control' a much larger number of shares. We get more bang for our dollar.

A less well known and less frequently used form of leverage is price leverage. It has a nasty reputation because it is most powerful at the disreputable end of the market – amongst the penny dreadfuls that now include dot-coms as well as the classic speculative gold stocks. Price leverage comes from a psychological weakness when shares are very low-priced. Buy them at $0.01 and a half cent rise does not seem astounding. Translate it into percentage terms and the 50% return is worth investigating. Many people ignore the opportunity because they are frightened by tales of low liquidity and difficult exits. There are some specific short-term trading techniques applied to this type of market and we consider them in Chapter 10.

Price leverage should not be so easily dismissed. It also applies to stocks trading at $0.30, at $1.00 and up to $3.00 or higher. These price levels capture the bulk of Australian listed stocks. Most provide steady trading, good daily volume, and consistent market depth. We use price leverage to maximise short-term returns for trading opportunities found in this large pool.

AUSTRALIAN TRADING APPLICATIONS

The structure of our market is different from markets in the United States. Many day trading techniques covered in American books are simply not relevant here. Others require extensive modification and adjustment before they can be applied successfully. There are also some techniques that take advantage of the Australian market's unique features and these techniques do not work in other markets. We explain these as they arise.

In some chapters we draw on techniques or approaches first created by traders like Robert Deel, Tony Oz, Oliver Velez and others. We do not claim these as our own. Our interest is in the way these are applied, and where necessary, subtly altered, to provide effective trading solutions in our markets. We provide an overview of the original trading technique, and then explain how it has been modified. The results are all illustrated with a case study. We encourage readers to obtain the original books by each author. Study their approaches. You may find wrinkles we have missed and which may set you on the path to trading success.

In each chapter we start with a general introduction and overview of the topic. Our intention is to highlight each application in short-term and intra-day timeframes, alerting readers to special risks. Where appropriate we include the database search formulas used to locate these opportunities. Some apply to end-of-day charting packages like GuppyTraders Essentials and MetaStock. Others come directly from real time data suppliers including MarketCast, AOT Online Trading and Hubb Data who provide real-time data screening.

Many chapters include a detailed example of the technique in action. Some of these examples are blow-by-blow, tick-by-tick, narratives of real-time trades. This is unavoidable in this timeframe because traders must focus on the detail of price behaviour. Sometimes, literally every trade counts and a tick up or down can mean the difference between profit or loss. We have chosen these 'fishing' stories carefully to ensure they fully illustrate the implementation of the tactics under discussion. Success in short-term trading demands attention to detail so we encourage readers to follow the detail in the trading approaches they are interested in.

Let's look at what you can expect to learn from each part of this book.

Part I – TRADING TIME

The first few chapters are a wrecker's ball designed to demolish some popular misconceptions which stand in the way of success in these short-term timeframes. They include the supposed advantages belonging to inside traders, and to their close relatives who are those who know exclusive market moving news. The single most powerful self-defeating excuse for poor trading performance is the idea that success depends on exclusive news. It is an antiquated hangover from the turn of the nineteenth century. The myth of the insider has pervaded and distorted market analysis throughout the twentieth century. There have been some spectacular examples of successful insider trading and from these the popular press have succeeded in convincing many people that insider trading is rife in every stock.

Yes, there was substantial manipulation of IPO pricing in the dot-com and tech stock boom of the late '90s. This did not prevent traders from making very good money by trading the stock on the day of listing. We show some examples of these tactics in later chapters.

These news reports easily grow into a conspiracy theory that explains our failure to make money. "We was robbed" is the plaintive cry of the unskilled, the lazy and the gullible who bought insubstantial internet companies that had risen from $4.00 to $400 in a few months. Too stupid to recognise a scary ride, they were taken for a ride. Willingly captured by greed, they were not interested in developing the skills necessary to turn the ride into real money. Yet successful management took just one surprisingly simple instruction to their broker – a sell order.

There is no room for conspiracy theories in this book. Both day trading and short-term trading are built around the idea that every fast ride ends suddenly, but we control when we get on, and off. The ride is widely advertised. We join an eager crowd who all have access to the same news and facts we do. Success does not depend on exclusive access. This is not a private ride. It is a public fairground.

Survival and success depends on skill and not on some secret knowledge of prearranged events. Traders of all types steered clear of corporate collapses like Enron, WorldCom and HIH Insurance because one look at the chart of price action showed a strong and solid downtrend. Many of the general public continued to hold, or buy, these stocks. The same news was available to everybody, but success came to those who assessed it objectively.

The wrecker's ball hurts when it hits. You may feel some pain as some popular misconceptions are demolished but please pay attention to the detailed corrective surgery.

We use real examples to show the difference between popular myth and trading reality. Most are real trades and you can use the same methods to enhance your own trading approach to the same types of situations.

Part II – FINDING OPPORTUNITY

Once we move beyond the first section, each chapter is designed to introduce and explain one or two important concepts that underpin short-term trading success. Each includes a case study trade to highlight the application and impact of the concepts, be it trading surprise news, increased volatility or a breakout to a new high. A number of the case studies are personal trades. The remainder are drawn from trades examined in real time in our weekly newsletter. These examples are carefully selected to highlight the relevant issues being discussed in each chapter. They pass the test of real trading so you can have confidence the issues and methods discussed are relevant to the markets you trade.

At the end of these chapters we include a summary of the techniques discussed. Readers in a rush can take a shortcut by simply flipping to the end of each chapter to read the summary. This is useful, but it ignores the subtleties involved in the application of short-term trading techniques. The case studies explore the twists, the inferred clues in order volume, and the skill required to effectively apply the technique. It is detailed reading but the difference between your golf swing and Tiger Wood's is also in the detail. Day trading looks like a quick fix but it takes time to prepare.

Day trading is similar to a battlefield routine – long periods of boredom punctuated by moments of intense activity. Some trades fall into your lap, but most are carefully ambushed after a long period of observation. Trades based on scalping approaches represent the boring day-to-day routine. The driving factor is volatility. This is not the general public's concept of volatility used to describe markets that go up and down instead of trending steadily in a single direction. Price volatility is a measure of the daily range of prices. Do prices tend to move by just a few cents each day, or does the stock have a history of $0.12 or $0.20 moves? Translate these into percentage calculations and we have a way to identify the most effective scalping opportunities.

The Americans call this 'nickel and diming' the market and it accurately describes the way frequent small profits are harvested quietly from the market. Returns run from a few hundred dollars to around a thousand on a good day, using trades of around $20,000 each. These returns are the core of professional day trading techniques and are generally considered too boring for those who only want to dabble in this type of trading.

This is the media's idea of day trading and it was helped by the inefficiencies of the US market. At the turn of the century the US market traded in fractions – quarters, eights, sixteenths and teenies. The minimum tick size translated into $0.065. Imagine buying a $0.10 stock knowing the next minimum price bid could only be at $0.165. Few US stocks traded at this level, although when Enron traded at $0.41 the minimum tick represented a

16% return. I would be happy to 'nickel and dime' the market for these types of returns. Many US day traders turned this type of scalping into a high frenzy of trading, reputedly making 20 or more trades a day.

Sorry, this trading style does not cross the Pacific because our minimum tick size is $0.001.

The dabblers, and other professionals, are attracted to momentum trading opportunities. Momentum describes the way prices move consistently in one direction and it captures the acceleration of this process. We call it rally trading and one approach involves riding the tiger. These trades are identified as they begin to move, or are captured shortly after the initial price rise. The ride to the top is fast, and often the collapse is even faster.

There are great profits and even greater losses available in these rallies. We look at one example that returns over 1,000%. Buy it at the wrong moment, trade it without discipline, and the loss is substantial. It is important to distinguish between traders who chase prices and traders who trade rallies. The two activities look similar, but only one is successful. Those who chase prices are like dogs who chase cars. Very few dogs catch the car, but when they do they are often killed.

Skilled rally trading relies on recognising opportunity, and developing the wisdom to wait for slower but safer trades built after the rally.

These are rapid short-lived opportunities. By the time we see them they are often either just making a top, or already gone. This is not a total disappearing act. Many excellent short-term, but slower paced opportunities are found in the patterns developing after a rally. These include our personal favourite, the bullish flag, along with upward sloping triangles and other rebound patterns. These are short-term three to seven day trading opportunities which call for patience while the price action sets up the rebound conditions.

Short-term trading does not necessarily mean fast trading. A good snapshot is not fired in haste. The best snapshots are taken by those who are prepared for the opportunity and wait for the best sight picture to emerge. Preparation and planning captures profit. Throwing money at runaway stocks is always gratefully accepted by other traders with more skill.

Part III – PRODUCING PROFIT

The instruments of leverage – derivatives like warrants, options and futures – supply the very profitable edge of short-term trading. Success looks easy from the outside with warrant prices moving from $0.05 to $0.13 with apparent ease. This is the magic of price leverage in action and it attracts many new and unskilled players. But make no mistake. These sophisticated markets call for high levels of skill. This is not a modern version of haggling over the price of a batik with a stall holder in Bali. The stock market most closely emulates this direct haggling between buyer and seller, but not the derivative market.

We focus on warrants. This market is better understood by thinking of how successful you are in haggling with a used car salesman. No matter how far you beat him down on price, when you drive away there is still a sneaking suspicion the salesman has done very well out of the transaction. The used car salesman stands between you, the buyer, and the person who originally sold the car. In the warrant and option market the third party is a professional, full-time, skilled market maker. I avoid knowingly trading against them whenever I can.

The organisation acting as market maker is required by regulation to maintain a market for each warrant when the general public shows no interest. When the public actively trades the warrant, the market maker may intervene at times to restrain the growth of prices beyond what they consider to be a fair value range. In most active warrant markets the market maker stands to one side and for a while the trading truly reflects the haggling between buyer and seller. At times like this the doors are open to market inefficiency driven by crowd despair and enthusiasm.

This inefficiency makes warrants an appealing short-term trading instrument. We are not interested in working on the market maker's theoretical terms when it comes to pricing and volatility. We are interested in observing the activity of excited crowds. This is where we trade, but to trade effectively requires an understanding of the order the market maker seeks to impose on the action.

We can simply plan to buy at $0.05 and sell at $0.13 but this demands more skill than first meets the eye. We take you through the necessary background to reveal the structure and mechanics of the warrant market before showing you how a short-term trade is identified, managed, and finally closed. We include trading screens and show how the market depth, volume, and tick trading clues appear in real time and how traders react to them. The examples we use are of personal trades and the analysis notes were originally written in real time.

The same leverage is used to slingshot earnings and dividend announcements. What may be an inconsequential move in the parent stock translates into significant short-term profits from warrant trading. These instruments provide the ability to capture the short, sharp, but expected swings, in crowd excitement as earnings are announced.

Part IV – LETHAL WEAPONS

Stocks and trading instruments which offer price leverage open the door to very useful trades. This is a long section because success depends on the detail.

Depending on where you stand, a gap in a price chart is a feature of beauty, or terror. Gaps indicate a substantial and significant change in crowd opinion. A gap is beautiful when the trader already holds the stock and watches it gap upwards on the open. This is most often related to skill rather than judgement. Traders waste a lot of time, and a lot of dollars, chasing gaps. There are some successes but the returns are inconsistent. We explore the structure of gaps to explain the implementation of a two-day gap strategy designed to capture crowd excitement.

These chapters are the first of those dealing with specific short-term techniques. These are bread and butter trades. Returns are 5% to 15% in a 24-hour period. Like most day trading strategies they look easy at first glance – and they are when all the conditions are set up perfectly. The details of pattern recognition and the evaluation of the order screen structure make the trade possible.

It is the detail of the intra-day price action, with tightly placed stop loss conditions, that makes these trades profitable. Not all traders have the patience required to micro manage the detail so the rewards are likely to slip through their fingers.

When we paint with a broad brush the detail counts for less. When we try to paint a miniature on the inside of a small glass perfume bottle, like the glass painters in Guangzhou, then the detail is vital. Small mistakes have major consequences. The same scale of detail and disaster applies with day trading. The successful results look impressive but do not let them blind you to the detailed craftsmanship required to produce them.

Accidents are inevitable so we end this gap discussion by exploring a defensive gap trading strategy developed by US trader Oliver Velez.

Some downward gaps rebound, providing opportunities for trades in ordinary stocks and for trades which use price leverage to exploit the short-lived recovery. These chart patterns are created and driven by repeated crowd behaviour. They set up rebound and breakaway trades which have a high level of reliability. This is snapshot trading with precision. Success is not guaranteed, but it is highly probable.

One set of patterns captures the resurge in excitement. The bullish flag pattern is often part of a larger move. Prices hit the projected target and then often continue to move higher. Successful trading calls for the short-term trader to cap his greed and ignore the larger trend developing. It is not always a comfortable decision.

The next set of patterns, the rebound or finger trades, are based on crowd resentment. There is a nasty, disappointed crowd at work. They have lost faith so when prices reach back to their most recent highs this crowd sells. No good aiming for a better price in this pattern. Once the target is reached, prices fall away very quickly. Traders snatch a 20% to 40% return in two or three days, but it is fatal to hang out for more, or to ignore the first signs of price weakness.

The collapse of these finger trades has unpredictable consequences. Some stocks just keep on falling. Others are part of a larger pattern and offer additional short-term trading opportunities. In one of the case studies we show how the initial successful rebound trade and collapse is part of a longer-term chart pattern. This upward sloping triangle offers another short-term trade on the triangle breakout that captures 30% in less than a week.

These simple, reliable and dependable chart patterns reflect the emotional behaviour of crowds. They are not popular hunting techniques for aspiring short-term traders who are attracted to the glitz of action. This is a pity because these patterns set up the conditions for successful snapshot trades that hit right on target.

The Australian banking industry builds massive profits from the small fees extracted every time we stand in line at the local bank. Similarly the day trading techniques based around the work of US trader, Tony Oz, take small profits from the market on a regular and consistent basis. Returns average 2% a day but some trades, as we show, return 10% to 30%. They are icing for the day trader's cake and they highlight the judgement required to use intra-day screens to manage entry and exit conditions.

It will take some time to reach this section on intra-day trading. Read this book from beginning to end and we take you through short-term trades spread over three to five days, overnight techniques and then, finally, the intra-day trades lasting just a few hours. Your venture into short-term and day trading has a greater chance of success if you follow the same path. Shorter time frames call for better judgement. Build this judgement in slower position trades. As experience improves judgement, you move to shorter time frames and meet the demand of faster execution with more confidence and success. Speed starts with slow paced practice – as our military weapons instructor knew.

Part V – PROFIT TAKING

This section looks at short-term timeframes where success depends more heavily on good trade execution than it does in position trading or investment approaches to the market. Time and timing is critical. A delayed order can mean the difference between a successful trade and a failure. Direct access to accurate, real time price and trading data is not an optional extra. The ASX trades as a fully electronic market so there is no excuse for delays in information delivery. When a stock trades we expect to see the 'print' on our screens in much less than a second. I run several data feeds, each claiming to be real time. Some are delayed, with price action consistently reported by other data suppliers three to five seconds earlier. In day trading this makes a difference.

Recently on a suburban street I spotted an XJ Jaguar for sale. The asking price was a mere $6,000. It had a number of mechanical problems, not the least of which was a leaking brake system. It was an accident waiting to happen, but the gentleman would have been happy to take my money. After all, he wasn't going to be in the car when it crashed. Brokers who do not offer stop loss facilities present us with the same problem. Without the most modern safety equipment, there is a higher risk our day trading or short-term trading will crash and burn.

We take readers on a detailed tour of the safety equipment currently available. This includes the full range of electronic and hybrid stop loss execution systems. Once you plug in a stop loss order facility to a fully electronic market like the ASX then the next logical step is to expand the range of contingent orders. This is intelligent use of computer technology but it appears few brokers believe their clients could benefit from this.

The choice of brokerages that offer contingent buy orders is limited. Yet this facility makes the management and monitoring of all trading approaches so much more effective. All traders have a choice between using tools or toys to trade the market. Investors and some position traders get by using toys. In shorter timeframes, survival depends on choosing tools. It is specialised shopping.

We close the section with an overview of the computer screens used for monitoring and managing short-term trades. It is not a complete collection. In keeping with the rest of the book, it is a selected survey of the screens and data providers we currently use. They may change in time as systems improve. One broking service mentioned in previous books has already disappeared – the victim of a takeover by a rival.

The cost of brokerage is one of the most significant factors in short-term trading. The cost of order execution services is much more significant. When selecting a broker to work with we look for speed, reliability, and a stop loss service. Brokerage cost is the last item considered because one poorly executed trade can cost a lot more than a year of brokerage fees. Discounts attract those who do not know the role that effective brokers play in trading success. Your capital depends on your choice so choose carefully.

Day trading is virtually impossible without access to real-time data supply and desktop computers to display the information and to lodge buy and sell orders. We assume these computers already sit on your desktop and that you are prepared to take the time to monitor and manage these day or short-term trades. In the final chapter we show examples of the data supply, trading and order screens we use. They are a guide to the screens available.

WORKING WITH CREDIT

Writing a book is not a short-term exercise. It is a lengthy and demanding process. Although the book carries my name as author, the truth is it could not have been written without the help given by many people. These include the private traders who attend my workshops and ask penetrating questions. Workshops with industry professionals in Singapore and Hong Kong provide a wider perspective on market trading activity. The people who read my weekly newsletter and send email questions and suggestions provide an ongoing challenge to explain more clearly the planning and processes required to understand trading. Visitors to the website raise issues and force me to clarify my techniques. Trading colleagues Robert Deel and Tony Oz have helped fine tune trading applications. All of you contribute to the ideas included in this book and I thank you for your assistance.

None of this is possible, writing or trading, without the support of my wife and son who put up with the side effects of my long periods of intense concentration while the first draft is created.

Getting ideas onto paper is just the first step. Just as important is the challenge to avoid repetition. The material in this book builds on many of the ideas and concepts covered in my earlier books, but we do not repeat them. This book contains new material and ideas.

The words and ideas demand editing and proofing before they are offered to outside readers. Leehoon Chong armed herself with highlighters and rigorously slashed poor expression and the numerous spelling and typographical errors in the early drafts. My mother Patricia found herself again hunting down mixed metaphors and imprecise sentence structure in the final proof draft instead of relaxing on holiday in the tropical Darwin winter.

The end of day charts in this book are created by the GuppyTraders Essentials charting package, or MetaStock. A few charts are created by Ezy Charts. The intra-day charts are created by the GuppyTraders Essentials charting package or by the MarketCast Windows Market Detective program. End of day data comes from JustData and is downloaded with their Bodhi Freeway service. Real time tick data comes from MarketCast and is delivered via a reliable broadcast system. We also use AOT Online Trading and Hubb Data for real-time data delivered via the internet.

Beersheba was the scene of the last great cavalry charge in modern history and I, like my great uncle, was proud to serve in the same regiment that still carried those battle honours. Their success rested on monotonous training and the experience gained in small skirmishes. Officially they were mounted infantry and battle victory depended on accurate shooting once they were deployed for action.

We are not engaged in the same endeavour, but we draw on the traditional cavalry tactics of fast action, precision and swift defensive extraction and apply them to the market. When market conditions are appropriate, we raid the trading screens for profit and our survival depends on consistent skill.

Train hard and raid well.

Daryl Guppy
Darwin
October 2002

PART I

TRADING
TIME

Chapter 1

TRAINING NINJA TURTLES

When a group of young turtles were dumped into a New York sewer they emerged as the martial arts phenomenon, Teenage Mutant Ninja Turtles. They are largely forgotten now, but at their peak every ten year old wanted to duplicate the snappy martial arts moves of these cartoon heroes and Taekwondo clubs experienced a burst of interest. However, it was only temporary because few children had the discipline required to develop the skills they craved. They wanted instant solutions but instead they found hard work and slow, steady progress.

The way to martial arts speed is not via a frenzy of imitated actions. It is achieved through the disciplined repetition of slow-motion drills. Instructors taught the movements of the Kichohyung form at a snails' pace. As training advanced the students worked on improving the speed of these basic moves. Their training started with slow-motion practice drills and laid the foundation for lightning fast moves.

Day trading and short-term trading use the same trading principles as longer-term trades. Working in shorter timeframes calls for skill which is based on the experience gathered while trading at slower speeds. Trades managed over weeks and months call for the same basic collection of skills as trades managed over hours or days. Successful short-term trading starts with slow-motion practice and lays the foundation for lightning fast moves built on effective analysis of the balance of probability, stop loss discipline and a comfortable relationship with greed. Some short-term returns are spectacular but they are the reward for staying with a consistent string of small-time trades with small profits. Like a beggar picking up small change abandoned on the street, every now and then the trader stumbles across a $50 note. It is unwise to rely on this happening every day.

You have a choice in exploring short-term opportunities. You could be a loser by emulating the behaviour of ten year olds who used a frenzy of imitated actions learnt from television and the popular press. There are many brokers and brokerages who are happy to take your commissions as you flail away at the market. Specialist day trading centres were established at the height of the public day trading bubble at the turn of last century. In the United States they provided hopefuls with a modern version of a seventeenth century London coffee house where traders met to make a market and speculate on uncompleted voyages to the spice islands. The modern version was complete with live screens, a collection of other day trading hopefuls, and some attempts at basic education. All you had to do was bring your money. These operators and the markets would take it from you.

These mug punters were market fodder and an irresponsible financial and popular press built their foolish antics into a mythical status. There were some big winners but few consistent winners amongst this crop of new traders. We have no wish to emulate the antics of those who had a 95% failure rate. If you are after a fast dollar without work then this book is not a good choice.

During the media's boom in coverage of day trading, the established and experienced day and short-term traders continued to milk the market. They still do so, even though the day trading boom is just a distant memory. They provide you with a second choice. A selection of their skills and techniques is the focus of this book. There are no quick answers, although there are fast trades and fast trading techniques. Our intention is to bring together sound decision making, price leverage and capital protection to capture the benefits of good trading and apply them to shorter-term timeframes.

The skills of a successful short-term trader are similar to the skills the rifle marksman brings to target shooting. When the conditions are just right he snaps off a shot with lethal accuracy. The market marksman applies similar skills to locate a target, capture the perfect sight picture and snap-off a successful, precision trade. Snapshot trading is not about photo opportunities – unless you count the happy family snaps of successful traders.

We apply these skills in nervous, unstable and volatile markets when it makes more sense to snatch profits from short-term trades than to buy stock for the long-term. These are defensive strategies because speed offers protection and limits risk by reducing the time the trade is open. It is up to you to choose between the careful application of these techniques when appropriate, or to use them as a consistent part of your total trading strategy. The choice, and responsibility, is yours.

Our focus is on price and its behaviour. We use daily and intra-day charts of price action to understand the nature of the trading opportunity. Even news-driven events are tracked by price activity which is captured on a chart. Our preference is the bar chart, although many traders also use a candlestick chart to display the same information. Which you use is a matter of personal choice. Some traders find it easier to assess price relationships with a candlestick display, while others collect the same information with a glance at a bar chart. A selection of working screen layouts is included in Chapter 28.

Fundamental analysis based on company reports, balance sheets, market share, strategic market analysis and the company management team are largely irrelevant to short-term traders. When a seller agrees to your bid for his stock he does not take a moment to consider the current PE ratio or the debt to equity ratio of the company. His only interest is completing the sale of his shares as quickly as possible, at what he believes is the best possible price. Some buyers you compete against make their decisions based on fundamental analysis, but their buying is unlikely to provide enough impetus to attract you as a short-term or day trader.

Our success rests on understanding the emotional content of price. It is created by the combined activity of many people – both buyers and sellers – who strike an agreement for a split second about the price at which they are prepared to do business. We track the growing excitement in the market and as short-term traders, we understand the opportunity it offers. Emotional people make mistakes and pay more than they should for shares. Our objective is to wade into the midst of this emotion, calmly buying and selling while others are losing their heads. We pit our judgement and skills against theirs and there is no guarantee we will succeed.

In the long-term a short-term trader may appear to fail. Where is the satisfaction in taking 5% from an explosive price move which then develops into a longer-term trend capable of delivering a 40% to 60% return? There is little satisfaction if the short-term trader pretends he wants to become a long-term trader. Short-term trading sets its own rules, its own time horizons and surrenders the possibility of long-term profits in favour of quick returns. By accepting the rules of this game we avoid the corrosive impacts of envy. There are always better opportunities than the one we are currently trading. Somewhere in the market others are winning while we struggle to exit a losing position. It is a fact of the market, and if we allow it to distract us from our chosen task then we are lured into forever chasing someone else's wins without collecting any of our own. All trading rests on discipline and focus.

Intra-day trading is the more infamous of the day trading techniques. It involves micro trading approaches where the trader intends to buy stock during the day and to sell it before the end of the day. There is no intention to carry the trade – or position – overnight. These trades may be as short as a few minutes in hectic and deep American markets. More typically in Australia they last several hours because we do not have the same high levels of trading activity. These are scalping techniques and we look in detail at these in later chapters.

Short-term traders identify price patterns and behaviours they expect to develop completely within a two- to five-day timeframe. This is sometimes called 'swing trading'. The objective is to trade high-probability developments, such as a bullish flag pattern or a rally trend created by an anticipated news release. Other opportunities include trading the impact of a defined or known event. Finding these opportunities calls for tracking volatility and identifying bullish strength. We consider several approaches and Australian adaptations of techniques based on work by American traders Robert Deel and Tony Oz.

Straddling the timeframe between intra-day and short-term trading is a collection of overnight trading techniques. These include trading overnight gaps and the one-day continuation of price breakouts. These trades are controlled with intra-day stop loss techniques and require constant monitoring. American trader and founder of Pristine.com, Oliver Velez, calls these 'guerrilla trading techniques'. The success of many of these techniques, like those of US trader and author, David Nassar, rest on exploiting the behaviour of market makers. Ours is an order-driven market where traders come together without the interference of a market maker. This makes some American techniques irrelevant to the Australian market and calls for the modification of others. We examine a range of guerrilla-style techniques later.

For convenience we group these approaches in the following way through this book.

➡ Short-term trading includes intra-day, overnight, and two- to five-day trades. Where we discuss specific techniques we specify which type of timeframe is best suited.

➡ Position trading includes trades designed to span weeks or months. Entry and exit decisions are based on end-of-day data and designed for execution in the next day's market. The skills learned here form the basis of short-term trading success.

➡ Investing approaches use months or years as a timeframe for performance and decision making.

DEMANDING TIMES

Some short-term trading techniques are applied on an end-of-day basis. It is possible to trade many short-term patterns while still working full-time. We need the help of a good electronic broking service which accepts contingent buy and sell orders, and supplies an effective electronic stop loss service.

Intra-day trading success demands full-time attention. It is simply not possible to work at a full-time, or even a part-time job, and give these techniques the attention they deserve. Most traders incorporate some of these techniques into their trading at specific times and in specific market conditions. In some cases it is more appropriate to trade a short-term opportunity. Pattern-based trades can be managed effectively while occupied with other work. When markets grow nervous near the top of trends we reach for short-term trading tactics because they provide a defensive mechanism. Selecting short-term trades is an effective way to manage this broader market risk.

Traders who apply these techniques as part of a broader range of market trading techniques need to take the time to monitor and manage these short-term trades with a higher level of attention. It does not always mean sitting in front of the screen all day, but it does mean having access to updated prices in real time on a regular basis. Your monitoring may include real-time alerts via email, text messaging or pager.

With some of the techniques discussed there is no escaping from the computer screen. Access to a real-time data feed is a necessity, along with fast internet access for the placement of orders. We look at the types of data suppliers, trading screens and brokerage requirements in later chapters and show how they are combined in some sample trades.

It is fun to pretend – ask any ten year old who wants to be a ninja turtle. But, as an adult, it is very expensive to pretend to be a day trader or a short-term trader. When reality meets desire in this market segment, the results are sometimes very bloody.

SLOW MOTION BUILDS SPEED

Short-term trading is inevitably built around fast-moving price action. The objective is to capture a profit in hours or days. The profit comes from changes in price and just as the market can quickly deliver a capital gain, it will snatch it away with frightening speed and ease. Short-term trading starts with long-term planning. All trades start with a chart of daily price action. We show later how a search through daily data highlights the potential short-term and day trading opportunities. Even those techniques which rely on news and price momentum are more effectively applied within the context of the daily price action. News that drives price up by a few cents does not necessarily provide a day trading opportunity. News that powers a low-priced stock to significant percentage gains delivers an excellent opportunity. The daily bar chart tells us which has the greater probability of success and profit.

While there is a temptation to flip forward to the chapters dealing with trading news, dividend announcements and overnight gap trading, we suggest you resist. Turn to these sections now if you must, but long-term success with these techniques rests on understanding the analysis and trading skills that form the foundation of all trading. They start with the balance of probability and our reaction to what happens when the balance changes. When it comes time to move with speed in the market, we do better if we first understand how to work with probability outcomes.

PREDICTION OR FORECAST?

Chart analysis is often confused with predicting or forecasting the market. This confusion is enhanced by those who confuse trading and investing. Chart analysis uses the action of price and volume to clearly show how the market has behaved. For traders, the past pattern of behaviour helps to identify market situations with a high probability of a specific outcome. Traders then develop a plan to cope with the probability.

When we cross the road we pause at the kerb, check left and right, then cross. The kerb tells us there are changed conditions ahead, but it tells us nothing about the actual events on the road. We prepare to behave in a particular way depending on what the road reveals. The trader prepares to act one way if certain conditions are met, and another way if different conditions are met.

Forecasting uses the higher probability situations to project future price action and acts in anticipation of this. It straddles the boundary between trading and investing. Here we stand at the traffic lights, stepping out confidently when the walk sign flashes. Sometimes we get wiped out as a car crashes through the walk signal, but most times the signal is reliable. When we see the signal we forecast the action for a selected period of time.

Prediction is a different beast altogether. It carries a high level of certainty about the occurrence of events at a specific time. This is like saying: I know there is a set of traffic lights at the end of the block, and at 10:38 a.m. the signal will be flashing 'walk'. This leaves little room for probability, although there are times when such predictions match the co-incident events and the predictions come true. Separating the co-incidence from accurate predictive ability is difficult.

WORKING WITH PROBABILITY OUTCOMES

As short-term and intra-day traders, we work with probability and it does not always go our way. We considered closing this chapter with an example of a successful short-term trade. Instead we examine a trade to highlight the relationship between probability and our need to be right. This example is a long-term trade, but in slow motion, it highlights the issues we face at speed in any short-term trade.

Consider the sample AGH trade in Figure 1.1. Entry was at $0.71. The trade objective was to ride the continuation of the trend. Instead the trend collapsed very rapidly, and an exit was triggered at $0.66 as prices dipped below the straight-edge trend line used to define the trend. Later the trend resumes and prices soar to $0.86. The early, and false, exit means we miss out on a 21% return.

If you believe trading is about being right then the exit based on trend weakness is a 'wrong' decision. If you believe trading is about working with the balance of probabilities, then the exit is a valid decision followed by a low-probability outcome. It is an annoyance, but not a fatal analysis or trading error. In short-term trading we must accept a higher propensity for shakeouts, or for missing out on a larger price or trend move. If we cannot accept this annoyance it grows to become a significant irritation and limits short-term trading success.

After fear and greed, regret is the most common emotion in the market. We regret having sold, or not having sold. Part of the process of developing trading discipline is developing the ability to accept regret as a minor trading emotion and to move on. So how do we handle the subsequent action with AGH? These are important issues because they impact on how we view our trading and how we measure success.

This AGH trade makes a small loss. It is a successful trade in terms of limiting the loss to within the 2% risk rules. It is a successful trade in terms of staying within a trading plan and taking a disciplined exit. We should accept several inevitable features of trading.

Figure 1.1 – Probability Knocks

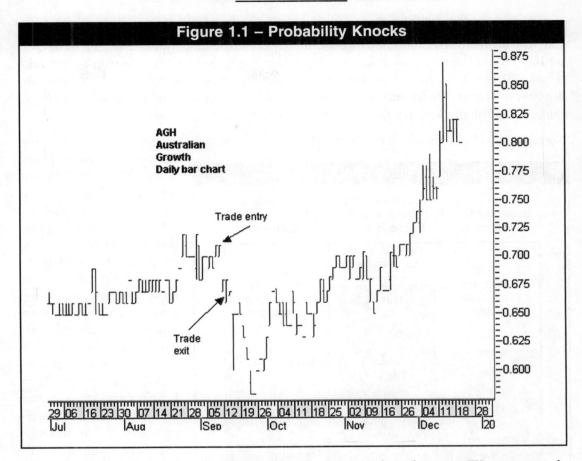

The first is the balance of probabilities aligned in any trading decision. We consistently look for trading entry points where the balance is tipped in our favour as indicated by our preferred combination of indicators. We also look for a change in the balance as the trade continues. Although the indicators and price action provide the signal for an exit, it is our judgement of the balance of probabilities that encourages us to act.

Our view of the balance is distorted by our emotions. On entering a trade, we tend to be optimistic. What is objectively a 60/40 balance in our favour, we see as a 70/30 balance emotionally. When we exit we are still optimistic which is why many exits are failures. The objective situation may show a shift in balance to 70/30 against the trend continuing, but we are inclined to see it as 60/40. As our trading improves we take a more realistic and less emotional view of the balance of probability at these significant decision points.

We all understand the idea of probability in a theoretical sense, but we are often less comfortable with it in a practical sense. In the market we confuse having the balance of probability on our side with guaranteeing our preferred outcome.

The diagram in Figure 1.2 shows a trading decision where the balance is 70% in our favour and 30% against. The combined signal from our preferred indicators are telling us to take action. This is the objective balance. Our subjective assessment is shown in the second column. When we commit to action we emotionally expect the balance to dramatically shift in our favour. We unconsciously shift the balance once our trading decision has been executed in the market. We believe our action further tips the balance.

Nothing could be further from the truth. The balance of probability remains exactly as it was before our decision. There is still a 30% probability we will make the wrong decision – as occurred in the AGH example. How does this relate to trading success? The AGH trade was not profitable, so in measuring its success we may be concerned with how much additional profit we could have made, or how much we missed by taking an early exit. Perry Kaufmann in *Smarter Trading* uses a trade efficiency approach to measure this. He compares the actual exit with the best theoretical exit. We find it both a depressing and fruitless exercise and one we ought to avoid.

Figure 1.2 – Emotional Probability

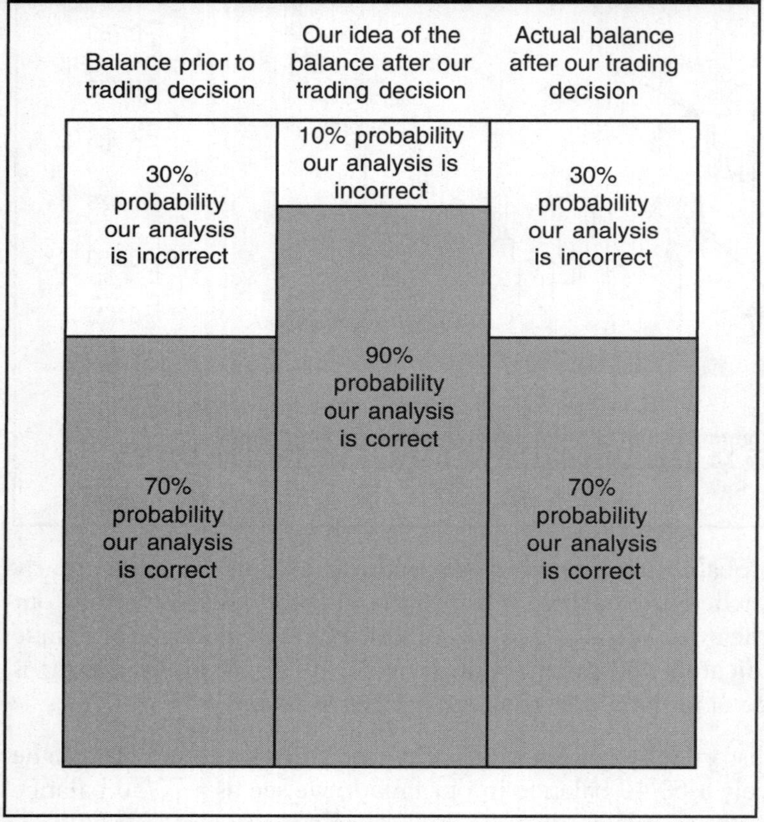

Balance prior to trading decision	Our idea of the balance after our trading decision	Actual balance after our trading decision
30% probability our analysis is incorrect	10% probability our analysis is incorrect	30% probability our analysis is incorrect
70% probability our analysis is correct	90% probability our analysis is correct	70% probability our analysis is correct

It is extremely difficult to exit at the exact top of any price or trend move. Obviously there are traders who do this, but experienced traders acknowledge it as luck. Traders find they cannot do this consistently, although they may have a streak of luck extending over several trades and giving them near-perfect exits. Very few traders are able to enter the trade at the very lowest point and then exit at the very highest point.

Even though this is a very unlikely outcome, many traders castigate themselves with the belief that the best trading strategy should deliver a perfect result. They believe trading is about being 'right' and this becomes more important than being profitable. Typically these traders hold falling stocks because they cannot admit they have made an error.

Ultimately trading success depends on being able to sell the stock you own. If you cannot sell then you cannot realise any profit from a trade. When it comes time to exit a trade we tend to concentrate on our own motives and position. This is fine from a technical perspective but it misses an important point. We also need to consider why anyone else would *buy* this stock from us.

There is only one reason. The buyer believes she can make money when she buys your parcel of stock. Most traders try to buy at a lower price and sell at a higher price. When we come to sell AGH at $0.66 we are looking for a buyer who believes AGH is going to keep rising. This means we must find someone who thinks exactly the opposite to the way we do. We are selling because we believe the balance of probability is 70/30 in favour of a trend decline. The buyer must believe the balance is at least 51/49 in favour of a trend continuation.

The buyer is not a fool. She makes an informed decision. You believe your decision to sell is a better decision. If your assessment of the balance of probabilities is correct then, in this example, 70% of the time you will be right. If your sell decision locks in a profit then you must also accept that 30% of the time you will be wrong and the buyer you sold to will make additional profits.

There is no problem here. Unless the buyer believes she can make money she will not buy from you. Do not begrudge her this profit, even if it is substantial, because it is she who hands the profit to you in your trade, even though as a short-term trader you might collect 10% while she goes on to collect 50% from the same stock.

When we come to identify a trade we must maintain our focus on the objectives and structure of the planned trade. It is difficult to be objective. It is important to try. If we allow emotional judgement to cloud our decisions we invalidate our analysis. Our subjective, or emotional, application of these concepts has the ability to gnaw away at trading success.

The advantage comes from slowing down the action in practice training so mistakes are more clearly seen. It is easier to eliminate these in slow motion than it is to see them at speed. Position traders are sometimes sloppy traders. There is time to cover up and recover from small mistakes. Not so in short-term trading so it pays to develop a better understanding of the little errors in longer-term trades before they grow to become a major obstacle to success.

Chapter 2

SABOTAGING
SUCCESS

Start with half a million dollars and it could take a long time to go broke trading the market. Along the way it is possible to have a lot of fun, to experience some great emotional highs and flirt with dark depression. Many new traders never get beyond this emotional roller coaster so they succeed in losing almost their entire trading stake. Their loss is not always a result of inexperience. It may take many years to drive a sizeable portfolio into bankruptcy and permanent inactivity.

The loss comes from their inability to learn from experience. They repeat the same mistakes time and time again, with just slight variations and with different stocks. At heart they do not want to win in the market. There is a range of reasons for this, as complex and personal as each individual who walks along this path. It is not our intention to delve into these. We want to note the powerful impact of this self-sabotage because when trading gathers speed these traits rapidly undermine success. If we learn to recognise and understand them in a longer-term trading context we give ourselves the opportunity to avoid them in a shorter-term timeframe.

Undetected, these position trading traits provide a faster way to lose money when we turn to the short-term trading arena.

If trading were as simple as selecting a stock on a technical basis and trading it, then more traders would be successful. Trading is difficult because although we insist on conducting prolonged and often accurate analysis, we then twist the entry decision to match our own particular biases and fears. Often the entry decision ends up discounting the original analysis. As a result we miss out on profitable trades, or buy into unprofitable trades. Both outcomes are despite initially sound analysis that, if followed, would lead to a successful and profitable trade.

Some psychologists and traders believe self-sabotage fills some deeper need. Trader, Ed Seykota, featured in *Market Wizards,* believes everyone gets out of the market exactly what they want. If you lose many trades perhaps it is because you subconsciously want to lose. This may satisfy some traders, but for traders who want to improve their success it is important to recognise where the problems may lie and to develop strategies to overcome them. Most times, discounting our analysis turns out to involve betting against the trend. We show how this works in the next section.

RESPECT YOUR ANALYSIS

Consider this straightforward trend trade as an example of how this analysis discount process works. The uptrend is defined by the accurately placed straight-edge trend line. The line has successfully defined a trend in place for many months. Prices find support on the line and bounce away. This is a very easy trend to trade. In this example the trader waits for prices to pull back to the proven trend line before entering at the best possible price. It is a sound strategy based on good analysis.

Our trader uses end-of-day data. She watches the close, and formulates her buy order for execution in the market the next day. Her entry signal is generated on the chart in Figure 2.1 by the price dip down to the trend line. The day closes higher as prices rebound away. The key question is: How much will she pay tomorrow?

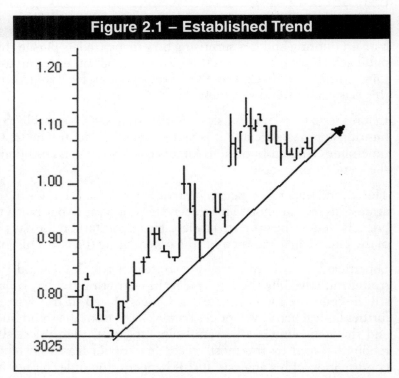

Figure 2.1 – Established Trend

The trader has three choices. The one she consistently chooses has a significant impact on her trading success. Some traders set their buy order in the zone shown by circle A in Figure 2.2. They want to buy this stock at yesterday's lows, or even lower. They look for temporary weakness in the new uptrend. Their order, placed below the current value of the trend line, totally discounts their trend analysis.

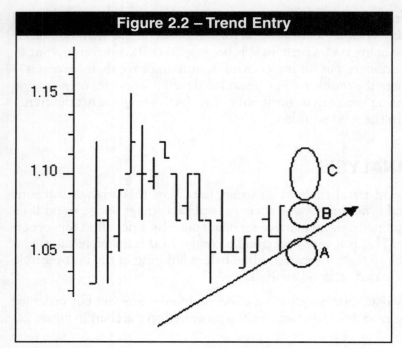

Figure 2.2 – Trend Entry

They want to buy the stock because it is bullish, but they will not do this until the stock stumbles below the very trend line they are using to define the trend. Their analysis and their action are inconsistent. Once the trade is open they plan to use a close below the trend line to generate an exit signal because there is an increased probability of a trend collapse. Yet this is the very condition they want to see before they agree to buy the stock in expectation of the uptrend continuing.

Now success depends on the trend behaving exactly opposite to the way her analysis suggests it should. This is bargain hunting and it is surprising how many traders pursue this strategy. If prices do not pull back to yesterday's lows then they miss out on entering the very trend they want to join. If prices pull back, these same traders often hesitate to buy because now they worry this is a sign of trend weakness.

In long-term trend trades – slow-motion trades – it is possible to get away with this bargain hunting approach because it is more difficult to define the trend exactly. In shorter-term timeframes bargain hunting is fatal because success relies upon a very tight definition of the trend or price activity.

The second trader who puts an entry order in area B has taken some steps to avoid betting against his own analysis. This trader does not want to pay much more than yesterday's high price. Preferably he wants to pay less. He might start off the day with an order at the bottom of the circled area and then lift the order during the day if his initial order is unfilled.

Superficially this is an attractive strategy. Look deeper and it is just a variation of the strategy followed by the first trader. In restricting the buy orders to area B, the trader is still discounting his own analysis. Orders placed in this area cannot take advantage of further bullish activity as prices bounce away from the trend line. If his analysis is correct, and the trend line is a powerful support point, then prices should rebound. The price rebound shown by the most recent bar should lead to a rebound continuation and a confirmation of his analysis. If this happens, the order placed in area B is not filled.

Again, this trader discounts his own accurate analysis by betting against the strength of the trend. He wants the strong trend to weaken so he can get on board. Often the trend leaves without him.

There is more room for error in longer-term trend trades. Success does not depend upon the precise entry point, as generally the trader aims to participate in a trend taking weeks or months to fully develop. In many cases an error of a cent or two on the entry has little impact on the total return from the trade. If the trader misses the buy opportunity shown in area B he may chase prices a little higher on the next day.

The short-term trader does not have this luxury. Miss this entry and he misses the trade completely. Short-term trends and price patterns are traded on their own terms and not as part of a wider trend pattern. Waiting for prices to return to area B deprives the short-term trader of an opportunity.

The trader who respects the accuracy of his analysis places an order in area C. He expects prices to keep on rising as they rebound from the trend line. This expectation is consistent with his analysis. He may use a variety of order structures or timing to get the best possible entry on the day. He is happy to pay market price, or a price higher than yesterday's high. The rebound is additional evidence his analysis is correct so if necessary, and within limits, he chases the price.

Obviously we have handpicked this example to highlight the issues. However the general conclusions remain valid and Figure 2.3 shows how it unfolded. The trader who discounted his analysis with an order in area A has around 45% chance of making a successful entry. The stronger and more established the trend, the lower this probability. Prices simply do not linger at these levels once the level has been hit and the rebound has started.

Traders who place an order around the high and close of the previous day have a better chance of joining the trend. We show this at 60%. The figure varies depending on the strength and

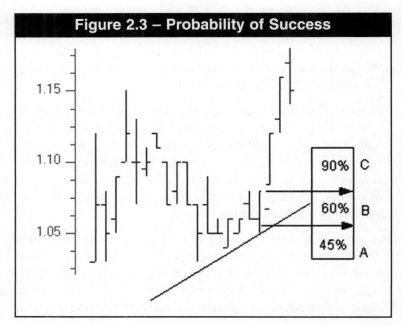

Figure 2.3 – Probability of Success

consistency of the trend. There is a greater probability of a pullback towards the value of the trend line so orders in this area are often filled.

The most successful strategy uses an order placed in area C. This is the only successful strategy in this example. The trader is prepared to accept the consequences of his analysis so he buys the stock at the best price available during the day, irrespective of how the price compares to the previous day's activity. He might pay more, or less, than the previous close. He trades the character of the rebound in a way consistent with his analysis. He has confidence in his analysis, and his buying strategy reflects this.

This strategy has a 90% probability of success. The times when it fails are when prices falter and move below the uptrend line. In this circumstance he may buy the stock today, but he then sells on the next day because the close delivers a sell signal. Trend lines are powerful tools, but they are not infallible. A small percentage of these trades fail, although this percentage is reduced when the trend is well established.

We do not have to pay market price when we enter a trade. We use strategies designed to get the best entry price on the day. However these strategies should not be confused with buying intentions that effectively discount our initial analysis. When our analysis of a strong trend is confirmed by price action behaving in the way we anticipated, then we should buy without hesitation. We trade today's price action, not yesterday's confirmation close.

PLEADING FOR RECOVERY

The fully equipped saboteur has a tool pack stacked with nasty tricks. Your personal sabotage kit has some tricks which you may not be aware of. Not respecting your analysis is just the beginning of a short course on effective ways to inflict financial damage on yourself. In normal trading and investing, the entry point is important for trading success. With short-term trading the entry point is critical.

We expect, or hope, every trade will turn out successfully. We accept some of our trades, perhaps 40% of them, will develop into abject failures. These may be a result of poor analysis or unexpected developments. The reasons are not excuses for inaction. We all know, in theory at least, what we are supposed to do. Every trade starts with a stop loss point designed to limit the financial impact of these errors. The most effective stops are built around the 2% rule which limits the maximum loss on any single trade to no more than 2% of our total trading capital.

As the trade develops and moves to produce a profit we believe the balance of probability remains permanently weighted in our favour. The longer the trade is profitable, the stronger this belief becomes. This hampers our reactions when a price shock ripples through the market. On a long-term trade it is possible to ride out the shock and implement a range of recovery strategies. In short-term trades this option is not always available, and nor is it sensible. The position trader loses when he converts trades into investments because he lacks the discipline to act on stop loss conditions. The short-term trader loses in the same way if she converts short-term trades into position trades. By doing so she respects neither her analysis nor her techniques. This sabotages trading discipline and makes it even more difficult to close these extended trades. It is a good way to start building a losing portfolio.

Consider how we react to price shocks when they hit open long-term trades. By understanding this process we can work towards avoiding it when it comes time to act in short-term trades.

When bad things happen we automatically close our eyes. When markets fall there is a tendency to do the same thing. When we open our eyes again, we hope the bad news has disappeared. We hope the price collapse has turned into a rally so there is no loss to our position or portfolio.

When prices fall significantly they may be reacting to a temporary dip. How do we know if this is temporary? Prior to the price dip we know the balance of probability is clearly weighted in our favour. This is the relationship shown in the charts in Figure 2.4. Unless something very dramatic happens we reasonably expect the uptrend to continue. There are many indicators to help identify this balance of probability – BOP. For this example we stay with a 10- and 30-day exponential moving average – EMA. In both stocks shown the spread between the two moving averages is well established, and confirms the weighting shown on the balance of probability scale.

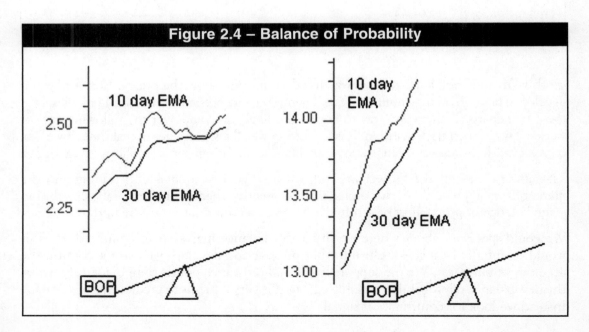

Figure 2.4 – Balance of Probability

What happens when we get a price shock? The most important effect is the balance of probability shifts as shown in Figure 2.5. We know there is now a strong probability the uptrend is finished. We know there is a good probability a downtrend could develop but we do not know how severe this may be. The moving average relationships for the two stocks show what happens at this balance point.

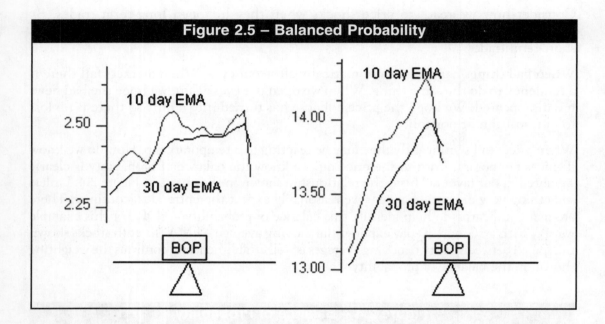

Figure 2.5 – Balanced Probability

Truth is, there is simply no reliable way to tell in advance how the price action is likely to develop. The uptrend may resume or the downtrend may become dominant. Look closely at these two charts. Is there any way to decide the likely outcome over the following days or weeks? This is not a trick question. It is a question we all ask ourselves in real time. If we fool ourselves with the answer in this trade we are likely to do the same in even shorter-term trades.

The effectiveness of the answer depends on how well we understand trading and the market. If we approach it from a probability perspective there is only one valid conclusion – the balance of probability has shifted away from a continuation of the uptrend.

We could speculate about where we think this balance may shift in coming days. This would essentially be a guess. Until further price action develops we cannot confirm the accuracy of our guess. We use support levels and resistance points to help identify where the new balance of probability has shifted, but it is very difficult to predict this in advance. Instead we look for confirmation signals.

Examining the chart activity as shown we must conclude we simply do not know what is most likely to happen. This doesn't mean we panic. It means we have to take action to protect our profits and capital until we have a better idea of how the balance of probability will shift.

When the balance of probability shifts it makes sense to implement new stop loss, protect profit and protect capital strategies. There is a cost involved. It includes brokerage and, if necessary, the need to re-enter the new uptrend at perhaps slightly higher prices. These are the costs of insurance.

If the uptrend continues we take a new trading position. If the downtrend develops then we already have our capital, and profit. This is put to one side until a new uptrend is established and proven.

Figure 2.6 shows how these two stocks developed. The balance of probability shifted in favour of a downtrend as FCL continued to fall. The bank, WBC, recovered and started a new uptrend. The balance of probability shifted back to favour us. The trader who held on with WBC has a smirk on her face because she believes her faith in the future, or hope for the future, was justified. The trader who adopted the same approach with FCL has a very large hole in his pocket.

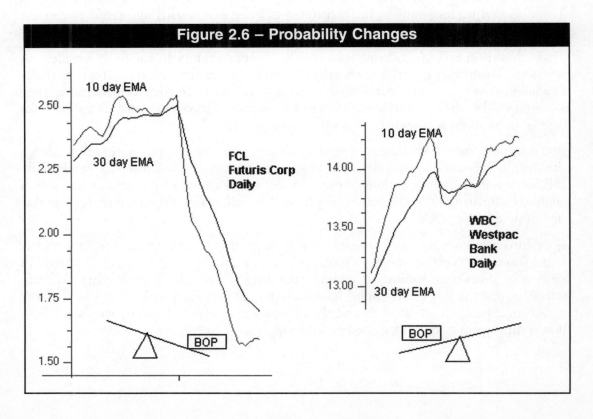

19

When the balance of probability shifts in open positions it is always a good time to reassess the stop loss and protect profit strategies. A defensive exit protects the trader and the investor against the possibility of a new dominant downtrend.

Until we are able to identify where the balance of probability is located it is unwise to pretend we can predict the future, either in the near-term or the long-term. Safety in the market comes from the effective management of risk by using defensive exits. It does not come from holding on to stock in the naive hope everything will be alright some time in the future.

REJECTING SABOTAGE

Good traders understand the role the balance of probability plays in selecting a trading opportunity. It plays a larger role in short-term trading. Better traders also understand the need to continue active monitoring of changes in this balance. When large events hit the market the balance changes quickly.

A short-term trade magnifies the impact of events. The shorter timeframe enhances emotional reactions. The FCL chart is unusual in its severity, but shift the timeframes to minutes rather than days and the price collapse becomes distressingly more common. These shorter trades are more finely attuned to price movements and profit targets are more sensitive to attack. Hesitation is often fatal.

Trades based on end-of-day price data give us the opportunity to carefully consider our reactions. The market is closed when we get the data. If necessary we have all night to sit up, to analyse, to worry, and to decide what we are going to do. Even given this additional time we often yield to the temptation to calculate the balance of probability where we would like it to be rather than acknowledge a significant shift.

In a day trade there is no time for lengthy analysis. We must recognise and acknowledge the shift in balance immediately. Even in short-term trades lasting three to five days the call for action is urgent. Failure of price to move as suggested by classic chart pattern analysis confirms a shift in the balance of probability. Failure to act turns a slightly profitable trade into a losing trade.

Look into your own trader's backpack. Is it better suited to a saboteur than to a trader? Until you throw out the saboteur's tools and explosives you give yourself little chance of success in short-term trading. Poor understanding of the role of probability on trade selection, and the way the changing balance is used to manage a trade is often at the core of our successful self-sabotage. In the next chapter we shift our focus to success to show how a short-term trade is identified and managed.

Chapter 3

MAGNIFYING

ERROR

Some modern trading approaches rely on the fuzzy logic of neural networks to make better trading decisions. Many traders rely on their own brand of fuzzy logic to identify trades and manage them. They are broadly successful because the timeframe they select for the trade provides room for non-critical errors. A trend lasting weeks or months is not abandoned because of small intra-day price movements, or even on the basis of an intra-day dip in prices below a major moving average line.

It is not appropriate to fine tune these trend trades to this level of management. The trend is more robust so it takes much larger price moves, or combinations of price activity, to signal an end to the trend. In shorter-term trades the trend is often more fragile and the intended return on the trade is more sensitive to comparatively minor price changes.

Many shopping malls are paved with tiles. Next time you visit take the time to select a line of tiles. It is an easy task to walk and stay within the narrow width of the tiles. If you wander slightly out of line there is no penalty. Now imagine walking the same narrow line on a steel beam. It's the same width but it hangs three metres above the ground. The task is exactly the same – walk within the line – but the tolerances are much finer. There is a larger penalty for any miss-step, just as there are larger penalties for errors in short-term trend trades. The principles are the same as those of longer-term trading but the risks make recovery more difficult.

There is less room for fuzzy thinking in short-term trading. The previous chapters have shown how to tighten our thinking about applying the balance of probability and respecting our analysis. These are two areas where common trading approaches lead to disaster in short-term trading. A third area is profit taking. After a brief discussion, we bring these factors together in a successful short-term sample trade.

The temptation to grab early profits is one of the major barriers to trading success for position traders. Instead of riding the trend as it develops just as their analysis suggested it would, these traders cannot wait to ring the cash register. Instead of substantial profits, they collect small profits.

In a trade planned as a short-term opportunity this lack of discipline severely reduces the returns available. The nature of short-term trading calls for the trader to allow the trade to develop fully as planned. Early exits limit rewards without changing the risk. Success demands good stop loss discipline and a better understanding of the relationship between trade planning, and stop loss exits to protect capital, and profits.

FINDING YOUR DEPTH

The entry price is critical in short-term trading because the duration of the trade, and hence the profit potential, is more limited. This does not mean the trader chases market prices. At times the trader must meet the asking price to be sure of getting into the trade. Some techniques rely on catching minor pullbacks after an initial opening burst of extreme excitement.

Deciding the best entry point involves two disciplines. The first is analysis of the opportunity and a decision about the best entry price in relation to the expected return from the trade. The second is the effective use of the depth of market information. This is a fleeting snapshot picture in time and is sometimes quite misleading. During the day the balance of buyers and sellers changes as orders are filled, or pulled, or altered. Prior to the open of trade the order lines fill up with planned, but unexecuted trades. This balance helps set the tone for the day and immediately suggests which strategies or potential trades may be more successful.

Before we take on short-term trading we need access to full depth of market data and a good understanding of what each of the three levels of depth is telling us. Consistent success in these timeframes is not possible using only the first level of data and a delayed data feed. The Stock Exchange Automated Trading System (SEATS) provides Australian traders with excellent access to vital market data.

Depth of market figures come in three levels. The first is Level 1 data. It tells the trader the number of buyers at the highest current bid and the number of sellers at the current ask. The second component of these figures – Level 2 data – is usually shown on a different screen as in Figure 3.1. It shows the consolidated volume at each price level. When the term 'undisclosed' or 'u/c' is added to the volume figure it normally means a very large order. These are consolidated summary figures.

The third SEATS screen – Level 3 data – shows a summary of the number of buyers and sellers at each price level below and above the current market price. It also shows the volume of orders at each level. This is used to confirm chart support levels. This is full disclosure of depth of market, or Level 3 data. This information is the most useful for traders.

We are all accustomed to using charting as a means of timing better entries and exits into trends. When we come to open the trade then there may be advantages in buying at particular times of the day. These advantages are created by the way the ASX order system works, and the way the opening of trade is handled.

Figure 3.1 – Level 2 and Level 3 Depth of Market

	99 Bids		**LEVEL 2 DATA**	555 Asks	
Buyers	Volume	Price	Price	Volume	Sellers
▶ 13	749627	1.260	1.270	434718	4
22	321200	1.250	1.280	674024	11
5	20914	1.240	1.290	230000	5
5	82250	1.230	1.300	358339	10
2	111300	1.220	1.310	147501	4
5	30000	1.210	1.320	41584	3

All orders are consolidated or combined at each price level

	103 Bids		**LEVEL 3 DATA**	552 Asks	
Buyers	Volume	Price	Price	Volume	Sellers
▶ 1	21627	1.260	1.280	6000	1
▶ 1	15500	1.260	1.280	25000	1
▶ 1	7500	1.260	1.280	388415	1
▶ 1	25000	1.260	1.280	75000	1
▶ 1	100000	1.260	1.280	20000	1
▶ 1	5000	1.260	1.280	21000	1
▶ 1	50000	1.260	1.280	50000	1
▶ 1	10000	1.260	1.280	12209	1
▶ 1	250000	1.260	1.280	413000	1
▶ 1	250000	1.260	1.290	20000	1
▶ 1	5000	1.260	1.290	50000	1
▶ 1	10000	1.260	1.290	20000	1
▶ 1	4000	1.260	1.290	100000	1
1	2500	1.250	1.290	20000	1
1	1000	1.250	1.300	231339	1
1	1200	1.250	1.300	20000	1
1	20000	1.250	1.300	50000	1

These are the individual orders from buyers at $1.26

Prior to the start of trading all shares go into a pre-open sequence. This means buyers and sellers place their orders before the market opens. Using the Level 3 depth of market screens, other traders see how many shares are available to buy, and at what price.

When the market starts trading several procedures are followed. The first is a rolling open where shares in larger blue chip companies start trading immediately along with a call of the board starting with A and finishing with Z. This means your proposed trade in Zylotech is delayed for 10 to 15 minutes.

The second feature is the way orders are matched on the open. In some cases the first sell order may be at $12.00 and the first buy order at $12.90. Traders use the ASX matching procedure on the open to get the 'opening price' for the share. By bidding ahead of his rivals, the trader is the first order filled when trading opens. It is filled at a price determined by the volume weighted average of the difference between the seller's price and the buyer's bid.

What is important is the way these procedures give a character to the opening of trade. On a bullish day the overnight excitement of the market is reflected in the opening of the market as these excited orders are matched on an alphabetical call of the board.

In *Share Trading* and *Better Trading* I suggested traders should wait until 20 minutes after the open so the market has time to set its direction for the day. Times have changed because we are now seeing many more market openings carry prices to extremes. In the first 10 to 20 minutes of trading the volatility of the market is excessive as shown in Figure 3.2. Quite simply, it overreacts, often dramatically, driving prices to their high or low for the day.

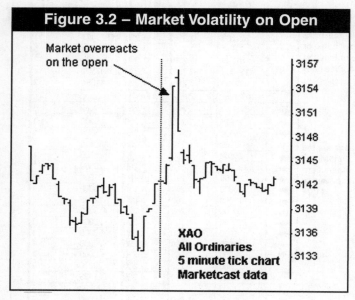

Figure 3.2 – Market Volatility on Open

Market overreacts on the open

3157
3154
3151
3148
3145
3142
3139
3136
3133

XAO
All Ordinaries
5 minute tick chart
Marketcast data

This is a market at an extreme and we use this to develop trading strategies. Depending on our objectives as buyers or sellers, there are advantages in waiting for the price to hit its extremes before taking action. Sellers have a decided advantage when they sell into a rising market in the first 20 minutes of trading. In contrast, bullish buyers have an advantage if they wait until the second hour of trading when the market typically pulls back from the rash excitement of the open. The combinations of time and opportunity are shown in Figure 3.3.

As more of the general public gains access to what used to be restricted information about the depth and structure of the market, and as more people understand how the opening mechanisms are implemented, we see increased volatility on the open and, to a lesser extent, on the close. Understanding this developing behaviour is an advantage used to improve our trading returns by managing a better entry decision.

PLANNING FOR FAILURE BRINGS SUCCESS

A sound profit strategy, a good eye open for risk, a fine judgement of the changing balance of probability and good entry management are all combined in a single successful short-term trade. Some of these trades are built around specific chart patterns and the sample BMS trade in Figure 3.4 illustrates both the success and shortcomings of these approaches. The trade returns 28% and opens the door to all the common trade emotions of fear and greed and introduces a third to torment short-term traders. It is regret and unless we learn to live with it, the short-term trader is in for an uncomfortable and unsatisfying experience.

The trade uses a price projection to measure previous price action and project future targets. It is most effective when used in conjunction with chart patterns which have a high probability of developing in a consistent way. Generally the base of the chosen pattern is measured and used to set a target based on the level of the subsequent price breakout.

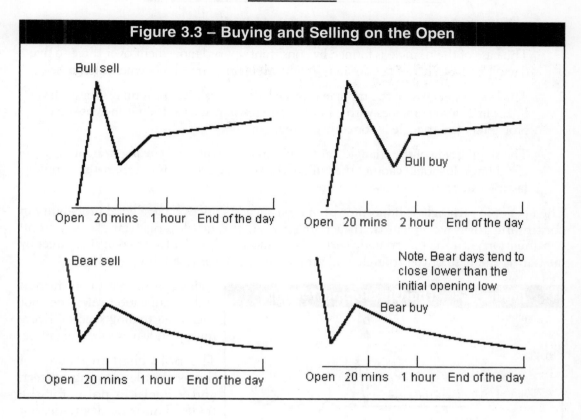

Figure 3.3 – Buying and Selling on the Open

There is a small collection of chart patterns which identify high probability outcomes. Although there are many fancy, and some fanciful, explanations for why they work, the truth, I suspect, is we do not know the exact reasons for their high level of success. Pattern trading is the basic starting point for short-term trading. Like many trading techniques, it is most effective when the chart patterns are clear and when they are carefully defined. Price patterns which closely *resemble* the carefully defined pattern, but do not match, are simply not good enough. The further the current pattern moves away from the stereotype pattern, the lower the level of probability the current pattern is a useful trading opportunity.

Some traders are perplexed when the pattern fails to develop as anticipated. They sometimes conclude the technique has failed when in fact it is a failure of their trading plan to take into account the full range of probable outcomes.

The trader's task is to identify the balance of probability. This also means recognising the conditions leading to the development of the least probable outcome. One of the more useful patterns is the upward sloping triangle.

The construction rules come in three parts:

1.   The base of the triangle is formed by consistent upward movement over three to five days. This base should not contain significant counter trend movements or pauses.

2.   The horizontal edge of the triangle is placed along a valid short-term resistance level. If this level also coincides with a longer-term resistance level then it increases the probability the triangle is correctly plotted.

3.   The sloping side of the triangle must conform to the rules for placing straight-edge trend lines. It should capture the bulk of the price action. This is a short-term trend lasting one to three weeks or more.

The up-sloping triangle is important because it suggests prices have a good probability of continuing to move upwards. In a rising trend, the up-sloping triangle is a trend continuation pattern. The triangle pattern also allows the trader to set an upside target by measuring the base of the triangle and projecting this measurement upwards.

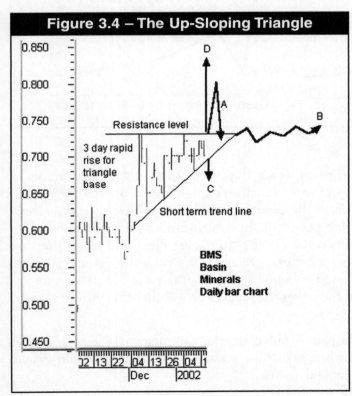

Figure 3.4 – The Up-Sloping Triangle

Following the exact construction and identification rules does not guarantee trading success. Every trade plan leaves room for failure.

The BMS chart in Figure 3.4 shows the developing pattern and a decision point for the trader. This is no day trade, but an entry in the next day or two after the last bar shown has the potential to develop into a powerful short-term three- to five-day trade. Breakouts from these patterns can be explosive. The short-term opportunity rests on longer-term and standard style analysis of daily bar charts.

Traders who want to use this pattern are expecting prices to breakout above the resistance level at $0.73. They are not expecting prices to collapse into a new downtrend, but in their trade planning they must make allowance for this possibility. If this pattern has an 80% probability of leading to a price rise, then there is a 20% probability it will not.

The range of probabilities in this 20% zone include:

a)   a breakout failure

b)   an insignificant pattern

c)   a trend collapse.

Each of the first three conditions, A through C, proves an exit signal because the trade has not developed as planned. Each shows the high-probability trade has become a dud.

The breakout failure is shown as line A in Figure 3.4. Price initially starts moving as expected, but then collapses back to, or below the resistance level. This price action suggests there is a reduced probability of the immediate uptrend continuing to meet the planned targets. Trades based on the triangle price projection are closed quickly, and often at a small profit. In some cases prices recover and go on to reach the projected targets. Rather than rely on luck and extraordinary events, experienced traders exit under these conditions. Their exit reflects a change in the balance of probabilities.

Despite this bullish pattern there are times where the pattern turns out to be insignificant or unimportant, as shown by line B. This type of failure also provides a time limit on how long the trade is held. The intersection of the horizontal resistance level and the up-sloping trend line is defined as a point in time. In this example, the tip of the triangle appears on 7 February. Traders who buy into this type of pattern before this date are expecting the price breakout to occur before 7 February. If prices do not move upwards, but continue to drift sideways beyond 7 February then the trade is classed as a failure. The inability of the pattern to develop delivers an exit signal. After this date there is very little chance of the trade developing as a triangle breakout. Depending on the time of entry, the trade may be showing a small profit. The trader is able to exit at breakeven or at a slight profit.

Short-term traders concentrate on line C as a measure of failure. A close below the trend line suggests the trend is ending. An exit under these conditions is usually at a loss.

Although the upward sloping triangle is a bullish pattern with a high probability of success it is also important to identify carefully the price conditions which suggest the pattern is failing.

MEET REGRET

Regret is usually partnered with success. Within a few days BMS reaches the triangle price projection target. How we react to this type of situation when price targets have been reached rapidly, plays an important role in developing short-term trading discipline.

We measure the base from the point where the start of the short-term sloping trend line intersects the vertical price bar at $0.63 to the resistance line at the top of the triangle. The value of this line – $0.13 – is projected upwards above the horizontal line forming the top edge of the triangle to set a price target at $0.86. This potential trade development is shown as line D.

Aggressive traders who entered this pattern development at $0.70 collect a 22.8% profit. Conservative traders who wait for confirmation of the pattern cannot enter until the day after the breakout, at around $0.80. This reduces their target profit to 7.5% and makes a good trade into a much poorer trade.

Not all traders set their sell order in advance, so when projected targets are hit so quickly greed and regret come knocking at the door. How much higher could this stock go? There are no past resistance points to work with so the trader must rely on projection techniques and tight stop loss conditions to manage this type of trade.

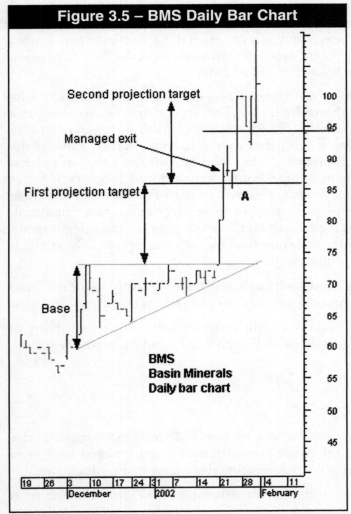

In a very strong general bull market there is around a 60% probability the target level will double once the first triangle target is reached. This takes the original target measurement, $0.13, and projects it above the first target at $0.86. This sets a new target at $0.99. This beckons with a 41.4% profit for the aggressive trader, and a better 23.7% return for the conservative trader. It is very easy to give into greed.

A 60% probability sounds enticing but this is not the strong bull market of 1999. The probability of achieving the second target is much lower so sensible trading suggests we should manage any further price rise very carefully with a tight stop loss.

The trade opens at $0.88 and keeps moving up as shown in Figure 3.5. We place a close stop just a tick below the opening price at $0.87. Once the trade moves to $0.90 the stop is shifted to $0.89, equal to the previous day's high. Beyond this level, the trader looks for continued signs of strong buying and weak selling. Sellers build a road block, increasing the number of sell orders at $0.92. It is time to sell out.

The most likely outcome of this close management is an exit at $0.90. This provides a 28.5% return for those who entered at $0.70, and a 12.5% profit for those who entered on confirmation of the breakout.

The price action in BMS continued to accelerate past the initial targets, reaching a high of $1.00. Double triangle target projections are infrequent outside strong bull markets. As traders we are percentage players. When the probabilities slip towards a coin toss outcome, we exit the trade.

We must accept the outcome and walk away. Or we can regret the outcome. This has important consequences because it eats away at our trading discipline. In this particular case the balance of probability drops from around 80% to around 50% after the price retreat.

REGRET IS NO SUCCESS

Traders who did not act on their stop loss – traders who froze at the wheel – survived not only to tell the tale, but to bring home a larger profit.

Or so the story goes, but for one important question. The trader who held onto BMS as it dipped back to $0.85 had abandoned his trading plan and ignored stop loss points designed to protect an open profit. Prices lift and in this example, the gamble pays off. When prices peak at $1.09, what trading plan, what stop loss approach, what consistent discipline is going to come to his aid to get out at $1.09 and lock in the open profit?

He has no method other than luck. Luck and greed got him through the pullback in area A. Does he rely on luck and greed to get out at the very top in the following day or does he wait until the day after?

On the chart it is easy. From the comfort of our armchair we point to the retrospective price on the chart, to achieve the best exit. But can we do this in real time? The answer is "Probably not". The trader who ignored stop loss discipline midway through the rise is the least likely person to rediscover stop loss discipline at the top of the rise. Without a stop loss strategy, and without the discipline to act to protect profits, he has no clear mechanism to determine which price retreat – 24 January or 30 January – is the signal of trend collapse.

Most likely he holds on, hoping luck comes to his rescue. When it does not and prices move back down towards the old targets around $0.92, he changes his thinking. Regret sours to revenge. Instead of taking what profit remains, typically these traders decide to get out when price moves up to $1.09 again. It can be a long and costly wait.

Without planning, trading slips easily into gambling mode. Without stop loss discipline the trade is built on hope and hammered together with greed. There are times when freezing in the trade delivers an unexpectedly good result. When this happens we need to develop a strict stop loss mechanism to lock in the bonus profits. I use an electronic stop loss service to do this.

Look hard enough and regret appears on every chart. Our task as short-term traders is to learn to live with it by concentrating on well planned and disciplined trades delivering profits on our terms.

HIGHLIGHTING WEAKNESS

Successful short-term trading highlights any weakness in our long-term trading strategies. What is a minor irritation in position trading has the potential to become a major weakness when trading timeframes are shortened. Walking the line in the mall is easier than walking the beam suspended above the ground because mistakes are rarely fatal.

Trading has always been about managing risk and this understanding distinguishes the novice from the professional. It is fashionable to talk about the rewards of trading but the realists talk about the risk and how it is managed. Short-term trading challenges us to explore these relationships in more detail and with greater precision. We can choose to examine this voluntarily, or let the market examine our approaches and highlight our weaknesses for us. The latter approach is a fast route to financial ruin.

Some traders fail to develop the skills, techniques or discipline necessary to consistently manage short-term trades. Traders whose discipline is corroded by regret are not satisfied with taking a small bite out of a much larger trend move. They look at the BMS trade above and cannot accept that an entry at $0.70 and an exit at $0.90 represents a successful short-term trade. The missed profits from the trade irritate and annoy traders, so when it comes time to capture another short-term or intra-day profit they abandon their trading plan and turn the trade into a longer-term trend trade. Sometimes it works but most times a planned short-term trade delivers only short-term profits. Success in shorter timeframes means shutting out regret and greed. Without this discipline short-term trading becomes ill-disciplined gambling.

Those who want to start from ground zero and step straight into the world of day trading have a very small chance of survival. Our objective in the remainder of this book is to examine a selection of techniques and approaches to extend your current trading skills into a tighter timeframe. It calls for an honest assessment of weaknesses in technique and emotional constraints. A few ideas, cherished by newcomers in search of a fast dollar, are also thrown overboard. We start with the idea that insider trading is a fast track to success.

PART II

FINDING

OPPORTUNITY

Chapter 4

INSIDE

RUNNING

A persistent rumour suggests true market success rests on inside trading. It is a pervasive idea infecting investment theory as well as trading. At heart the concept suggests advantage comes from knowing something before the rest of the market is aware of it. In investing this means finding undervalued companies before the market discovers them. In trading it implies access to confidential company information before it is released in a note to the stock exchange. In short-term trading, it is supposed to mean catching the news minutes or seconds before it breaks.

When we start to trade the market there is a sneaking suspicion information counts and that we can turn this into a profit. There is a little bit of Warren Buffett in all of us. Somewhere in the back of our mind lurks Benjamin Graham and his belief about buying sound companies that are temporarily undervalued. We believe if we identify a bargain situation when we have access to news before other market participants, then we have a profitable trade. All we do is buy ahead of the crowd. This is a useful investment strategy for stocks.

Access to this early information is considered so powerful that it provides an unfair opportunity for a small group to profit at the expense of the broader market. Our Exchange regulations reflect this concern with heavy penalties for inside trading. The inability to achieve many convictions for insider trading suggests the problem may be more complex and difficult to define than the simplistic rumours suggest.

The true insider, perhaps a company executive, acts by himself and tells no-one. The nasty insider allows family and friends access to shares at preferential prices prior to the listing of a new company. This practice was widespread with IPO – initial public offer – launches in the United States at the height of the technology boom at the end of last century. Neither of these insiders interest us. Our concern is with the insider tip which is one variation of the early release of market moving news.

Insider trading is not the same as informed trading. The difference between insider trading and informed trading is slim, but important – the former is illegal. In the real world some people start to suspect important information before others. This opinion is insignificant until they take a market position. When people back their suspicions with cash, or by taking unnecessary losses, then other traders listen. The informed buyer or seller has, at best, a one-day advantage because as soon as he takes a market position it shows up in the volume and price information. Other traders read the intent more quickly on a price chart than in the morning newspaper. Chart interpretation is a profitable skill and is worth developing.

If we believe short-term trading success rests on early access to news then we spend a lot of time, and money, searching for the most effective news delivery service. We subscribe to CNBC, pay for a live news feed, pay close attention to stock exchange notices, and cultivate friendships with brokers and analysts whom we believe have good relationships with company insiders. We dress this up in a fancy costume and call it in-depth research. Or we could call it at face value and admit we are trading on hot tips.

Getting fast news may be a problem, but the real problem is knowing what to do with it. Success in short-term trading rests upon using the news, or rumours of news, as the basis of further management of a trading opportunity. This is very different from traders who treat inside news as a complete trading solution – a guaranteed path to financial success.

News-based trading does offer short-term advantages if we use the news as a component of our trading plan. In the next few chapters we look at some successful strategies. The strategies mean little if we are still burdened with the popular perception that success depends on early access to news or some form of hot tip. We consider two examples below.

FROM THE INSIDE

This real story starts with a weekend backyard BBQ and we can speculate how some participants may have behaved. The BBQ was attended by a small group of friends, and a company insider. In the course of conversation over burnt sausages authorities alleged the guests were told of a news release timed for the coming Wednesday prior to the open of market. We need to be realistic about news. It does not spring ready-formed from thin air. Somebody is responsible for creating the news and company PR officers prepare the news release. By the time we get the news it has already passed through many hands and been available in one form or another for many days, or even weeks. Top-secret government agencies leak news on a regular basis despite the best security that taxpayers' money buys. When we talk of company secrecy and news embargoes we kid ourselves if we believe news comes as a surprise to everybody when it is released.

The proposed news release informed an unsuspecting market the company had signed agreements in principle to create a global market for its product. This is the stuff of giant profit dreams and, not unexpectedly, some of the people who attended the BBQ probably reached deep into their wallets and purchased stock when the market opened on Monday.

Our concern in this example is not with morality, but with the impact of this alleged insider trading. If this technique is successful then it is worth our time legally chasing news and news sources. If the technique does not yield a substantial advantage, then we employ our time more effectively by learning to use the news in different ways.

Imagine how the BBQ participants react. They jump into the market on Monday, buying the open. They worry that if they do not buy the open, other people may come into the possession of this same knowledge and take advantage of it. They fear paying a higher price on the open. Even with inside information, speed is an advantage. This is the way the novice trader, and even sometimes the experienced trader, thinks.

The chart shows exactly how the market has reacted to this development. This chart extract in Figure 4.1 covers the period before, and after, the news release. Take a moment to identify the point on this chart where you believe the news was released to the market. Work back three days from this bar, identify the Monday open and the date of the weekend BBQ.

You have a choice of leading price action at point A with a 20% increase in price for the day, or point B with a 29% rise. Perhaps point C is stronger evidence of this excitement with a 41% rise. Point D, with 22%, is only slightly worse than point E with a 23% rise for the day. Choose point A and you get to ride a 254% rise which would truly illustrate the advantages of inside trading, despite its illegality.

Somewhere on this chart is the inside advantage. Can you find it? The answer is over the page.

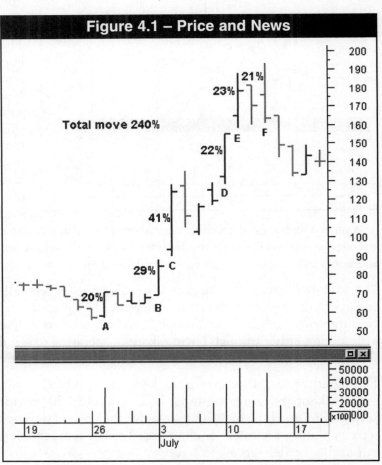

Figure 4.1 – Price and News

The news hit the market at point F, shown in Figure 4.2. Prices climbed rapidly on the release, and then fell back to close lower than the open. They continued falling over the next few days.

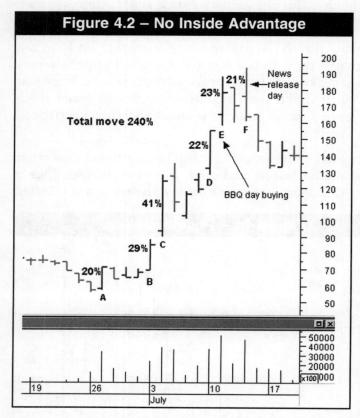

Figure 4.2 – No Inside Advantage

The total price move from point A to the high at point F is 254%. Those armed with the inside BBQ information entered some time during bar E and captured around 23% based on their hot tip. Even capturing this return called for good trading skill to exit at the very top price of $1.95. Failure to act on the day of the news announcement drops their hot tip insider trade back to around breakeven.

This example highlights three important points. The first is the non-exclusive nature of news. Many people knew, or suspected, good news was developing for this company. Their buying started around $0.55 and drove prices up to $1.50 before the insider's BBQ occurred. Does this mean all the previous buying was based on inside information?

It would be highly unlikely. It is a fair assumption some of the buying made use of specialist knowledge not available to the broader market. This does not disadvantage other buyers, and nor does it confer a major exclusive advantage on those who knew the information first.

This leads to the second point. The last traded price reflects all that is known, or rumoured, or suspected, or proven about the company. The price incorporates the thoughts of the most informed and the least informed investors who are prepared to back their judgement with money, either through buying shares, or refusing to sell their existing share holding. Their emotions are reflected as crowd psychology and captured in the activity of price.

The significance of this news is tracked, not by a BBQ invitation, but by chart analysis. The breakout above the resistance level around $0.70 provided ample evidence of a new rally. It confirmed the bullish break above the upward sloping triangle. Based on this price activity alone a technical or chart-based trader joins the developing trend at $0.80. An exit at the top delivers a 143% return.

The impact of news does not depend on its exclusivity. News is rarely unexpected or exclusive. Most times it is comprehensively leaked by rumour, or deliberate release, before the formal announcement to the market. We have the opportunity to follow the progress of this leak by closely observing price action. This provides an important day trading and short-term edge. We look at trading leaked news in the next chapter. News leaks provide a fruitful hunting ground and introduce the trading skills required for short-term trading.

The third point shows clearly how those who trade on hot tips play a loser's game. It is a fair assumption many of those who bought after the weekend BBQ still held shares when they dropped back to $1.30. Why? They entered the trade based on information from a third party without undertaking any real analysis for themselves. Typically they wait for the same third party to tell them when it is time to get out. Usually it's a long wait. Those who follow buy tips tend to wait for sell tips but, as brokerage records show, buy recommendations outnumber sell recommendations by ten to one.

The most important lesson from this chart is that inside information or hot tips, even if they are accurate, very rarely give us a significant advantage in the market. We should assume there are always others who have far better knowledge than we do about what is happening, and that their buying and their rumours show up in the price action long before we get to hear about it. We need to know our place in the information chain. Accept this and we turn our attention to areas where we get a real edge in the market rather than wasting time chasing an imaginary edge.

SUSPENDED INFORMATION

Early access to news poses one set of problems. The reverse situation occurs when a company is suspended from trading pending news and we use a real suspension announcement to examine how news, or lack of it, is incorporated into a trading plan. The company name is changed to MDHU and the price activity illustrates how an inside trader *might* react and considers the advantages he might enjoy.

On Thursday MDHU commenced trading after a short suspension, pending a news announcement. The news announcement was not received favourably by the market and price rapidly fell to a close at $0.47 as shown in Figure 4.3. It is true buying the

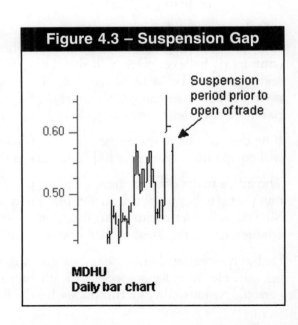

Figure 4.3 – Suspension Gap

Suspension period prior to open of trade

0.60

0.50

MDHU
Daily bar chart

rumour – if one existed – prior to the news announcement returned a useful profit. However, it is also true it is difficult to sell at or near the high of the day, at $0.58, once MDHU started trading on Thursday. There is a 20% return available for those who bought around $0.48 and sold at around $0.58. Those who sold at $0.55 saw returns shrink to 14%.

Let us assume for a moment at least one of those who bought at $0.48 prior to the price rise on expectation of a news announcement was an 'inside trader' using information not known to the wider public. How well could this fictitious person have done? Did this knowledge give the fictitious trader an advantage over the rest of the traders?

I suspect the answer is likely to be "No" for several reasons. This trader did not hear about MDHU until it started to recover after the collapse. This sudden recovery suggests the possibility of some informed buying. He buys at around $0.48. The best exit, at $0.66, returns a 37% profit. By comparison, a simple trend trade based on chart analysis collects 42% by following easily defined trading rules. Our inside trader is relying on the hot tip to be accurate and has no plan other than hoping his hot tip works.

How likely is the inside fictitious trader to exit MDHU at $0.66? He bought MDHU in anticipation of a news announcement. At the time MDHU hits $0.66 the news announcement has not been made. This trader believes price will skyrocket when the market gets to know the news he already knows. As a result he does not sell before the temporary MDHU suspension, pending a news announcement.

When the announcement is made, and MDHU starts trading again, the price dips quickly to $0.58 and then lower. This is the opposite reaction to the one the inside trader expects. How is he likely to handle this?

If he has spare cash he may become a buyer again. He fools himself by rationalising that the market does not yet fully understand the importance of the news. Once it does, he confidently believes prices will rise above the old high of $0.66. This is a classic mistake and a common belief in all types of novice trading. Normally the novice hopes a falling price will rise so he can get his money back. The inside trader thinks the same way, but he has more confidence because of his hot tip.

If he does not have spare cash, then he is still likely to hold on to the stock believing it will go up once the market fully appreciates the impact of the news.

The inside trader does not have a trading plan. All he has is a hot tip. The person who gave him the tip to buy is unlikely to give him a new hot tip to sell. The hot tip vendor also believes MDHU will react positively to the news. They wait, often in vain, for the price to rocket upwards again. If it does not then how is our inside trader going to decide when to sell?

He has no trading plan, so he is most likely to wait for another hot tip to tell him when to get out. He waits for somebody to tell him what to do because he has refused to take personal responsibility for this trade when he first brought it. Outsiders think inside trading is smart, but most times it is a dummy approach encouraging people to hold onto stock until someone tells them to jump.

With a close on Thursday at $0.47, do you think our fictitious inside trader who purchased MDHU at $0.48 is going to sell? Probably not. If prices drop further it is even more unlikely he will sell. Acting on a tip, or inside information, suggests he does not have good trading discipline. This is the type of trader who rides the price all the way to the bottom and then sells in disgust.

CATCHING THE RUMOUR

If we assume this rise in MDHU is a rumour-driven rise in anticipation of a news event, then how is it best traded?

Smart traders identify news-driven events from the way price behaves. The equilateral triangle alerts them to a stock waiting for a news event. Traders do not have to know what the news event is, or the reliability of the rumour. Once they see the price start to run the smart trader buys. Many traders follow these tactics when they look for unusual price increases. They trade rallies based on rumours of news events.

The news event trader looks for these rumour run ups. On an intra-day basis he buys in the area shown in Figure 4.4. The smartest of these traders aim for a defined return from the trade in situations like MDHU where there is no chart support for a news event. By taking a defined return, shown in the rumour sell area on the chart, the trader protects himself against the adverse effect of a poorly received news event. The rumour is often more enthusiastic than justified by the real news.

We see this overreaction with MDHU as prices opened much lower after the news announcement. The danger in all rumour and news-based trading is a suspension from trading. It is a danger because it cools the ardour of the crowd. There is time for the excitement to subside and when this happens other traders make a more rational judgement. The rumour-based trader aims to capture exuberance, not reality. This often makes the news-based exit less successful because much of the potential profit is surrendered.

The legitimate news and rumour-based trader does not use any 'inside' knowledge

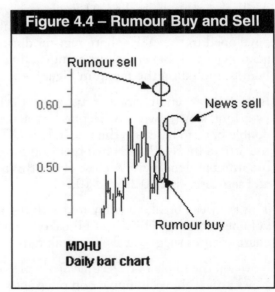

Figure 4.4 – Rumour Buy and Sell

Rumour sell

News sell

Rumour buy

MDHU
Daily bar chart

of news events to make this trade. He uses his knowledge of price behaviour to recognise the impact of rumour on price, and to trade the resulting rise. These skills are available to anybody who uses chart analysis. The information is available to anybody who collects end-of-day price data. The advantage enjoyed by the illegal inside trader is limited because as soon as he buys in large enough numbers to change the market price, his secret is out in the open.

READERS' DUMPS AND BUMPS

Every week I receive a number of well-intentioned tips about stocks. Some come from reputable sources such as brokerage reports and newspapers. Some come from less reliable sources, such as emails and phone calls, and some come from suspect sources, such as chat rooms. The worst are unsolicited emails recommending overseas listed stocks or those which plead; "Please send money – cash only – to Nigeria". These I throw in the bin and ask their ISP to block further spam mail.

A few tips I subject to further charting and technical analysis and this sometimes tells me about the impact of the report on other readers. These bumps or dumps provide short-term trading opportunities because the report attracts an emotional crowd in search of easy money without hard work.

There are nearly 2,000 listed companies, and only a handful receive coverage from the financial press, or from brokerages. Naturally our attention is attracted to those mentioned, and we are more likely to take a look at them. This can develop into a readers' bump which is a temporary change in the overall trend and a fast trading opportunity.

The Speculator column in *The Bulletin* is used by many people as a source of 'tips'. For a while the column tracked AI Engineering and the coverage had an undoubted impact on individual stocks. "This column probably had a lot to do with the instability that developed in the AIE's share register during the past 12 months," the column's author acknowledged. Several short-term trading opportunities developed from these readers' bumps, including the bump in Figure 4.5.

Is this rise a trend change or just a short-term opportunity? The AIE chart is dominated by a long slow downtrend defined by a straight-edge trend line moving towards a new double bottom based on the low in June. We assess this without knowing anything about the article in *The Bulletin* by observing the resistance level at $0.185. Prices are likely to run into problems here. A close above this resistance level suggests the breakout is for real and sets targets at $0.22 and $0.26.

This is a weak breakout compared with the June rise supported by a significant increase in volume in area A. The current breakout is a weak up move with low trading volume. Basic chart analysis suggests this is a weak rally.

Now add the impact of *The Bulletin* article. The rise starts on *The Bulletin* publication day. News articles have an impact on price activity and this can be a trap. When we are aware of these 'tips' we should treat the price activity with additional caution as with low-priced and low-volume stocks, the impact is often short-lived. If we are not aware of the news story then good chart analysis still protects us by distinguishing between a trend change and a rally. The downtrend was confirmed in the following weeks with prices slipping to $0.11. Readers' bumps are very short-term opportunities.

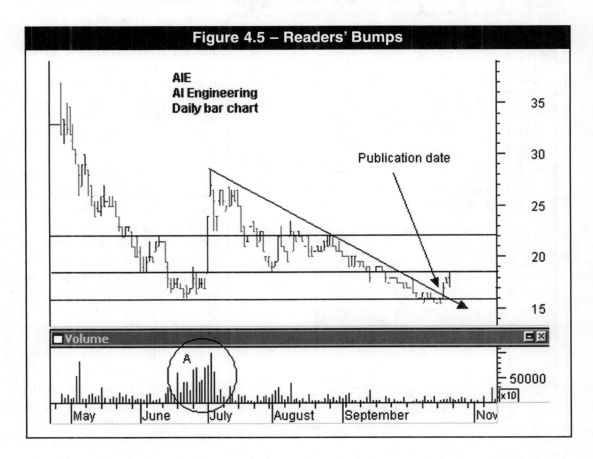

Figure 4.5 – Readers' Bumps

NASTY NEWS

The opposite of a readers' bump is a readers' dump after nasty company news. The readers' dump inflicts severe financial damage so there is an important protective advantage if it is recognised early. This brings together those who follow the financial press, the relationship between rumour and news, and the sudden rumour-driven price drops which catch the uninformed and unskilled by surprise. News often leaks and we do not need to be an insider to catch the leak early.

We use SOH in Figure 4.6 as an example of this process. SOH had been in a steady downtrend for ten months and many thought it was drifting into bargain territory. The temporary support levels provide important signals. The dip below support at point A is the first warning of significant problems.

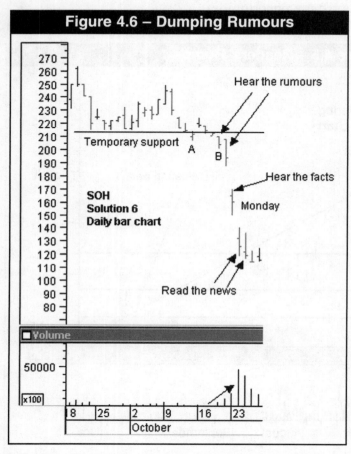

Figure 4.6 – Dumping Rumours

The financial press speculated about SOH and this shows up in the beginning of the readers' dump pattern with the break below temporary support at point B with accelerating volume. People read the rumour and decide to act. The rumour is the first confirmation of their worst fears.

The second stage of the readers' dump is when the facts are actually released to the market. SOH made its announcement on Monday and those with access to intra-day screens, live news feeds, or who had read the well-informed article in *The Australian Financial Review*, were ready to exit SOH at almost any price.

These well-informed people are not the general public. They are professional, or semi-professional traders. They are valued clients who have been contacted by their brokers. They are probably not you, or the mums and dads. We get to hear the facts as a news report on the TV, or read about it the next day.

This is when the readers' dump really accelerates. We see substantially increased volume and a significant gap down in prices. This action confirms the new and accelerated downtrend. The dump is a three- to five-day pattern. It starts with rumour, accelerates with the release of facts, and plummets as the news spreads more widely in the general public.

This is not a conspiracy. It is a typical reaction to rumour and news. The fall below the temporary support level on increased volume is like a flashing ambulance light. We know there has been an accident but we do not know the details. It is a signal to take defensive action if we own the stock. If we ignore the chart signal we run the risk of being dumped as rumour turns into fact and then into news. In short-term trading we try to act before the news and often there is no shortage of advance warning shown in the charts.

Chasing early or inside news distracts the trader from more effective trading methods. Rather than jogging down the inside trader's path and attempting to find unexpected news events before they happen, the trader benefits from news events which companies are happy to leak in advance. Our short-term trading advantage comes from the way we use our skill to exploit the same information known by everybody else. Our edge is not short-lived and fleeting. It is consistently applied to exploit short-term opportunities. We look at how to expand this edge in the next chapter.

☰ MARKSMAN'S NOTES

➜ Inside news provides a limited advantage.

➜ Inside news leaks and this shows up in price action days, or weeks, before the official news release.

➜ Hot tips give only the buy side of the trading equation and do not answer the question, "When do I sell?"

➜ Learn to identify news rumours from chart patterns or changes in price ranges.

➜ Buy the rumour and sell when the news is released.

➜ Use the financial press to identify readers' bumps.

➜ Readers' dumps are dangerous. Protect yourself by using a chart to identify them as they develop.

➜ Avoid conspiracy theories. They are a distraction from real trading opportunities.

Chapter 5

LEAKED
NEWS

News is the lifeblood of the market. It colours our view of the future prospects of the economy, of industry sectors, and of the companies we choose for investment or trading. When news was difficult to come by there was an important advantage in getting early access. In the nineteenth century, China traders grabbed the advantage by posting lookouts on Hong Kong's mountain peaks and sending a fast boat to meet the incoming mail ships. Collecting the mail and papers early provided an important trading edge.

In the nineteenth century brokerages built offices near the stock exchange so runners could dash across the street to deliver trading instructions based on breaking news. The traders' advantage was found in the area A on the diagram in Figure 5.1. The slower spread of news gave an advantage to those who had it first.

Despite fibre optics, cable news and internet trading, some brokerages still find prestige in being physically close to the stock exchange. Many people still believe news provides the most important edge and they attempt to apply the precepts of the last century to modern markets that demand, and get, continuous disclosure. Now our news trading advantage is confined to a small window of opportunity, shown in area B. News spreads more rapidly – almost instantaneously – so there is less time for opportunity to develop. By the end of day one we assume most of the general public is aware of what happened.

News of victory at Waterloo in 1815 took 24 hours to cross the channel to England. The noise of the 1883 volcanic explosion from Mount Krakatoa in the Indonesian Archipelago took 35 hours to circle the globe. News of the terrorist attack on the New York World Trade Center sped around the world in minutes.

When our trades are based on first access to breaking news we go head to head with full-time professionals trading other people's money. We also deprive ourselves of important advantages delivered by increased desktop computing power.

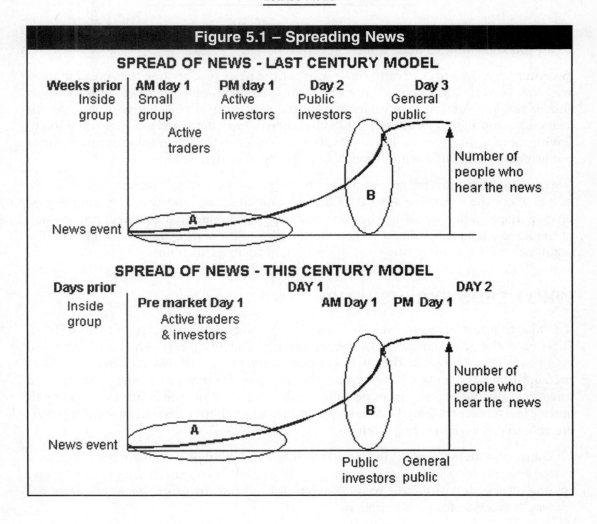

Figure 5.1 – Spreading News

The advantage comes from the way we use information rather than from when we get information. Desktop charting and analytical packages provide the power to analyse markets with as much speed and efficiency as our professional competitors. We move in smaller size trades, spending $5,000 or $50,000 rather than $500,000 or more when we trade. It is an important advantage and provides us with access to market segments closed to the institutional professionals.

The professionals have many advantages in short-term markets. Perhaps the most important is their ability to know what to do with the news when they hear it. Sure, we think we know what to do but the truth reveals a different reality. How often have you followed a good dividend announcement expecting to see a price jump only to watch a price fall? You may be part of a large group of traders who lose money trading dividend announcements when the market reacts in a contrary fashion. Knowing the news in advance does not mean you know how to trade it most effectively.

A century ago the prizes went to those who got the news first because the spread of news was slow. Now the prizes go to those who most effectively apply the news. This paradigm shift is the key development underpinning the explosion in personal trading in recent years. The shift has taken us from not having enough news delivered in a timely fashion to having more real-time news and information than we can handle. Instead of finding news our attention shifts to sorting through news for news of significance.

We can reasonably assume any significant news spreads so quickly that most people know of it at about the same time as we do. Use this assumption and the keys to trading success change shape. When we all use the same news, apply the same analytical techniques, look at the same charts and indicators then victory goes to those with the most trading skill – and nowhere is this more true than in short-term trading timeframes.

WHO NEEDS EXCLUSIVITY?

The idea that first access to exclusive news underpins trading success is a powerful belief. It is one of the most significant of the market myths standing between us and successful trading. It is so ingrained that it is difficult to overturn, and yet its defeat is a vital precondition of success. Move beyond this myth and a vast panorama of short- and long-term trading opportunities becomes visible. Stay within the confines of the myth and we feel forever frustrated by the way it appears that others, with exclusive news access, are able to defeat our trading attempts.

Of course the financial news industry, from financial journals to cable television, has a vested interest in convincing us there is a direct link between news, opportunity and trading success. It may be true to some extent for full-time institutional and professional traders. It is less so for private traders.

Our focus is on short-term trading techniques, but stand back for a minute and consider the chart of the American power company, Enron, in Figure 5.2. I have two questions for readers. The first is based on your purchase of stock in this company when it was trading at $80. At what price and at what time would you make a decision to get out of this losing trade?

The second question relates to the entry opportunity in September. Would you buy at this time?

The trader takes one look at this chart and immediately concludes this is a stock in a downtrend. He does not buy into it at any time in this twelve-month period.

The investor never looks at this chart. Instead he relies on recommendations made by those who use fundamental analysis. Goldman Sach's top analyst, Abby Cohen, called this stock 'Good value' in September. Other analysts had called Enron, America's seventh largest company, "one of the most innovative US companies" only weeks before the collapse.

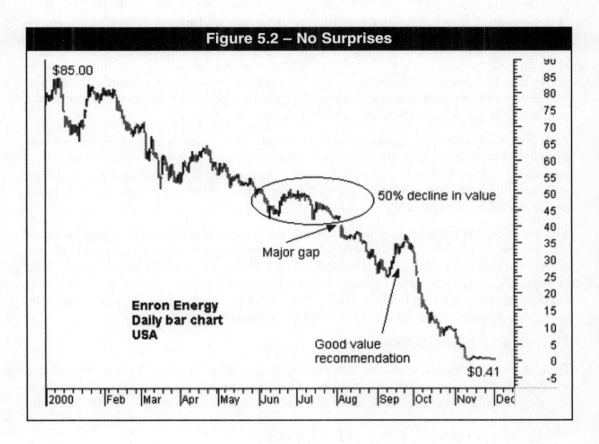

this stock 'Good value' in September. Other analysts had called Enron, America's seventh largest company, "one of the most innovative US companies" only weeks before the collapse.

The collapse was described by financial commentators as "stunning in its speed and severity". This is one comment about Enron that is absolutely false. Even if we held onto our shares purchased at the highs in January, by July it is clear this stock is headed in only one direction.

How do investors explain this sudden collapse? The fundamental analysts warn of a high P/E ratio, but only after the stock has collapsed. They point to insider selling as a warning sign. By June 2001, 16 members of Enron's top management had sold $164 million in shares. At the time analysts said this was a bullish signal. After the collapse they said it was a bearish signal.

Management was tight lipped about financial performance, delivering hard-to-understand reports. "It's a complicated business" seemed to be the excuse that satisfied most analysts

– at the time. Then there were unusual related party transactions appearing in the financial reports. Highly paid analysts seemed to miss those at the time, but found them when the price dipped towards $0.50. Finally investors were warned of the collapse by the departure of the chief executive. The analysts spin on this event told investors new management blood would take the company to new heights.

How do traders explain the slow collapse of Enron or WorldCom? Quite simply, they do not bother because a simple glance at the Enron chart at any time between March and November tells them this stock is a dog. Later they read of the reasons with detached interest. It does not hurt them because they did not buy the stock.

The investors who buy Enron on brokerage advice in March or September expose themselves to greater risk in the market because once they have made their choice they believe no further action is required. Rather than just blindly buying and holding, they seek out the best advice available and then buy and hold. They see risk as primarily being in the selection of the stock.

The point of this exercise goes to the core of the relationship between information and action. The chart is available to everybody. The price action shown for Enron, WorldCom or any other stock, is objective and verifiable. It is not manipulated by analysts' projections, by guesswork based on sloppy accounting, or subject to fair value calculations. It is simply a record of prices actually paid for Enron shares over the twelve-month period shown on the chart, as the company slipped from $85.00 to $0.41.

There is no exclusive information here.

Yet one group of traders and investors rode this stock from the very high of $80.00 and still held it when the company was delisted. They claim insiders knew what was happening and they should have warned investors. Another group took one look at the chart and refused to buy the stock simply because it was in a downtrend. A third group sold short into this massive downtrend and made a fortune.

The difference in results is not due to access to exclusive information. It is a direct result of trading skill. We all have access to the same information, but only some are able to use it effectively. Success in short-term trading depends on your ability to deal with market reality and not be blinded by market myth.

News is important, but assume everybody has it.

HURRAH FOR MARKET INEFFICIENCY

It is easier to trade the impact of news when we know the news events in advance. The opportunity to hone our skills here develops the ability to trade surprise news and in Chapter 7 we look at these methods. In this chapter we examine methods for trading news everybody knows is coming. We start with dividend announcements and later look at tactics for trading earnings announcements. If we believe early or exclusive access to news is a prerequisite for trading success then the widespread knowledge of dividend dates appears to provide no trading opportunity. If we accept it is what we do with news that counts, then dividend dates provide a variety of short-term trading opportunities.

The efficient market theory says all known information is already discounted by the market. Information is immediately reflected in the price due to participants acting in a rational way upon the information. This theory claims it is not possible to beat the market because price already reflects what is happening. This theory ignores market inefficiency.

This theory is often teamed with the random walk theory which says each traded price is an independent event, similar to a coin toss. This means yesterday's price has no relationship with today's price, or tomorrow's price. This theory also claims it is not possible to beat the market. The theory ignores the emotional content of price.

Traders and others who outperform the market recognise the emotional content in price and the repeated behaviour of crowds. These factors are what distinguish technical and charting analysis from the efficient market theory. Chartists believe all that is known, unknown, rumoured and suspected is reflected in the last traded price – but they do not assume market players are rational. The emotional content of price provides the margin exploited by short-term trading. When dividends are announced they arouse emotions and this drives price beyond its previously traded levels.

Fortunately for us, the efficient market theory is just theory. The regular market inefficiencies allow traders to beat the market. Market inefficiencies include emotionally driven prices, the distortion of price activity as a result of greed and fear, and the impact of crowd psychology.

APPLYING THE DATES

The core of success in these strategies depends on market inefficiency. This inefficiency also applies to dividend announcements where the impact is widely known and felt. This applies in a bullish market and is built around the widespread confusion about the ex-dividend date. In the example in Figure 5.3 we assume the dividend is announced on 1 June. The stock goes ex-dividend on 10 June. The stock continues to trade without the current dividend until the next dividend is announced. The record date is 15 June.

The key question is this: At what date do we lose the entitlement to the dividend? Experienced traders know shares purchased on 9 June carry an entitlement to the dividend. The entitlement period ends prior to the *start* of the ex-dividend trading day – effectively it ends with the close of trading on 9 June. Shares traded prior to 10 June are technically cum-dividend. On 10 June the stocks are quoted ex-dividend. This means stocks bought on 10 June no longer give the buyer an entitlement to collect the dividend.

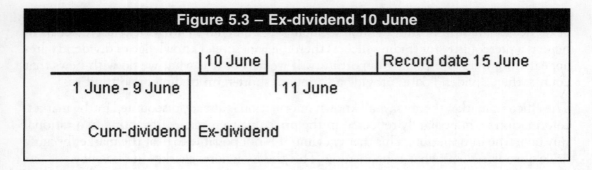

Figure 5.3 – Ex-dividend 10 June

| 10 June | Record date 15 June |

1 June - 9 June | 11 June

Cum-dividend | Ex-dividend

Inexperienced traders and investors often think the stock loses the entitlement to the dividend at the *end* of the ex-dividend date. They believe if they buy stock on 10 June – the ex-dividend date – they are entitled to the dividend. They believe if they buy stock on 11 June, the day after the stock goes ex-dividend, they are not entitled to the dividend.

Experienced and quick traders see the opportunity inherent in this confusion. On the opening of trade on 10 June there may be a few buyers who still believe they can buy the stock and get the dividend. This misconception means they bid the same price, or sometimes even a higher price, than yesterday's closing price of the stock. They believe they are getting an extra $0.30 dividend when, in fact, they are losing it.

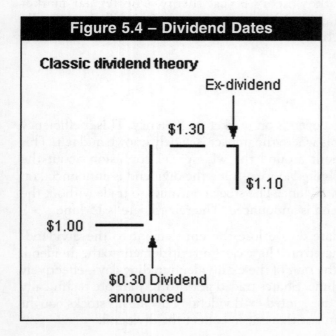

Figure 5.4 – Dividend Dates

Classic dividend theory

Ex-dividend

$1.30

$1.10

$1.00

$0.30 Dividend announced

Inefficient markets provide trading opportunities. Information and skill is not evenly dispersed and the disparities are more pronounced as we move away from the top 100 or 200 stocks that are closely followed by herds of analysts.

For the trader who purchased stock at $1.00 this provides an opportunity to collect a 60% return on the trade as shown in Figure 5.4. She does this by selling on the open as soon as the stock goes ex-dividend. Her final trade is made up of two components. First she collects a $0.30 dividend she is entitled to. Then she collects a $0.30 profit based on her purchase price of $1.00 and her exit price at $1.30. In this example her total return is $0.60 from a trade entered at $1.00. Even if the opening price falls to $1.28, $1.25, or even $1.15 the trader is still able to combine her dividend entitlement with a healthy capital gain from simply buying and selling the shares.

The record date shown in the previous diagram is a hangover from the days when trades were completed with paper scrip. It sometimes took weeks for the scrip for trades completed on 9 June to arrive at the broker or the share registry. Until the share registry received the scrip for all trades on 9 June they were unable to determine who was entitled to the dividend. The record date is the last date for recording who owned what shares on 9 June. These days, with electronic scrip this process is completed almost immediately. However the record date is usually still set around 10 days after the stock goes ex-dividend.

DIVIDENDS AND PRICE

A dividend announcement is a unique market event. It is one of the few times when traders and investors know, in advance, the exact date of a major news event which changes the market price of a stock. Dividend announcement dates are generally known, or guessed at. The data provider, JustData – www.justdata.com.au – provides a rolling list of last year's dividend announcement dates as shown in Figure 5.5. The size of the dividend is subject to well-informed rumour and speculation. This is our opportunity to make the dividend work for us.

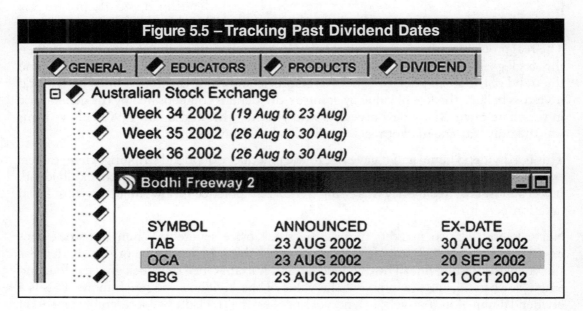

Figure 5.5 – Tracking Past Dividend Dates

SYMBOL	ANNOUNCED	EX-DATE
TAB	23 AUG 2002	30 AUG 2002
OCA	23 AUG 2002	20 SEP 2002
BBG	23 AUG 2002	21 OCT 2002

Before we develop an effective trading or investment strategy for capturing the value of dividends we need to clearly understand the impact of dividends on market price. The theory treats the value of the dividend as a bonus to the existing market price. A $0.10 dividend is expected to increase the market price by $0.10. When the stock goes ex-dividend the theory suggests the price will pull back to the same level as it was before the dividend was announced. This theoretical relationship is shown as the thick black line in Figure 5.6.

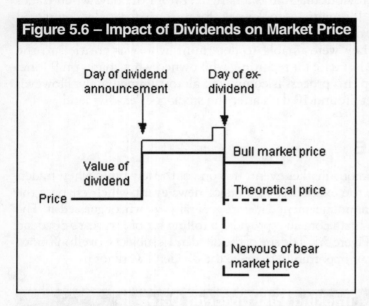

Figure 5.6 – Impact of Dividends on Market Price

Sometimes markets are easily excited so this strict theoretical relationship is distorted as people are carried away with the value of the dividend as shown by the thin line. This is the emotional content in price and adds a fillip to short-term profits.

However the theory remains valid because once the dividend is announced, the existing share price is adjusted to reflect the new additional value of the dividend. This excitement on the day of the announcement, or in the days leading up to it, provides a number of trading opportunities.

The real problem with the theoretical behaviour is at the other end of the process – when the stock goes ex-dividend. In a bull market the stock price typically falls just a little and the trend of the stock price continues as before, as shown by the dotted line. Traders and investors believe the loss of value by going ex-dividend is compensated by the general rise in the share price. Many new investors who watched this in the late 1990s believed this was the only way the market reacts to dividend announcements.

This is a dividend bump and it gave rise to the practice of dividend stripping. Here, traders bought the stock on the day of the announcement and sold it on the day it went ex-dividend. It was almost risk-free money in a rising trend. This practice is now subject to substantial taxation penalties.

Nervous and bearish markets punish the stock price severely. When the stock goes ex-dividend the market price falls by much more than the lost value of the dividend as shown by the dashed line. The dividend is a last hurrah. Once the stock goes ex-dividend a new downtrend starts, wiping out the value of the dividend and much more. This is a dividend dump. Alternatively, in a nervous market, the stock drops considerably in market price and then trends sideways. The theoretical value of the dividend to stock holders is destroyed by the collapse in price and shareholders are worse off than if they had sold the stock before the dividend announcement.

The challenge for traders is to capture the full value of a dividend with smarter trading. There are three strategies and all rely on the price activity before the stock goes ex-dividend.

1.   Trading the bump with price leverage

2.   Trading the bump or dump with derivative leverage

3.   Making the dividend work when we already own the stock as an investment.

We examine the first two strategies in the next chapter. Although it is not, strictly speaking, a short-term strategy, the notes below consider the third strategy – to make the dividend work when we already own the stock as a position trade.

RETAINING DIVIDENDS

The danger in nervous markets is that the market price fall when the stock goes ex-dividend is so large that it wipes out the dollar value of the dividend. A dividend of $0.05 is poor compensation when the ex-dividend price falls by $0.15.

An effective short-term strategy captures the emotional lift in prices created by the dividend announcement. The position is sold just before the stock goes ex-dividend. This is similar to dividend stripping and captures the value of the dividend as reflected in market price in this example with Australian Stock Exchange in Figure 5.7. The difference is in the timing. Selling to capture the dividend after the stock goes ex-dividend attracts a tax penalty. Instead we sell before and in nervous markets this approach captures the full value of the dividend. Those who follow a buy and hold strategy may find the value of the dividend is completely destroyed by subsequent market action.

A more effective strategy is to hold onto the stock and apply

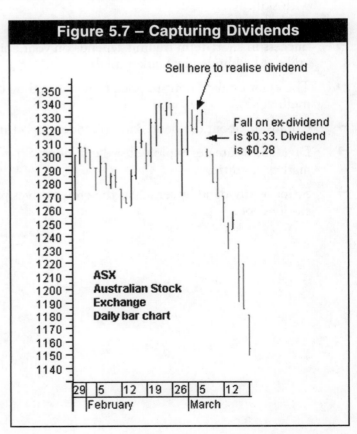

Figure 5.7 – Capturing Dividends

Sell here to realise dividend

Fall on ex-dividend is $0.33. Dividend is $0.28

ASX
Australian Stock
Exchange
Daily bar chart

derivative trading strategies using warrants or options. This requires additional capital and not all investors are comfortable with this because they believe it increases risk. The leverage offered by these derivatives means a small dollar amount quickly generates a large dollar return equal to or greater than the dollar return expected from the dividend on the underlying stock position. With this cash in hand, the investor is protected against the loss of the dividend due to extreme adverse price movements. We step into the world of derivatives in the next chapter.

SHARPSHOOTER'S NOTES

→ Exclusive news is an illusion because news spreads so quickly.

→ News is important, but assume everybody has it.

→ Leaked news is available to everybody so the advantage goes to those who trade with skill.

→ We all use the same charts for analysis, so trading skill makes the difference.

→ Success in short-term trading depends on your ability to deal with market reality and not be blinded by market myth.

→ The emotional content in price provides trading opportunity from market inefficiency.

→ Confusion about dividend dates provides opportunity.

→ Dividend strategies exploit crowd emotions. Strategies change in bull or bear market conditions.

→ Strip the dividend by selling as the crowd drives price up before the stock goes ex-dividend.

Chapter 6

EARNING A

DIVIDEND

News does not have to be exclusive to be profitable and this chapter uses a real trade to explain how common news is used to generate uncommon profits. Dividends and earnings announcements are the bread and butter of leaked news and offer opportunities to collect four day returns of 70% or more. Earnings reports carry a dividend announcement. This presents us with two distinct types of short-term trading opportunities. The first is built around the earnings announcement and includes the days before the official news release. The second opportunity is structured around the dividend dates and the day the stock goes ex-dividend. Emotional excitement builds on these dates because many people feel they will somehow miss out if they do not get the stock before it goes ex-dividend.

I love emotional trading and emotional markets. The behaviour of greedy people is more easily anticipated and this provides many short-term trading opportunities. The market conveniently groups this behaviour into a regular timeframe most commentators call earnings season. Companies tend to report financial results at about the same time twice a year. This herd behaviour concentrates a particular type of emotional behaviour into two relatively short time periods. People who give only passing attention to the market start to pay close attention as earnings results are released. There is a larger crowd for traders to play with.

Many people like to believe there is not a level playing field in the market. It is a handy excuse used to explain away their inability to trade. When it comes to carefully leaked news events, some traders point to the so called 'whisper number' as evidence the insiders have the best running. This number was purported to be generated by 'the street' and kept secret from the general public. Here's how people assumed it worked: A company may announce a public figure based on a 20% earnings increase. In the bull market of the '90s, just meeting this figure was not enough, particularly as many companies were beating their earnings forecasts. In carefully managed private briefings, the company told selected analysts the real earnings result would be 25%. The intention was to surprise the general public. The analysts' figure of 25% became the whisper number.

The public was happy when the company reached the forecast 20% figure but the institutions sold off because earnings failed to reach the whisper number.

The discussion about the whisper number is based on the idea there is an objective truth or reality behind market activity. It denies the emotional content of price in favour of a rational pricing model. "If only I knew the whisper number then I could make a better decision about the correct pricing of the stock." Such approaches are doomed to miss the real trading opportunities that develop around these events. These are crudely summarised in the market epigram "Buy the rumour, sell the news". In the notes below we show how the rumour and news approach does not rely on knowing anything of whisper numbers or other inside information.

As short-term traders we need to understand how the crowd reacts to the information available to all. We do not need to outsmart the crowd by knowing information unknown to them. We only need to out-trade them. We do this by being alert for these leaked news events and applying strategies designed to ride the emotional coaster. The objective is to jump out at, or near the top. Our interest is not in the earnings, or the dividend, but in the capital gain created by an emotional crowd, swooning over the prospect of future wealth while we generate current income.

ADDING LIFT

Earnings come before dividends. Both announcements offer the opportunity for short-term trades and are traded in similar ways. Some of the announcements are an opportunity to apply leverage to the trade. Leverage is gained when you have a mechanical advantage. You lift very large objects by using a lever and a fulcrum. A small weight lifts a very heavy weight. Financial leverage works in the same way. The first form – instrument leverage – is based on derivative instruments, like options, warrants and futures contracts. For a small amount of cash – good faith money or option premium – you control a large block of shares. We introduce some warrant techniques below, but discuss them more fully in later chapters.

The second form of leverage – price leverage – is based on low price and relies on common misperceptions about value. It does not seem to matter if we pay four cents or five cents for an item, but we are not prepared to pay five dollars when we were quoted four dollars. The percentage difference is the same but the psychological difference is very large. As a result, low prices move easily while high prices move slowly. This gives low prices a leverage advantage.

When we turn analysis into opportunity we have a choice. We can trade the price action directly, or look for a derivative instrument to magnify the impact and extent of the anticipated price move. Many traders reach for a derivative instrument wherever it is available, but these solutions carry their own specific type of risk. They are often a very profitable solution, but not always the best. Factors including liquidity, trading activity and time decay may increase the risk beyond limits compatible with the proposed reward.

Other traders compensate for low leverage by trading the stock using a very large position size. This is a scalping approach, discussed in Chapter 9. Here a lot of money is used to generate a small percentage return that translates into substantial dollar returns. When a 1.67% return is equal to $50,000 many traders are satisfied and forget they need a three million dollar trade to achieve this result.

Our objective in this chapter is to examine how the known news event – a dividend or earning result– is traded effectively on a short-term basis. We start with direct trading of the stock, and then look at how a derivative instrument – a warrant – is used to magnify these returns to 92% over four days. This trade shows how end-of-day data is combined with real-time intra-day trade management to manage the opportunity.

We assume you are familiar with the basic terms of short-term trading from your experience as a position trader. Warrants are a derivative trading instrument similar to options. They are traded on the ASX in the same way as ordinary stocks. We are interested in the leverage they offer. Warrants are issued by third parties, usually banks or financial institutions. To ensure an active market, the third party is required to maintain a market for each warrant by offering to buy and sell warrants when no other trader is interested. This market is created by market makers.

Finally, price action during the day is monitored using a real time screen and the course-of-trades information. This shows the time, price and value of every trade for any stock during the day. American traders call this time-and-sales data. Each recorded trade is called a 'print' and the term dates back to the days when ticker tapes conveyed this information. Traders 'print the tape' when their personal trade appears in the time-and-sales data flow.

REAL DIVIDEND INCOME

The dividend announcement, like an earnings report, provides several trading opportunities:

➜   The time of the profit and dividend announcement – the dividend bump.

➜   The period approaching its ex-dividend date.

➜   The moment when the stock goes ex-dividend.

Our interest is in the first opportunity – the dividend bump because this is a known, and to some extent, a predictable news event. We know when it is likely to be announced, and we generally know the likely outcome through newspaper reports. In this example we look at a mid-week earnings and dividend announcement by Telstra. It did not come as much of a surprise. Traders were prepared for it in many news reports leading up to the announcement day. Sometimes the announcement may be disappointing because earnings and dividends are less than the market expects. Other times they are more than the market expects. We generally cannot predict these details with any degree of precision. Nor do we need to. What is useful is the date of the announcement and the general market feeling, as reflected in news commentary, about the direction of the result – up or down.

Dividends and earnings reports are regular events cloaked in secret market business. Despite consistent internal company timetables for the collection and analysis of data, it is difficult to determine when dividend or earnings announcements will be made. Dates are announced a few weeks in advance in the Monday edition of *The Australian Financial Review*. Some brokerage websites provide a record of past ex-dividend dates. The best source is JustData – www.justdata.com.au – which provides a searchable rolling list of previous dividend dates. Companies are creatures of habit so past dates are a useful guide to future dates.

We are interested in the trading advantage offered by a rise in earnings and a subsequent increase in dividends. We expect to see a rise in the share price driven by crowd enthusiasm on the day, and perhaps continuing for another one or two days. There are several strategies used to capture this bump. We use similar strategies to capture a 'dump' on bad news and this hedges or protects our underlying stock if we already own it.

We use Telstra as an example and the first approach buys TLS on the Friday or Monday prior to the date of the dividend announcement on Wednesday. We buy in anticipation of a known news event and base the decision on the general market opinion which anticipates a bullish outcome. The best we do with a stock like TLS with relatively low-price leverage, is buy at $6.28 and then sell on the confirmation of the dividend at around $6.73 on the day, or if the stock looks very bullish, perhaps hold off until the next day. This strategy provides a 7.2% return as shown in Figure 6.1. This is not particularly satisfactory. It is suitable for scalping approaches that aim for small short-term profits.

The most effective way to capitalise on this anticipated dividend bump is to use a call warrant. The call warrant makes money as the share price rises. A call warrant is the right to buy shares at lower than current market price. A call warrant exercisable at $10.00, and which cost $0.50 to buy, does not make money until the share price is at $10.51 – the warrant price plus exercise price is greater than the current stock price.

The primary selection criterion here is a history of reasonable trading volume in the warrant. When we turn to the list of available TLS warrants there are just four competing for our attention. They are TLSWMM, TLSWDJ, TLSWZC, TLSWPF.

The key selection feature is liquidity. There are nearly 40 TLS call warrants available. Less than half of them have consistent volume. An even smaller number have consistent *good* volume. We want good volume because our intention is to buy the warrant on Friday and sell it again on Wednesday or Thursday. We need other traders to trade with.

In this situation it is more important to select the day of entry rather than the price of entry. We use Friday as the entry day. Our choice of entry prices range from $0.04 to $0.20. Here our choice depends on our attitude to leverage and to price leverage.

Leverage, as it traditionally applies to options and warrants, is created by the exaggerated link between the parent stock and the derivative. Price leverage is the

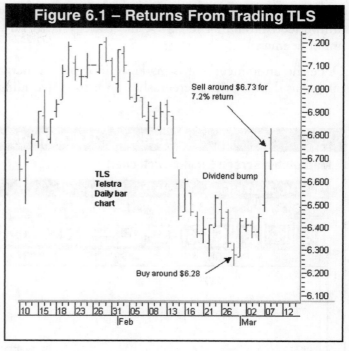

Figure 6.1 – Returns From Trading TLS

Sell around $6.73 for 7.2% return

TLS Telstra Daily bar chart

Dividend bump

Buy around $6.28

recognition of the way the market finds it easier to lift a stock from $0.04 to $0.08 than from $4.00 to $8.00. We select TLSWDJ as the best candidate for this dividend bump strategy. It is purchased on Friday at $0.13.

Our trading plan for the dividend bump is based on the news event. It is not based on any price targets, projections, chart patterns, or support and resistance levels. We are simply riding the momentum generated by an expected bullish announcement on Wednesday.

This strategy requires us to actively watch the live market screens on Wednesday as the announcement is made and as the market reacts to it.

We want to see several features in the warrant price activity since our purchase on Friday. The first feature is a general rise in the warrant price as the market rumour mill generates increased expectations of a bullish earnings announcement on Wednesday. This is important. If the warrant does not move in response to these bullish rumours we need to sell it on Monday or Tuesday because it is unlikely to react fully to any real bullish announcement on Wednesday.

On Wednesday morning we watch the order lines and the first trades. We expect to see the increasing bullish behaviour reflected in increasing prices. We want the general public to start thinking about buying TLS warrants because they are, by now, convinced the dividend announcement is going to be very good.

These are traders buying the news. They are the people who buy from us when the news is announced later in the day. Our strategy is to buy the rumour and sell the news announcement.

Once the announcement is made we look for an increase in buying and enthusiasm for buying as shown by the screen shot on intra-day trading in Figure 6.2.

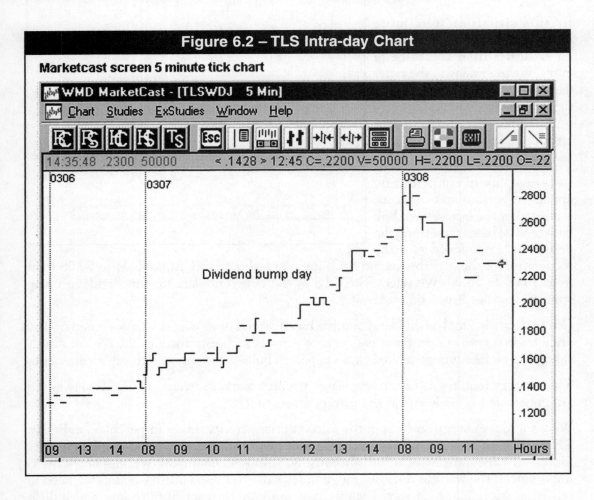

Figure 6.2 – TLS Intra-day Chart

Once we see this, our objective is to sell out at the high point. We are looking for any sign of a pullback in prices because this suggests market enthusiasm is weakening. This is a good time to take our profits. Ideally we should be simultaneously running several windows on our computer screens. They should include an order line for TLS, the parent stock, and the order line for our selected warrant, TLSWDJ. Moves in TLS translate very quickly into moves in TLSWDJ.

With our selected warrant the price closes on its high for the day. We take our exit at $0.25. We do this because our intention is to trade just the market enthusiasm on the day of the announcement. We want to sell the news and in a nervous market this is even more important because enthusiasm may be fleeting. In this example our strategy returns 92% over just four days. The daily chart in Figure 6.3 shows the entry and exit points.

Some traders choose to stay with the trade overnight and look for a better exit the next day. In a bullish market this is a good strategy. In a nervous market it has less chance of success. A defensive exit is designed to capture available profits on the day of the news release. It is not always the most profitable, but it is the exit with least risk.

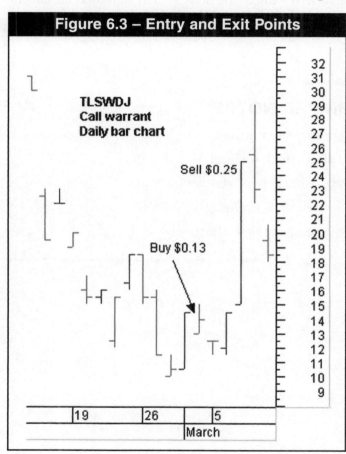

Figure 6.3 – Entry and Exit Points

TLSWDJ
Call warrant
Daily bar chart

Sell $0.25

Buy $0.13

This strategy has many advantages. For those who already hold TLS, it allows them to capture an additional dividend bonus. For traders who want to generate extra returns from effective trading strategies, this approach delivers good short-term trades with a high probability of trading success.

We started this example with four potential warrant candidates. The others perform at around the same level. The worst is a 75% return. The other results are 138% and 125% returns in less than a week.

NEWS FOR EVERYONE

It is worth repeating that news does not have to be exclusive to be profitable. The market provides the opportunity for traders to profit from news freely available to all. Modern trading does not seek an insider's edge. It uses an edge built on trading skill by selecting the best trading instrument to generate substantial returns from an emotional crowd. This is where opportunity is found.

News, by its very nature, contains surprises. It delivers information we were not previously aware of, but it is now delivered quickly and efficiently to most market participants. In the next section we examine how these surprise announcements are traded. There is a slight edge here, with an advantage to those who follow a live news feed and a live screen. If you are serious about short-term trading then these screens and services sit on your desktop. Even in this timeframe, and with this type of news, we do better if we assume everyone knows as much as we do at the same time as we hear the news. When all traders are caught by surprise, or by a rapidly breaking news story, it is those with superior analytical and trading skills who win.

SNIPER NOTES

→ Trade earnings and dividend pre-release rumours.

→ Trade with price leverage for direct stock trading.

→ Trade with instrument leverage using derivatives like warrants.

→ Ride momentum created by known news events.

→ Select trading instruments to leverage returns effectively.

Chapter 7

SURPRISE

NEWS

As a child interested in the news, I discovered the word was an acronym for North, East, West and South because news items came from every corner of the earth. It wasn't an entirely inaccurate idea and in today's markets news travels rapidly from distant places. This fact is partly responsible for the increased volatility of our markets. They react, sometimes violently, to overnight events which happen when our markets are closed.

Traders who play with dual listed companies take on substantial additional risk because they are exposed to ongoing 24-hour volatility. Consider PBL, a media company listed only in Australia, and News Corp which is dual listed in Australia and the US. Overnight news signals a massive increase in the price of newsprint. Here's an event which equally affects both companies.

Traders following News Corp in Australia have gone to bed. Traders in the US have time to absorb the news, play out their reactions, and by the end of their day, set a new adjusted price for News Corp. This new price fully incorporates their responses to the news event and is reflected in the price of News Corp as trading opens in Australia. The News Corp price shows a continuity.

Traders involved with PBL face two problems when they wake up and examine the Australian market. First is the impact of the price rise in newsprint on PBL. Hurried analysis may suggest a fall of a few cents on the open compared to yesterday's close. Their second problem is the reaction of News Corp to the same news event. Perhaps the reaction is greater than expected. This reaction carries across to the open with NCP in Australia and the shock transfers to all other media stocks. This, in turn, suggests the PBL reaction will be more significant, stretching to ten cents. Australian traders have to analyse and incorporate the impact of two news events – the newsprint price rise and the behaviour of NCP – into their trading strategy for the open of market.

They have one distinct advantage. Wake up early enough and they may have four hours to consider this analysis and develop trading strategies before the Australian market opens.

This is just one instance where a news event delivers a very nasty surprise. Trading surprise news calls for different techniques. Some surprises are genuine, while others are like the regular birthday present from a distant aunt – another starched handkerchief. Each surprise calls for a slightly different trading strategy. Each starts with an analysis of the daily charts and ends with the careful micro-management of the daily intra-day tick, or three minute chart.

In the previous chapter we briefly mentioned the impact of earnings downgrades. These are generally not leaked news. These are surprise news events, particularly under the continuous disclosure regime being enforced by the Australian Stock Exchange. Continuous disclosure delivers a mixed bag of benefits and drawbacks to investors. It swamps the market with unimportant news. We do not need to know when the company signs every minor price arrangement. This news is insignificant and helps to create an industry of newsletter writers and analysts who sort through the chaff to find the wheat.

More importantly, continuous disclosure creates a sense of false security. We assume every company complies with the rules so there are fewer nasty surprises. This is at odds with the natural desire of companies to protect commercially sensitive information until the last possible moment. It is also at odds with the regrettably strong Australian trait in public affairs, of reaching for the first available lie whenever any wrong doing is exposed.

Continuous disclosure is a type of news just as subject to management as any other press release. A recent study found an interesting relationship between stock exchange queries based on unusual price movements, the company response, and the release of materially relevant news. When companies were queried and asked to explain significant share price moves most replied in the standard format, "There is no new information to report". In a substantial majority of cases important market moving news was released to the market within five days of the initial denial.

This has many implications. The most significant for short-term traders is the way impending surprise news is reflected in price activity in the days leading up to the formal news release. We call this 'informed trading'. It is a mixture of rumour, suspicions, media hype, leaked news and perhaps some true inside trading. The exact nature of the mix is not as important as the message that price action delivers to observant traders. We get to see the price action building and we join the action, buying the rumour and selling the news as it happens. What is a surprise to the broader market does not have to be a surprise to us.

BAD NEWS TRAVELS QUICKLY

Have you ever been financially assaulted by a surprise earnings downgrade? It is a nasty experience being mugged by your own computer screen. In some cases this is truly a surprise news event, but in others the punch has already been telegraphed and it shows up in the price charts. It is no use looking to fundamental analysis for advance warning. These analysts try to trade the current market by looking in the rear-view mirror which is plastered with the most recent company reports compiled from data between three and six months old. No wonder corporate collapses like Enron, HIH Insurance, Pasminco and OneTel are able to sneak up on them.

Some analysts have special contacts. They are more informed than their competitors and this makes them appear more astute. They hear surprise news before the rest of the market. This can happen courtesy of briefings for selected analysts, and the continuous disclosure regulations have not been effective in preventing this procedure. This is informed trading but does it give these analysts, and their clients, a significant advantage?

The answer goes to the core of short-term and day trading success. If success depends on news then our focus should be on getting behind the news and cultivating sources, or at least, people who know these sources so we are amongst the first clients to be informed. If some of the surprise news events are already foreshadowed in price action then our focus turns to improving chart reading and analysis skills.

Our conclusion about informed trading, and whether it is a significant advantage, depends on a single question. How does the person who knows of this surprise news put the information to work? She does so by selling her shares ahead of an earnings downgrade announcement or by purchasing shares if she wants to go short. This trading activity leaves a trail in the market. Her footprints show up in the daily course-of-trades information. This record shows the time and price of every trade. Her footprints are captured in the daily bar or candlestick chart. The distance between the open and the close show who is running in fear, and who is propelled by greed. These messages travel more rapidly than the official exchange notices.

In the previous chapters we suggested news does not have to be exclusive to be profitable. We now want to suggest that, in certain circumstances, we do not have to know the content of news for it to be profitable. Instead we observe the building impact of an impending surprise news announcement.

TAPPING THE TELEGRAPH

We all know others get important market-shifting news before we do. A major Australian-listed company provides the material for this case study. We are interested in the way price information allows traders to tap this hidden market telegraph, so the name of the company is unimportant. These events occurred in early 2002 and we examine the way all traders can be aware of these events and deal with them. The company provided briefings to selected brokers prior to releasing bad profit news to the general public – after the market closed on Friday.

This activity raises two issues for technical and chart-based traders. First it underlines the failure of fundamental analysis which is based on guess-estimates. According to *The Australian Financial Review*, brokers and analysts were caught unaware by the size of the profit drop. When analysts rely on company reports and other fuzzy fundamental figures their conclusions are also fuzzy.

The second issue relates to the ability of the price activity shown on the chart to forewarn other market participants about the information being provided by the company to selected brokers and analysts. We tend to focus on the indicator and chart signals which suggest a new uptrend is about to develop or that a trend is likely to continue. We should also remember these same techniques are used to identify the end of an uptrend. This is always important when we come to exit an open trade. It is also important when we are thinking about buying a stock in a strong trend as prices dip downwards. We want to know if this is a temporary price weakness or the start of a new downtrend.

In this discussion our concern is not with the ethics of the action taken by the company.

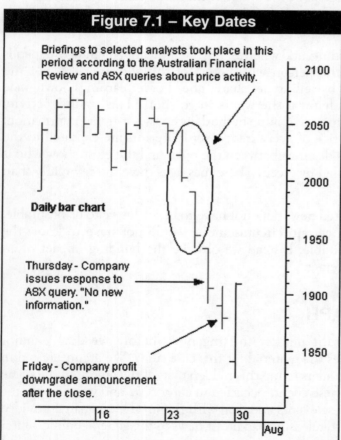

Figure 7.1 – Key Dates

Briefings to selected analysts took place in this period according to the Australian Financial Review and ASX queries about price activity.

2100

2050

2000

Daily bar chart

1950

Thursday - Company issues response to ASX query. "No new information."

1900

1850

Friday - Company profit downgrade announcement after the close.

16   23   30

Aug

Traders accept this action will continue to occur in the market despite continuous disclosure requirements. Our concern is to understand how charting and technical analysis helps us, as traders, to identify significant changes in market activity which may be driven by breaking news which we do not yet know about.

Using information from *The Australian Financial Review* we estimate when the first of these selected brokerage briefings took place. The key dates are shown on the chart extract in Figure 7.1. It is reasonable to assume the first analysts selected for the briefings passed the information on to their brokerage employers, and from there, to selected clients. This is the reality of the market. News trickles down from the few to the many. As more brokers were briefed over the next day or so, the selling pressure mounted.

The activity on Tuesday and Wednesday was unusual enough for the ASX to issue a formal query to the company. The company response came on Thursday. "On Friday morning" according to *The Australian Financial Review*, "as the shares continued to fall, the ASX got serious". The result was a formal company announcement to the market of a significant downgrade in profit results. This warning was released after the market closed on Friday. The chart extract shows the close-up daily market response as this news became more widely known.

The news release was a surprise but were the facts a surprise? Long-term analysis of the company chart prepares the trader for the possibility of bearish news. It also provides the information necessary to develop defensive short-term strategies.

Turning to a 12-month display in Figure 7.2, the chart shows three dominant trends across several timeframes. The primary trend is shown as trend line A. This is a failed uptrend. The first break in this long-term uptrend happened in April. It was an early warning of trend weakness. Prices recovered but the trend line, which had previously acted as a support level, now acted as a resistance level. The change to a resistance function is shown by the way the trend line changes to a thicker line.

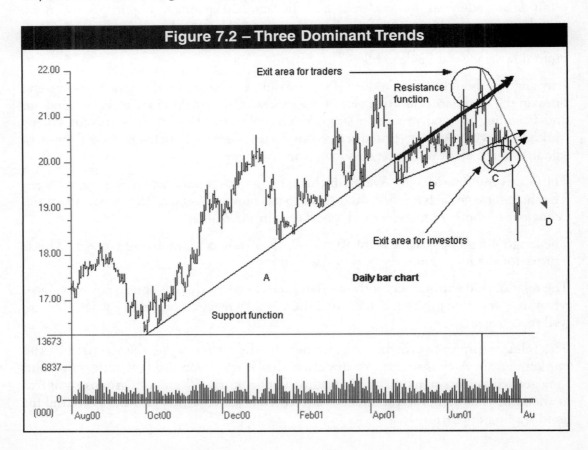

Figure 7.2 – Three Dominant Trends

This tells us the uptrend is weakening. Trend line B shows the new, weaker uptrend. Its failure to push significantly above the old trend line confirms the trend weakness. Traders use this information to make an exit in the area shown.

Investors take a lot more convincing that their blue chip stock is moving into a downtrend. Active investors took an exit when prices closed below the new short-term uptrend, shown as line B. The very short-term uptrend, line C, defined a very weak recovery. The drop below this trend line was an exit signal confirming trend weakness.

Traders using charts argue the poor company results were already suspected by the market. The growing failure of the uptrend combined with the new downtrend, as shown by line D, was clear evidence that it was a good time to take profits from this trade. For other traders who were interested in buying the company, the same charts suggested it was not a good time to buy into the stock in anticipation of a new uptrend developing. This is a bearish chart with a bearish outlook.

Drop this long-term analysis of an end-of-day chart into the mix of news releases and profit downgrades and the sudden and, at the time unexplained, drop in price, is not a complete surprise. The extent of the drop is unexpected but the drop is confirmation of an existing trend rather than the start of a new trend. Good traders took profits before the profit downgrade was made public.

Any analysis should be the product of several different types of indicators. Placing trend lines on the bar chart is just one part of the process. Our conclusion revolves around our understanding of trend strength. Our preferred tool in this type of analysis is the Guppy Multiple Moving Average first discussed in *Trading Tactics*. It delivers several types of signals and the chart in Figure 7.3 shows many of them.

The Guppy Multiple Moving Average includes two groups of exponential moving averages. The short-term group is a 3, 5, 8, 10, 12 and 15 day moving average. This is a proxy for the behaviour of short-term traders and speculators in the market.

The long-term group is made up of 30, 35, 40, 45, 50 and 60 day moving averages. This is a proxy for the long-term investors in the market.

The relationship within each of these groups tells us when there is agreement on value – when they are close together – and when there is disagreement on value – when they are well spaced apart.

The relationship between the two groups tells the trader about the strength of the market action. A change in price direction that is well supported by both short- and long-term investors signals a strong trading opportunity. When both groups compress at the same time it alerts the trader to increased price volatility and the potential for good trading opportunities.

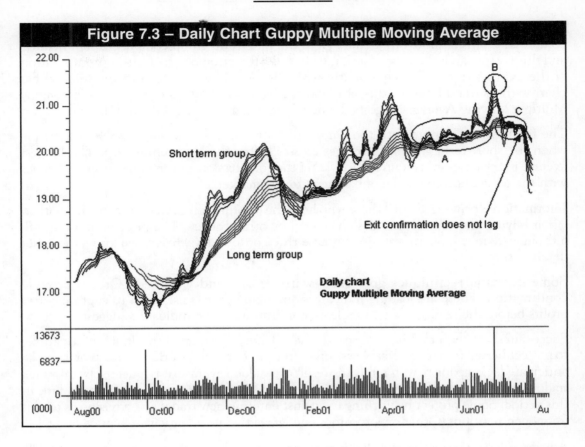

Figure 7.3 – Daily Chart Guppy Multiple Moving Average

The first indication of trend weakness is shown in area A. Here the long-term group of averages – the investors – remained unexcited about the company. When prices pull back they are not active buyers. The compression of the long-term group of averages shows there is no aggressive buying taking place on price dips. This tells us there is weakening support for the trend.

The second indication is area B. Here the short-term traders succeed in driving up the price. The long-term investors are not interested in this. There is no sudden surge in buying from this long-term group. They do not share the short-term trader's enthusiasm. The slight rise and expansion in this group is most likely caused by long-term investors taking advantage of these higher prices to sell the company. When a rally driven by traders is the start of a long-term uptrend, we expect to see increased activity amongst long-term investors. This shows up on this indicator as an expansion of the long-term group and a definite turn upwards. Most importantly, this upturn and expansion continues as the short-term rally inevitably falters and retraces. Now the long-term group sees an opportunity to get the stock more cheaply, and they outbid each other.

This doesn't happen. Instead as prices collapse, the long-term investors' group also compresses. This is shown in area C. Here the long-term group compresses significantly and this is often an indication of a change in trend direction or a new, strong continuation of the existing trend. To help confirm which is most likely we turn to the original bar chart with its trend lines. In this situation the bar chart analysis is bearish so the Guppy Multiple Moving Average suggests the development of a strong downtrend.

The final feature to note with the Guppy Multiple Moving Average display is the time when the short-term group of averages crosses below the long-term group. The longest average in the long-term group is 60 days. Yet the compression and crossover is simultaneous with the early selected release of bad news to the market.

Information is privileged until those who hold the information decide to act in the market. Their buying and selling provides clues seen by other traders. The price action tells all, although we may have to wait, in this case three or four days, before we know the exact detail of the news.

Some charting techniques give early warning of trend weakness. Others provide confirmation. These are leading indicators and many traders use them to capture better profits before the reality of a news release confirms what the indicators suggest.

Successful short-term trading depends, to a very large extent, upon the ability of the trader to protect herself from disasters. News comes from all round the world but much of it can be anticipated. Company news is rarely the result of a sudden event so it is reflected by informed trading some days before the formal news release. Many short-term opportunities lurk in this period. Some protect by warning us against entering new trades and advising us to exit from open positions. Other opportunities encourage traders to anticipate a price boost.

Adverse surprise news is the apocalyptic nightmare that wakes short-term traders in the middle of the night. Profitable surprise news provides the material of pleasant dreams. Just like their nasty cousins, profitable surprises are often revealed in price activity long before the actual news event is uncovered. We look at strategies for pleasant surprises in the next chapter.

≡ MARKSWOMAN'S NOTES

→ Surviving surprise news starts with the analysis of daily charts.

→ Fundamental analysis is not useful for short-term trading.

→ Even bad news is foreshadowed in price activity.

→ Combine indicators to analyse the scene and plan your reactions to surprise news.

→ Chart warnings allow traders to prepare defensive short-term strategies.

Chapter 8

FAST

NEWS

N ot all news is unexpected. Using our own analysis or the analysis of others, we reach informed conclusions about probable future events. An army calling up all of its reserves is a good indicator of increased military activity. When an attack comes it is no surprise. Markets may be caught out by the timing of an event, but not by the event itself. Markets are constantly factoring future events into today's prices. Short-term traders are not particularly interested in this longer-term function. As expected, they bring these analysis skills into a tighter timeframe to trade fast news.

This is the key skill required of traders who build strategies around news events. They must understand the impact of the event on pricing and position themselves in the market to take advantage of it. They run a pre-defined and tight stop loss condition, usually based on intra-day price action. Despite their best efforts, their analysis may be incorrect and the market may move against their position. They buy a stock in anticipation of a price rise, but instead the stock falls when the news event takes place. Investors and others may have the financial courage to back their analysis against the activity of the market. Short-term traders cannot afford to do this because their profits depend on the effective harvesting of short-term moves. Keeping hold of a losing trade, shifts from short-term trading to position trading and this calls for an entirely different approach to risk, risk management and capital allocation as discussed in *Better Trading* and *Trading Tactics*.

Fast, accurate analysis is useful only if it is effectively executed in the market. We need a brokerage order execution system with several features. The first is straight through processing. When we click the buy or sell button and meet the current bid or ask, our order must travel to market instantly. Success depends upon rapid execution so there is no time for a broker to accept the order and then manually relay it on his terminal to get the order into the Australian Stock Exchange SEATS trading system.

I recently executed a trade to close out a profitable superannuation position. The stock was making a long-term blow-off high and was unlikely to sustain its current prices. I was informed my sell order would be passed onto the funds' brokers and executed sometime within the next three hours! After some discussion I was able to get the timeframe down to thirty minutes. Others have reported brokerages who boast they routinely execute orders within three minutes.

For day traders and short-term traders these execution speeds spell the potential for financial murder, particularly in fast-moving momentum trades, or scalping trades that rely on capturing precise, small moves. Acceptable execution speed is under one second. This is achieved by linking your internet order directly with your brokerage, and then directly to the SEATS order execution system. The brokers' system electronically verifies your cash balance via a link with your nominated financial institution. If your order value exceeds the cash available in your account the order is not passed to market. The probity check is measured in computer time and is so rapid it exerts no appreciable delay in order execution. True straight through processing is a must-have feature for short-term and day trading.

A second required feature is an electronic stop loss facility. It is a regrettable reality that most brokerages do not offer any stop facility to their clients. They claim it is impossible to implement, or too time consuming, or too fraught with liabilities. Some use third-party order execution software but refuse to turn on the stop loss facility.

A brokerage who does not offer a stop loss facility is like a used car dealer who offers to sell you a very cheap, very fast car. It is cheap because the car has no seat belt and no brakes. Drive it off the show room floor and you are instantly at risk because you have no method of stopping the car other than your own willpower.

Legislators recognised that willpower and holding onto the steering wheel were not sufficient to prevent death and injury in car crashes. The result was compulsory seat belt legislation.

The brokerage industry is exempt from this type of safety requirement and yet a stop loss mechanism is the single most important and easily implemented feature adding significant additional protection for their clients. Just like a seat belt, it will not save them from death in all crashes, but it limits the injury and damage. A stop loss is required for trading in all timeframes, and for investors too. Had the service been widely available in the April 2000 market collapse there would have been far less financial damage inflicted on clients.

Once a brokerage implements electronic straight through processing then an order can be managed by a selected series of computer algorithms. The stop loss facility is just the start and this leads us to the third desirable brokerage feature – the contingent order. This order structure is used when the trader wants to wait for a set of market conditions to occur before he takes action. The most common contingent order is a stop loss order. It says "Sell this stock if the price falls below a certain level". A contingent buy order says "Buy this stock if prices rise above a certain level".

The most effective contingent orders are placed electronically. The computerised order system monitors the trading activity in the nominated stock. When the buy or sell conditions are met, the contingent order is activated.

The contingent buy order simply tells the brokerage computer system to execute a buy order if the stock trades above a particular price. It is further modified, if required, with a volume condition and with a start and finish time.

Contingent orders mean you do not have to be the fastest mouse click in the market to get the stock you want at the price you want. Instead your order lies in ambush and is triggered as soon as prices move to the relevant point. Put these features together into a brokerage system and the short-term trader has a powerful combination. I use AOT Online brokerage because it is one of the very few services currently offering all these features. Others use a hybrid service like DataTech to electronically monitor the market and use brokerage skill to manage the execution of the stop loss service. Each approach has its advantages and we discuss them in Section 5. Each is far superior to brokerages which do not offer stop loss facilities.

These order execution features help us trade surprise news and leaked news. We look at a case study below and then bring all the features together in a trade based on unexpected, fast-breaking news after a trading halt.

SPEEDING NEWS

Market news has many interesting features. Those economists who favour rational and efficient market models believe the impact of news is instantaneously factored into the stock price. Observation of news releases leads traders to a different conclusion. In most cases the market is relatively inefficient when it comes to acting on news events. News rarely explodes onto the market. Most times it seeps down from a narrow base to a wider investing and public base. This inefficiency provides traders with many opportunities.

This trade starts on a Monday and is built around a not-entirely-unexpected earnings report. Just prior to the open of trading, MIM announced a better-than-expected, substantial lift in earnings and profits. This is a good result, so we intuitively expect to see an increase in the MIM price. Traders watching the live news feeds received this information first, and in the first 10 minutes of trading, drove the MIM price from $1.35 to $1.37. This is not a remarkable price lift for such good news, and those traders who bought at these levels were disappointed as prices fell to a low of $1.32 before closing at $1.34. This was not a trade to tell your partner about.

We cannot know what really happened but we infer the probable course of events and, from this, develop a strategy to more effectively trade news events. We start with the inferred activity. The news-hound traders have two choices. They can bid well ahead of the sell orders in an attempt to get a good entry into what they believe is a stock that will move up during the day. Their excited early buying helps to make the initial price move.

The market often shows extreme movements in the first fifteen to twenty minutes of trading as shown in Figure 8.1. Sometimes on a strong, generally bullish day, the market continues in this direction. On most days, there is a correction. The initial uptrend is followed by a downtrend retracement, and then the new uptrend develops and stays in place for the remainder of the day. Individual stocks mimic the general market behaviour. MIM goes up and then falls. Later it rises slightly.

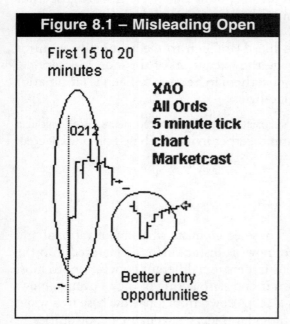

Figure 8.1 – Misleading Open

First 15 to 20 minutes

0212

XAO
All Ords
5 minute tick chart
Marketcast

Better entry opportunities

With the news-hound traders out of the way, other traders who watched the news but waited for the retracement buy the stock. During the day, other potential traders of MIM hear about the earnings release on the radio. The news trickles outwards, gradually reaching more people. This earnings growth is a good result for MIM but it is not headline news. Unless they listen to a specialist market report on TV or radio, it is unlikely people will hear about it during the day. But within 24 hours, as shown in Chapter 5 we expect all significant market participants to know the news.

The major general news impact comes from the TV news reports and the morning newspapers. This is when most of the general public get to hear about the good earnings results. They are the people who flood into the market on the day after the news release. This is market inefficiency and it is reflected in price behaviour. Any sustained rise in MIM is most likely to develop as a larger crowd comes into the market as buyers because they are pleased with the profit figures. Those who already hold the stock now become potential sellers but most often at higher prices. This has the classic potential to drive prices higher but, again, we need to avoid the potential mistake made on the Monday when prices rose initially and then collapsed.

The solution starts with a close examination of the bar chart. It concludes with the use of a contingent buy order, automatically executed electronically.

Chart analysis starts after the news has been released, either on the day, or the next day. We start with the news-hounds. As soon as the news is released the news hounds turn to the daily chart. MIM has enjoyed a substantial uptrend but in recent days it has sold off, resulting in the potential for a short downtrend. This is shown by the straight-edge trend line in Figure 8.2. The placement of this line generally defines the downward movement over the previous days.

If the news release is going to have a significant impact on the MIM price then we expect two things to happen. First, a price rise above this tentative short-term downtrend line. Second, a price lift above the previous day's high of $1.37. To add a margin of safety, we set a trigger price for action at $1.38.

If prices move in this way there is a good probability the MIM uptrend will resume. It also suggests the news-driven price rise has a better chance of continuing through the day, and over the following days.

This analysis allows the trader to set a buy zone for MIM. We have shown it as a zone $0.01 wide starting at $1.38. Once a trade takes place in this area, our plan calls for us to become a buyer. This calls for a

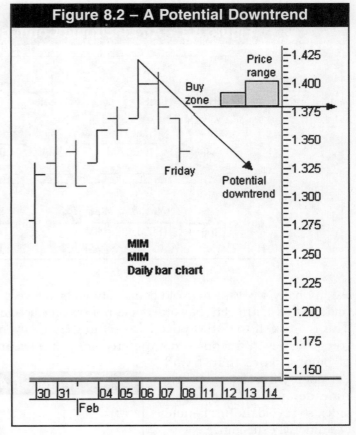

Figure 8.2 – A Potential Downtrend

contingent buy order where we take no action until our set of conditions has been satisfied. This plan can be implemented in one of three ways.

The first, and most difficult, calls for the trader to sit in front of a live market screen and monitor the price of MIM. On the first sale at $1.38 or higher, she immediately places her buy order. This plan is OK if you have the time to sit in front of a screen. It is not so good if you are working at another job.

The second option is to use an alert service, either via the net, or via a SMS service. The effectiveness of the plan depends on your ability to receive the message as soon as it is sent, and to be able to contact your broker to execute the contingent buy order.

The third option is to use an electronic contingent buy order as shown in Figure 8.3. This allows you to set the conditions of the buy order. In this example, we want to buy 18,000 MIM if the last sale price was at $1.38 or higher. This order could also be structured to trigger the buy when the highest bid is $1.38.

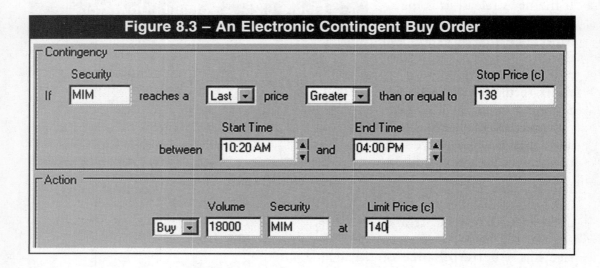

Figure 8.3 – An Electronic Contingent Buy Order

Additionally, we want to avoid being conned by a fake breakout in the first 20 minutes of trade so this contingent buy order does not become active until 20 minutes after the open. This is a risk. If the MIM price takes off in the first twenty minutes of trading and keeps going, our buy instruction is not triggered until after twenty minutes. The danger is the risk of paying more than $1.38. Personally, I prefer to use the time delay with contingent orders so I avoid the first minutes of irrational exuberance.

Once the contingent conditions are established, we set the buy instructions illustrated in Figure 8.4. Our trigger price is $1.38, but if we set our buy price at this level there is a chance we miss out. It is better if we calculate the maximum price we are prepared to pay for MIM should our breakout conditions

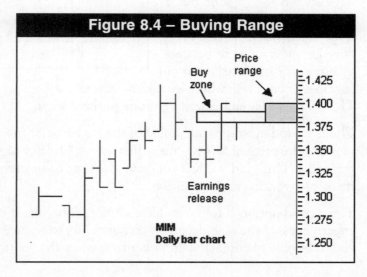

Figure 8.4 – Buying Range

be satisfied. In this example we set the price range from $1.38 to $1.40. This gives us room to move if prices hit $1.38 and then immediately jump higher to $1.39 or more.

This electronic contingent buy order is automatically monitored by the broker's system. It is not placed in the market. The system monitors the market, waiting for an alert signal – a trade at $1.38. As soon as this trade takes place, our contingent buy order is sent direct to the SEATS system using the straight through processing facilities. The delay between the trigger price and the placement of the contingent buy order is less than a second because the entire process is electronic.

In that second, prices may have dipped back to $1.37, or moved forward to $1.39. Our buy order is set at $1.40. This does not mean we pay $1.40 for MIM shares. By using this higher value it places our buy order at the head of the buying line. It is filled, or matched, at the prevailing lowest sell order. The order is effectively filled 'at market.'

The MIM price recovers on Tuesday, shooting above the buy zone, and reaching to the top of our acceptable price range. There are many trades at $1.38 which is the bottom of our buy zone. The contingent buy order is easily executed at this level getting us into the trade without the need to personally monitor the market during the day.

Contingent buy orders are also effectively applied to trading pattern breakouts. This gives the trader the opportunity to buy into the stock as the breakout takes place, rather than waiting for end-of-day confirmation with an order for execution in the market on the following day.

SUSPENDED BY THE NEWS

"Trading suspended pending an announcement" is a message to send shivers down the spine of every person who currently holds shares in the company concerned. In some circumstances it is an advantage if we already know or suspect favourable news. The suspension from trading gives the trader time to analyse the probable impact of the news and to select the best trading tactics. In rare situations traders have a choice of companies and trading instruments, and we use the case study below to highlight and compare the analysis and selection steps applied where the short-term opportunity is built around a surprise news event.

The bidding for the National Rail Corporation contract was a well-known event. The contract was not news but the winning tenderers were. The same situation applies to the release of interest rate changes by the Reserve Bank. The event and its time are known in advance, but the content of the news is only guessed at. An interest rate fall is traded in many ways. Many traders use bank stocks to trade the impact and they follow the same analysis steps outlined below. They do not have the advantage of a suspended trading period, so they must be ready to apply their prepared analysis quickly.

The announcement of the successful National Rail Corporation tender winners – LAC and TOL – was made just prior to the open of trade. Trading in these two stocks was halted and opened some 20 minutes after the general market. TOL gapped up 13% and LAC 17%.

The 20-minute gap was marked by intense order activity as the news filtered into the market. The most significant increase in order activity started when the official ASX alert was issued some 10 minutes after the news story broke on the main news providers like AAP, CNBC, Reuters and Bloomberg.

This activity revealed many traders simply do not understand the impact of news. Just as the announcement was made, the lowest seller for TOL wanted to sell 625 shares at $26.35. When trading opened, the sell price had dropped to $26.33 with 320 on offer. The LAC offer price remained the same at $11.10, but the volume grew from 300 to 3,269.

The story on the buy side was considerably different. Buy offers for TOL jumped from $28.00 to $29.40 or 5%. LAC jumped from $11.65 to $13.60 or 16.7%. How do traders choose between these two stocks to select the most profitable short-term return? Having a choice of two stocks affected by the same event is unusual, but selecting between competing stocks driven by different news events is a common task.

Deciding which stock to trade requires analysis of their depth of market data and price leverage. We could take a guess at which is the better buying opportunity, or we watch what the market is telling us prior to the commencement of trading. The changing order line tells us how the market is thinking and provides guidance to the most profitable trade. Our objective is to buy the stock at the best price possible after the open and to trade the initial news-driven enthusiasm, selling as close to the top as possible.

The first factor to consider is the buying volume shown in Figure 8.5. The more fuel builds up on the buying side, the greater potential for continued momentum. This screen shot extract taken from AOT Online shows the top 12 consolidated orders. The full screen display continues to a much greater depth than shown here. The volume of buy orders is significantly greater for LAC than for TOL. This suggests LAC may be the more profitable opportunity.

The spread between the original highest buying price, just prior to the news announcement, and the buying price just prior to the open of trading is also a useful guide. The TOL bids climbed 5%. In comparison, the LAC bids climbed 16.74%. Not only are there more buyers for LAC but they are also more eager. There is a more excited crowd than the group following TOL. The growth of the order line suggests LAC offers a better short-term trading opportunity.

The final factor is price leverage. In this case, where two stocks benefit from the same news event we expect each to perform at around the same rate. In a day trading environment the minor differences between the two performance levels are important. An additional point pays for brokerage and locks in better profits.

Figure 8.5 – Market Depth for TOL and LAC
Consolidated depth of market just prior to the open of trade

TOL Buy orders		TOL Sell orders		LAC Buy orders		LAC Sell orders	
Volume	Price	Price	Volume	Volume	Price	Price	Volume
1000	2940	2633	320	1000	1360	1110	3269
6000	2915	2635	625	4600	1350	1112	100
6000	2905	2640	987	37000	1340	1115	2530
1000	2901	2655	166	60000	1330	1117	669
15750	2900	2660	345	15000	1325	1118	900
500	2891	2675	275	500	1321	1119	1380
15000	2890	2680	179	51900	1320	1120	1000
14500	2860	2685	375	5500	1315	1125	2625
15000	2855	2700	3347	2600	1311	1130	400
26390	2850	2710	883	2000	1310	1149	585
20025	2840	2720	350	1000	1305	1150	200
300	2835	2749	375	50000	1301	1162	888

Screen shot from the Integral Trading Platfrom, AOT Online

Price leverage simply means it is easier to lift a low-priced stock than a higher-priced stock. With TOL at $26.00, the price leverage advantage lies with LAC trading at around $11.00. The difference is psychological and, when markets react emotionally, this becomes important. The higher buying volume with LAC confirms many others are thinking the same way.

We have a choice of trading tactics. We can join the line of buy orders near the top and hope to get an entry near the opening price. This strategy works well if prices continue to climb. If prices fall it is sometimes difficult to set a valid stop loss condition, particularly when prices gap considerably on the open.

The alternative strategy waits for a price pullback after the first buying frenzy is exhausted. Excitement is often followed by remorse so the pivot point reversal is often swift and definite. Prices fall rapidly after the initial highs and then reverse just as rapidly as more experienced buyers come into the market five to 15 minutes after the open. If prices do not pull back, the trade is abandoned. This is the strategy we apply to this example and is shown in Figure 8.6 along with several exit points.

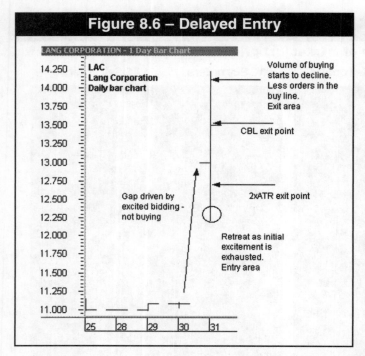

Figure 8.6 – Delayed Entry

Excitement is a characteristic of enthusiastic new players rather than professionals. After such an exciting open there is often a temporary pullback in prices as more experienced traders hover in the background. This is our planned entry area and we watch for a temporary pullback to $12.25 and buy 1,640 shares for a total cost of $20,090.

The TOL buy line does not show the same level of excitement as LAC. Buying is more sedate, and prices do not pullback after the open at $28.90. This confirms the better short-term opportunity is with LAC.

Traders manage this type of trade in two ways. The first is to shoot for a defined return. The very strong buying suggests a minimum target of 10% with the possibility of making 15%. Once the trade moves above 10% we monitor price activity carefully, looking to sell on the first downward move. In this real trade we took an exit at $14.09 a little after midday as buying volume declined. This delivers a 15% return and a $3,017.60 profit.

STOPPING OUT

The second way to manage the trade is to apply a trailing stop loss strategy after the trade is entered. Traders use a count back line applied to a five-minute tick chart for this as shown in Figure 8.7. This keeps the trader in the trade for around three hours. The exit is triggered by a move below the count back stop loss line. This gives an exit at $13.53 which returns 10.45%.

Some traders apply other stop loss techniques such as twice the average true range (2xATR). This method is detailed by Chris Tate in *The Art of Trading*. In this trade example the 2xATR stop loss exit is at $12.70. For news based trading this stop loss is too far below the high of the day.

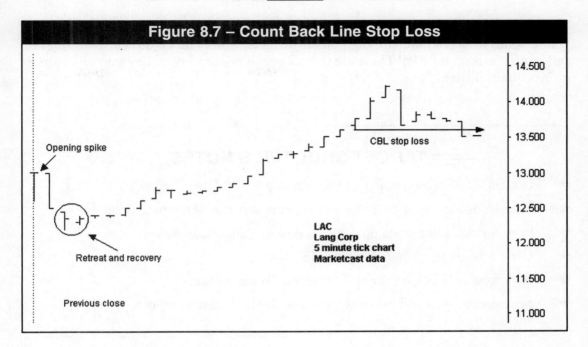

Figure 8.7 – Count Back Line Stop Loss

Both formal stop loss methods deliver a poorer return than the target trade method we actually used in the trade but they use a more clearly defined stop loss condition. When we aim for target returns we do not always achieve the target in these types of trades and it is sometimes difficult to manage the exit effectively. These types of stop loss calculations are used as a backup. We aim for targets, but if the stop loss is hit first, the trade is closed.

The enthusiasm, shown in the buy order line, and the price leverage lift LAC to a 16.5% for the day based on the low to high. TOL delivers just 4.6%. The success of this strategy does not rest on our ability to instantly analyse the impact and significance of the news announcement. We let others do this, watching their actions as they buy or sell in the market. These movements in the order line tell us what the market thinks and provide us with the opportunity for a quick profit.

The short-term strategies, discussed in this and the previous chapters, rely on reactions to fast-moving events. The impact on prices is often substantial and good traders collect handsome profits. Riding the news is the exciting edge of short-term trading. It has the potential to deliver good profits, and even better profits when we apply derivative trading strategies, discussed later. These fast trades are where the financial and popular media chose to focus during the dying months of the bull market. Their coverage gave day trading a glamour it does not deserve. By highlighting the lucky-strike mentality they ignored the hard daily grind in the life of short-term and day traders.

There is "gold in them thar markets", but there is also an awful lot of dirt to move. While some traders chase the big golden nuggets, others make do with the smaller and more common tailings. These are the scalpers who turn big money into real money in incremental slices.

TARGET SHOOTER'S NOTES

➜   Use end of day chart analysis to set buy triggers and a buy range.

➜   Use electronic contingent buy orders to manage the developing trade.

➜   Look for order line build up during a trading halt or suspension.

➜   Use price leverage whenever possible.

➜   Wait for a pullback on the tick chart after trading resumes.

➜   Set target returns and use other stop loss methods as a safety net.

Chapter 9

SCALPING
STRATEGIES

Scalping was a popular activity in many old cowboy westerns. In the financial markets, the world leaders in this technique are American and they succeed by cutting a thin slice from price action. Australian banks were quick to see the possibilities and their slice from every transaction is not enough to cause you pain but adds up to billion-dollar profits. Trade at the right size – millions of dollars at a time in currency markets – and the financial scalp also adds up to billions. Trade at our size and the returns are measured in hundreds, or at times, a few thousand dollars.

Scalping is the boring reality of day trading. This trading technique relies on making money from very small moves in price. The small percentage return is translated into a large dollar return because the position size – the cost of the shares – is very large.

Scalping is usually limited to institutional traders and market makers. In certain well-defined circumstances it is also used by private traders with limited capital. Scalping is a day-trading technique and we use day-trading style calculations to assess the trade. Scalping opportunities for private traders rely on strong support and resistance levels or fast-moving momentum blips.

The US markets are larger, deeper and more liquid than Australia's. Their small and mid-cap companies have larger capitalisations than many of Australia's top 100. When it comes to scalping opportunities, the US market provides a range of opportunities well beyond the capacity of the Australian market. As a result we need to closely examine US trading methods and adapt them to our smaller market. Additionally we need to remove the impact of market makers and the strategies built around them. When we trade ordinary stock, and some derivatives, we do not have to factor in market maker activity.

Scalping relies on volatility. Unless prices move in a consistent range between the low and the high we cannot take a profit. A range of a few cents means little in a stock trading at $30.00 but it offers more opportunity in a stock trading at $3.00. Volatility comes in many forms but those of interest to us fall into three groups.

The first is the normal volatility of a stock. Every stock has its own rhythm or range. The range is calculated using indicators such as Average True Range, or the Average Dollar Price Volatility calculation discussed below. Most stocks move in a price range too narrow to offer the opportunity for good profit on an intra-day or short-term basis. At times National Australia Bank has a low-to-high daily range of $0.30. This range suggests we could make a profit, but a move from $36.00 to $36.30 delivers only a 0.83% return for the day.

Trade with $20,160 and we buy 560 shares at $36.00. Capture the entire $0.30 range and we take home $168 for the day, before brokerage. Trade with $180,000, buying 5,000 shares and at the end of the day you take home $1,500.

If you sit on an institutional trading desk, you may have the opportunity to buy 30,000 NAB shares by spending $1,080,000 of other people's money. Capture the $0.30 range for the day and you deliver a $9,000 profit to your employer. The percentage return in all cases is 0.83% but the position size delivers significant differences in the dollar returns.

We assume readers do not have $1,080,000 to allocate to a single short-term trade. We work at the other end of the scale, trading with between $10,000 and $50,000 in a single trade. Scalping based on consistent price range activity of less than 1% is not a viable strategy. We need higher volatility to make the risk in short-term trading balance the reward.

The second form of volatility is short-term volatility, created by a news event or some other factor with a short-term impact. These news events include both leaked and surprise news, as previously discussed. Other factors include the development of short-term price patterns, such as gaps, flags and triangles which are covered later in Part IV. Success comes from trading a defined event.

The third type of volatility is sustained volatility where there is a high probability of volatility persisting for several days. The real problem here comes in separating temporary and erratic price moves from those likely to persist for days or weeks. We increase the probability of success if we trade a stock with a history of movement.

We could buy any moving stock and stay for the ride. These are momentum techniques and we look at them in Chapter 12. They are different from scalping techniques which rely on the volatility of a stock.

For the moment we concentrate on using sustained volatility as a means of scalping regular returns from the market. We draw upon the work of American trader, Robert Deel and some of the strategies detailed in his book *The Strategic Electronic Day Trader*. His methods form the basis of this scalping technique but we have made modifications which improve its application in Australian markets. We start with the concept of Average Dollar Price Volatility and then examine how it is applied to selected candidates in an actual trade. We have extracted a selection of Deel's techniques. We encourage readers who are interested in exploring the wider explanation of his strategies to buy his book and explore his website, www.tradingschool.com.

ANALYSING VOLATILITY FOR DAY TRADING

Analysing volatility is very useful in making trading decisions. It helps to identify points where new buyers or sellers are entering the market and to confirm existing support or resistance levels derived from the daily charts. Volatility is measured in many different ways. They all aim to capture the degree of expected change in prices given the previous history of the stock. One approach to understanding volatility is to consider the average distance the stock has moved over a given period of time. This timeframe may be daily, weekly, or monthly. A market which is highly volatile is characterised by large price ranges measured by the distance from the high to the low.

Short-term traders look for stocks with certain volatility characteristics. These include stocks where the rate of price change is very dramatic. Deel starts with a five-day period because the trading focus is short-term on day trades or micro trends – rallies – lasting for a few days. The direction of these trends is set by the relationship of the close to the median or mid-point price for the day. The chart display in Figure 9.1 shows the median price as a dot on each daily price line.

To create this display in MetaStock, first plot the bar chart. Then select the indicator called 'Median Price' from the MetaStock menu. Drag this onto the chart display and it is shown as a line. Select the line and then select 'Properties'. Change the thickness of the line to the maximum and change the display 'Style' to the thick oscillator. This puts a thick dot on each bar at the median price level as shown.

To establish the trend we count the number of days over the five-day period where the close is higher than the median price.

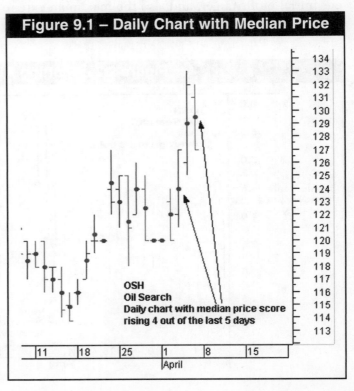

Figure 9.1 – Daily Chart with Median Price

OSH
Oil Search
Daily chart with median price score rising 4 out of the last 5 days

This establishes the level of bullishness, or bearishness. The objective is to trade with a strong trend. When all five days show a higher close than the median price the trend gets a top score of five. Where all days are lower than the median price, the score is minus five and indicates a strong bearish trend.

This relationship is transferred into a MetaStock Explorer search and the full details are at the end of the chapter. The filter in the exploration only shows those stocks with the strongest bullish bias.

The next step is to establish the average price volatility for the week. This is measured in two ways. The first is by a numerical calculation to establish the potential reasonable average move for the stock. This is how much, on average, we expect price to move during a single day. This is called average dollar price volatility – ADPV. It is constructed by taking the price range from high to low for each day and calculating the difference in dollars. A simple average of the total is calculated. This uses the MetaStock indicator fine-tuned by Patrick Macdonald and the formula is shown at the end of the chapter.

When the ADPV is plotted on a chart, as shown in Figure 9.2 we quickly know the potential each day has, on average, to move by a known dollar amount. This defines both our initial profit target, and also the maximum extent of our stop loss level. This dollar value defines the volatility of the stock.

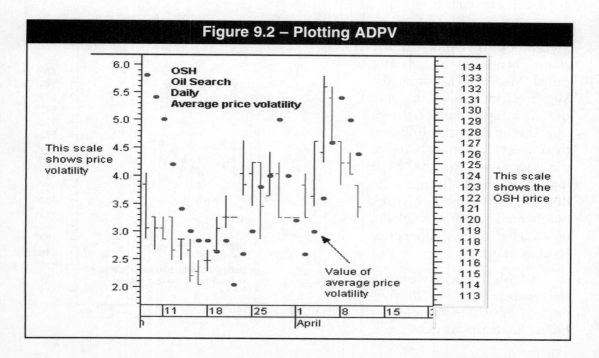

Figure 9.2 – Plotting ADPV

The stop loss is defined by a moving average of the lows. Deel uses a 7-period moving average on a five minute tick chart. He uses a 17-period moving average as an absolute stop loss. The actual stop loss exit point is set between the 7- and 17-period moving average values. A move below the 7-period average is an alert, and a move to the 17-period moving average is an exit signal.

We use the ADPV to provide a screening or filter parameter to select those short-term trends with the best potential for scalping.

SELECTING A SCALP

Scalping is a strategy which exploits short-term trading technique designed to generate a small, steady return. The objective is to use the volatility of price to capture $300 to $2,000 from the day's trading with a reasonably high level of probability. Successful scalping requires a consistently deep market where many trades take place each day.

Scalping works most effectively in stocks which offer some price leverage. Stocks trading at around $1.00 offer the opportunity to collect a reasonable return because there is a good probability the price range for the day is wide enough to capture a good dollar-based return.

Scalping is a function of size. It is very difficult to capture good scalping trades with only $2,000 in the position. Scalping becomes an effective use of capital once the size of each trade starts to exceed $20,000. Some scalpers do not apply these techniques to trades using less than $50,000.

The scalping trade has a dollar-based target return. It does not have a percentage-based target, although we select opportunities based on the best percentage returns. Traders aim for small target returns, perhaps $300 a day. On a $20,000 trade, a $300 return delivers a 1.5% profit. Increase the position size and the dollar return remains constant but becomes a smaller percentage of the capital employed in the trade. On a $50,000 trade a $300 profit represents just a 0.6% return and may be generated by a move of just $0.01.

Scalping success depends on low brokerage and effective trade execution. The DJS example in Figure 9.3 collects $855 based on a $20,007 trade with a move from $1.17 to $1.22. Traders shoot for specific entry and exit prices. The objective is to capture a rising trend and ride just a very small part of it. It is not suited for traders who do not have the time to sit in front of a live screen during the day. Nor is it a suitable technique to use with brokers who charge $80 a trade, or a percentage-based figure. This technique requires discount brokerage. Profits in dollar terms are low, so brokerage becomes a significant factor in the take-home profit.

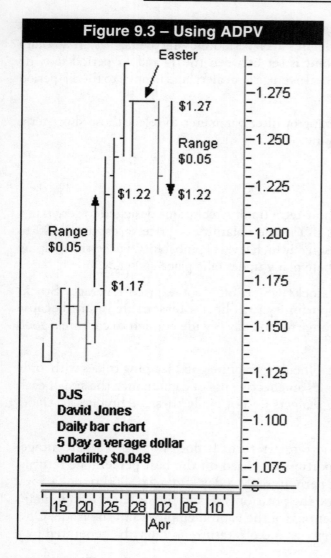

Figure 9.3 – Using ADPV

Easter

$1.27

Range
$0.05

$1.22 $1.22

$1.22

Range
$0.05

$1.17

DJS
David Jones
Daily bar chart
5 Day average dollar
volatility $0.048

1.275
1.250
1.225
1.200
1.175
1.150
1.125
1.100
1.075

15 20 25 28 02 05 10

Apr

With such low dollar returns these quickly become high-risk trades. Apart from analysis and execution risk, additional risk comes from the trading relationship between reward and risk. If $0.01 offers a sufficient reward, then a price fall of $0.01 – the minimum trading tick – has the capacity to wipe out all the intended profits in the trade. This is why it is so important for prices to be in a bullish, rising intra-day trend. The objective is not to wait for the best price but to take the current ask and ride the rise in prices during the day.

Managing these types of trades falls into two parts. The first is based on end-of-day analysis. The second is based on intra-day tracking. The end-of-day analysis is designed to identify those stocks which are potential candidates for scalping. The first list comes from a scan looking for stocks which have traded more than 1,600,000 shares on the previous day. This sounds a lot, but for shares trading at $0.01 this represents a dollar turnover of just $16,000. If our planned trading size is $20,000 then we really want minimum dollar turnover of $800,000 a day. This is 20 times the size of our intended trade.

Yes, the maths is correct. Our intended trade is for $20,000, but we want to make both an entry and an exit, so our combined trading size is $40,000. We need to ensure there is enough depth and liquidity in the market to allow us to buy $20,000 worth of shares and to later sell a $20,000 parcel.

Turnover of $800,000 a day is the minimum calculation based on the starting filter price of $0.50. At a starting price of $1.00 traders look for a minimum 800,000 shares traded each day. The $800,000 turnover absorbs our two planned trades of $20,000 each.

Consistent with our minimum planned trading size of 1,600,000 shares, we cut all those stocks below $0.50. Few of these consistently turnover $800,000 a day. When the scan is completed there are very few stocks meeting the liquidity conditions but they do provide the advantage of price leverage. At the other end of the price scale we cut stocks trading above $5.00. The objective here is to capture the best price leverage. Stocks trading between $0.50 and $5.00 tend to have a little more volatility and this helps boost the returns from the scalping technique.

Traders with larger size lift the upper cut-off point to $8.00 or $10.00. The search should return a relatively small number of stocks. We are looking for a specialised trading situation so it is unreasonable to expect a high number of returns. We look for the best combination of our planned position size with the best potential risk/ return ratio.

Once the first list is produced the next step is to establish the five-day average range of prices – the volatility. The results are used to sort candidates. Stocks with the highest volatility over five days offer a better opportunity for intra-day profits than stocks with a lower volatility. Here we are interested in the raw range – the difference between the high and the low for the day. They are ranked using their Average Dollar Price Volatility.

DIRECTION COUNTS

The Average Dollar Price Volatility search does not tell us the direction of the potential price moves. Successful scalping depends on selecting those stocks with a greater propensity to rise. We want to add $0.024 to our purchase price rather than lose it. Deel searches using a Deel Momentum Filter included in MetaStock. His objective is to identify those stocks which are most likely to continue trending upwards.

This filter is designed to alert you to stocks which have colossal momentum and extended trend. The number of stocks passing this filter depends upon market sector and strength. This filter is used by day traders and aggressive investors. Stocks screened by this filter have a tendency to trend for several days and even weeks in an upward direction.

Traders without access to the MetaStock search achieve a similar objective by examining the charts. This is not a sneaky business. We are not trying to out-fox the market. We just want clear chart evidence that prices are more likely to rise than to fall. We find the evidence in well established uptrends. Scalping is not appropriate for breakout-style trading. The returns are simply too small to justify the risk involved.

On the open the next day, we watch the way these trades develop as the order lines build prior to the market open. In particular we look for evidence in the order line structure that prices are likely to continue rising. This confirms the best scalping opportunity. We show how this is implemented in the next chapter.

MetaStock Exploration Formulas

Average Dollar Price Volatility exploration – Deel

This exploration is designed to provide the average dollar price volatility figure in column F and finds this figure for all stocks scanned. It is most useful to apply this exploration to a small group of stocks. It matches the steps in Robert Deel's book *The Strategic Electronic Day Trader*.

Col A:	day 1	HIGH–LOW
Col B:	day 2	Ref((HIGH–LOW),–1)
Col C:		Ref((HIGH–LOW),–2)
Col D:		Ref((HIGH–LOW),–3)
Col E:		Ref((HIGH–LOW),–4)
Col F:		(H – L + (Ref(H,–1) – Ref(L,–1)) + (Ref(H,–2) – Ref(L,–2)) +(Ref(H,–3) – Ref(L,–3)) + (Ref(H,–4) – Ref(L,–4))) / 5

Average Dollar Price Volatility indicator – Deel

This indicator plots the value on the chart display. It is useful only as a quick method of attaching the volatility value to the stock. Apply this with caution and make sure the new scale display is also included.

(H – L + (Ref(H,–1) – Ref(L,–1)) + (Ref(H,–2) – Ref(L,–2))+(Ref(H,–3) – Ref(L,–3)) + (Ref(H,–4) – Ref(L,–4))) / 5

Bullish Range – Deel

This default MetaStock exploration is designed to find those stocks where the close is above the median price over the past five days. It matches the steps in Robert Deel's book *The Strategic Electronic Day Trader*.

Col A:	1	CLOSE – MP()
Col B:	2	(Ref(CLOSE,–1))–(Ref(MP() ,–1))
Col C:	3	(Ref(CLOSE,–2))–(Ref(MP() ,–2))
Col D:	4	(Ref(CLOSE,–3))–(Ref(MP() ,–3))

Cont'd...

MetaStock Exploration Formulas *(Cont'd)*

Col E: 5   (Ref(CLOSE,–4))–(Ref(MP() ,–4)) Filter colA>=0 AND colB>=0
AND colC>=0 AND colD>=0 AND colE>=0

Filter enabled   Yes

The filter in the exploration only shows those stocks with the strongest bullish bias over all five days. By removing the filter all scanned stocks are shown. Ranking the first column sets the overall score for each stock.

Scalper's Exploration

Finds stocks with turnover of more than 1,600,000 shares trading above $0.50 and below $5.00 and ranked on Deel's Average Dollar Price Volatility indicator

Col A:	Volatil$	Fml("Deel – average dollar price volatility")
Col B:	close	CLOSE
Col C:	vol	VOLUME
Filter		colB>.50 AND colB <500 AND colC >1600000

≡ MARKSMAN'S NOTES

→ Scalping trades offer small percentage returns.

→ The Deel bullish range search finds volatile stocks which are candidates for trading.

→ Average Dollar Price Volatility sets the expected price range.

→ Use deep markets with price leverage.

→ Scalpers shoot for low dollar returns so low brokerage fees are vital.

→ Find candidates with an end-of-day search and filter for the highest potential percentage returns.

→ Visit www.tradingschool.com for more information on advanced techniques.

Chapter 10

LIFTING
THE SCALP

The Lord High Chancellor in Gilbert and Sullivan's *Mikado* is noted for waving a list of people, who, if they disappeared, would never be missed. We apply the same type of ruthless execution every time we complete a scan of the market. It is not enough just to come up with a list of all stocks that meet our specified trading criteria. Matching a mathematical condition, in this case within a selected Average Dollar Price Volatility range, reveals only one feature of the potential trading opportunity. Trading success depends on a range of other features.

This, incidentally, highlights one of the reasons for the failure of black box trading systems which claim to automatically identify trading and investment opportunities for users. The reports generated contain a list of shares meeting a set of defined mathematical conditions but they may, or may not, be good trading opportunities. The inability to discriminate between the good, the bad and the possible defeats these programs. In the final analysis, the user must make a decision about which of the recommendations he trades.

The same confusion about the nature of advice plagues financial industry regulators who are still deeply suspicious of any software that scans, or explores a database and returns a sorted list of stocks matching user-defined conditions. They suspect this is trading advice. In reality it is an efficient way of sorting and classifying stocks according to price behaviour. It is a *starting point* for further analysis. It is not a solution.

The scan or exploration is a quick way of separating those stocks which have risen for the day from those which have fallen. We might make the sorting slightly more sophisticated by looking for stocks where a short-term moving average has crossed above a long-term moving average. This condition helps identify rising stocks. The point of crossover does not, by itself, generate a buy signal, although in some trading approaches it is used in this way. If we are trading from the long side – buying at a low price with the intention of selling at a higher price – the list is further refined. Eventually the user makes a choice about which stock to trade. He may choose to make the decision himself, or he may take a short list of candidates to a licensed financial adviser and use it as a starting point for further discussion.

We have not strayed too far from the Lord High Chancellor's list. Ours is in hand, courtesy of the MetaStock explorations built around Robert Deel's search for volatility. On the day of the search shown in this chapter, the list includes 20 candidates. Like all traders we face one important limitation. We only have enough capital to trade one of these. Deciding which stocks to cut involves several selection steps and we explore them below.

The first sorting is built around volume. We set a minimum dollar turnover which is large enough to incorporate, or hide, our proposed trading size. We aim to spend $20,000 so it is no good buying a stock with an average turnover of $5,000 a day.

The second sort uses end-of-day charts to identify trends. Apart from identifying trending activity we are also asked to exercise our judgement. What are the chances of prices reaching our short-term targets? It is difficult to put a hard probability figure on this. Some chart features, such as an existing double top, make it more difficult for prices to push higher. There are no hard and fast rules. Here experience and judgement count. It is also an opportunity for hope to play a larger role than usual. In the case study we show the role each plays.

The objective of this screening combination is to reduce the list to just a single outstanding candidate. Most times we succeed in weeding out all except two or three. Which one gets the nod, and which gets the chop, depends upon the opening behaviour of price. We use live screens to follow the open of market, buying only the stock that moves favourably. We conclude this case study by showing how the daily screens are used to manage a successful scalp. This real scalp is 4.35% thick, adding $880 profit for the day.

RANKING TREND AND VOLATILITY CANDIDATES

The search for suitable trading candidates starts with a price and volume elimination process. We start with a list of stocks trading between $0.50 and $5.00. The objective here is to capture the best price leverage so stocks in these price ranges have more volatility and this helps to boost the returns from the scalping technique.

The search produces a list of 20 candidates, shown in Figure 10.1, that meet the price and volume requirements. The list is further filtered against three criteria.

1.   **Current trending behaviour.**

     The trend notes in the final column in Figure 10.1 provide a shorthand guide. Downtrends are shown with a '\' and uptrends with a '+'. Sideways trends are indicated with a ' –' and a '?' identifies those where price action is too confused to offer easy analysis.

Figure 10.1 – Trading Candidates

Security Name	Volatil$	close	vol	Ticker Syn	TREND
BORAL LIMITED.	7.6	362	1654781	BLD	\
BURSWOOD LIMIT	2.2	89	4053656	BIR	+
COMMONWEALTH	1	117	3036322	CPA	-
DEUTSCHE OFFIC	1.8	128	4776488	DOT	\
FGL	5.4	478	3956535	FGL	-
FUTURIS CORPOR	5	166	1864071	FCL	\
HARDMAN RESOU	2.6	70	3010653	HDR	+
IRON CARBIDE	12.8	274	3451662	ION	\
JOHN FAIRFAX HC	7	373	3430643	FXJ	\
LEND LEASE US	1.6	154	3344015	LUO	+
LIHIR GOLD LIMITE	5.4	117	11517916	LHG	\
MACQUARIE INFA	5.4	336	4734852	MIG	-
OIL SEARCH LIMIT	4	115	4715167	OSH	\
ORIGIN ENERGY	5	313	2834800	ORG	-
PEPTIDE TECHNO	28.6	320	3007347	PTD	+
QANTAS AIRWAY	6.4	440	2840854	QAN	-
SMORGON STEEL	3.6	132	3262646	SSX	\
STOCKLAND TRU:	3	434	1714422	SGP	-
WESTFIELD AME	1.8	194	9864389	WFA	-
WESTFIELD TRUS	2	326	2955360	WFT	-

2. **Average Dollar Price Volatility over five days.**

   Meeting volatility conditions does not mean the stock is trending upwards. It tells us little about the probability of prices rising. We apply trend analysis techniques to assess this balance.

3. **Leverage.**

   All other conditions being equal, our preference is for opportunities which offer the best price leverage.

We start with the trend analysis. The selection process is straightforward. We select those stocks showing a clear uptrend because this increases the probability of the uptrend continuing. Tomorrow's price action is more likely to move up, rather than down.

The MIG chart in Figure 10.2 does not show a clear uptrend. You might like to argue some of these charts show the potential for a breakout. This argument may well be correct, but this is not the type of trade we are looking for. A breakout from an existing downtrend, or sideways movement, has a lower probability of moving upwards than a stock already in an uptrend. Our objective is to capture a continuation of an existing trend. We are not interested in trading against the current trend in anticipation of a change in trend direction. On this basis stocks like MIG are eliminated from this search.

The same reasoning applies to stocks like BLD which are in an obvious downtrend as shown in Figure 10.3. There may be some useful downtrend rallies, but the probability of capturing one of these on the exact day we decide to enter the trade is quite low. Weak stocks are more likely to continue to weaken. Stocks in an uptrend have a better probability of continuing their upward movement for the next day when we intend to trade. There is no reason to add downtrend stocks to this selection list. Cut them out.

The next filtering step ranks the Average Dollar Price Volatility, calculated using the Deel formula shown at the end of Chapter 9. The results are included in the initial scalping market scan. The first column – Volatil$ – shows the range of price activity, on average, over the past five days. These results are pasted into a spreadsheet for further analysis. By adding the Average Dollar Price Volatility to the closing price we set a potential profit target price for the next day – assuming the uptrend continues. This is shown in the second-last

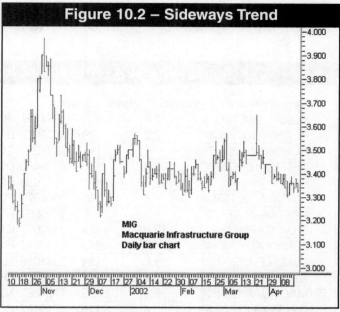

Figure 10.2 – Sideways Trend

MIG
Macquarie Infrastructure Group
Daily bar chart

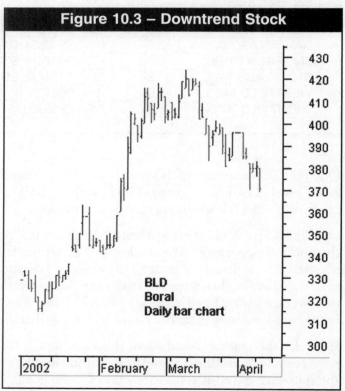

Figure 10.3 – Downtrend Stock

BLD
Boral
Daily bar chart

column in Figure 10.4. This is then recalculated to give a projected percentage return, shown in the last column.

Figure 10.4 – Results of ADPV Filter

Security Name	Volatil$	close	vol	Ticker Sym	target price	% profit
BORAL LIMITED.	7.6	362	1654781	BLD	369.6	2.10
BURSWOOD LIMIT	2.2	89	4053656	BIR	91.2	2.47
COMMONWEALTH	1	117	3036322	CPA	118	0.85
DEUTSCHE OFFIC	1.8	128	4776488	DOT	129.8	1.41
FGL	5.4	478	3956535	FGL	483.4	1.13
FUTURIS CORPOR	5	166	1864071	FCL	171	3.01
HARDMAN RESOU	2.6	70	3010653	HDR	72.6	3.71
IRON CARBIDE	12.8	274	3451662	ION	286.8	4.67
JOHN FAIRFAX HO	7	373	3430643	FXJ	380	1.88
LEND LEASE US	1.6	154	3344015	LUO	155.6	1.04
LIHIR GOLD LIMITE	5.4	117	11517916	LHG	122.4	4.62
MACQUARIE INFA	5.4	336	4734852	MIG	341.4	1.61
OIL SEARCH LIMIT	4	115	4715167	OSH	119	3.48
ORIGIN ENERGY	5	313	2834800	ORG	318	1.60
PEPTIDE TECHNO	28.6	320	3007347	PTD	348.6	8.94
QANTAS AIRWAY	6.4	440	2840854	QAN	446.4	1.45
SMORGON STEEL	3.6	132	3262646	SSX	135.6	2.73
STOCKLAND TRUS	3	434	1714422	SGP	437	0.69
WESTFIELD AMEI	1.8	194	9864389	WFA	195.8	0.93
WESTFIELD TRUS	2	326	2955360	WFT	328	0.61

One method of selection chooses those scalping candidates with the highest potential profit level. The best of these is PTD with an 8.94% return based on an average price range of $0.286. This is impressive, and attractive.

One look at the PTD chart in Figure 10.5 shows it is not the best trading opportunity for this intra-day approach. The stock is in a downtrend. This is a potential breakout trade, not a trend continuation trade. The breakout has already shown three days of very fast activity. Many of these types of trades run out of steam after three to five days. Based on the Average Dollar Price Volatility of $0.286, the target price is $3.48. This is achievable, but it calls for a very dramatic continuation of the rally.

Consider the market dynamics of this situation. If this rally had started at $5.30 – the previous year high – there would be few obstacles to it continuing. In the current situation, the relationship is different. Many people who bought PTD at prices between $5.30 and

$3.00 are sitting on losses and they form a very large crowd of potential sellers. They are most likely to take the opportunity to get out at a small loss, or a small profit. It is more difficult for this stock to punch its way through the crowd of sellers. There is a lower probability this rally will continue, even though it shows the best results when we filter for potential returns.

We drop this stock because it is not consistent with a rising trend. For the same reason we also eliminate three other candidates. These are the best performing stocks based on comparing the target price to the current close. Unfortunately, they are all stocks caught in substantial downtrends. This is not to say these stocks will not provide profitable trades during the day. It simply acknowledges there is a lower probability of success in looking for a rising day in a downtrend.

Ideally we want a match between a rising trend and a good profit return. We have just three candidates, BIR, HDR, and LUO suitable for further analysis. Which trade is executed depends on their performance as the market opens.

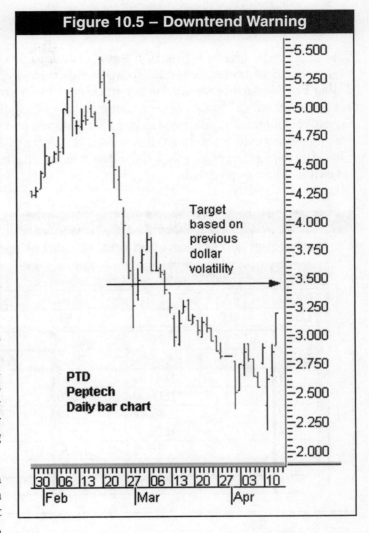

Figure 10.5 – Downtrend Warning

Target based on previous dollar volatility

PTD
Peptech
Daily bar chart

MANAGING VOLATILITY

The problem now is to choose which of these is the best trading candidate. The choice is not absolute. It requires judgement and is based on what we believe to be the most probable outcome. Each of these stocks has a high probability of going up, but this does not necessarily mean each will go up. We make the selection as the market opens the next day.

We start with the order lines because they tell us which of these candidates is poised for success.

The LUO order line in Figure 10.6 is not very deep, even though there is a consistently high number of trades each day. To make this trade work using the calculated Average Dollar Price Volatility we need to get an entry at $1.54 and an exit at $1.56. On a $20,020 trade this returns $260 for the day. Using this pre-open order line we need to assess if this is possible, or probable. We need to buy 13,000 shares, and this is achievable. The stumbling block in this trade is the large undisclosed sell order at $1.55. This has the potential to provide a cap on the price rise, for the day at least. This makes it more difficult to achieve an exit at $1.56 as planned.

Figure 10.6 – Order Line for LUO

Marketcast live screen - just prior to market open

MarketDepth - LUO - Second Level

Symbol	± %	High	Low	Prev	Open	Tot Vol	Trades
LUO	-0.6			1.540			0

		17 Bids			9 Asks		
Count	Buyers	Volume	Price	Price	Volume	Sellers
1	3	144105	1.530	1.540	238673	2
2	1	150000	1.520	1.550	75000u	3
3	3	4600u	1.510	1.560	5000	1
4	4	150543	1.500	1.600	8000	3
5	1	1500	1.490			
6	2	6000	1.460			
7	3	55701	1.450			

An alternative is to join the buy order line at $1.53, but this does not give us much of an advantage. It lowers our required sell level to $1.55 – shooting for the same size price move – but our sell order goes to the end of the line and this reduces its chances of being executed. Even if we can buy LUO at $1.53 it is still potentially difficult to exit at $1.55 because of the large undisclosed sell order at this level.

This candidate fails the last selection test because the order line does not allow us to implement our trading strategy.

The HDR order line in Figure 10.7 is more appealing. It shows a very high volume of trading with around 50 million shares wanted against 22 million shares on offer to sell.

This is likely to be a more active market with a higher number of trades for the day. This higher level of liquidity improves our chances of getting into and out of the trade. The estimated match price is $0.705. An entry at $0.70 and a planned exit at $0.73 offers a 4.29% return. On a trade size of 29,000 shares this returns $870 for the day.

Figure 10.7 – Order Line for HDR

MarketCast live screen - just prior to market open

MarketDepth - HDR - Second Level

Symbol	± %	High	Low	Prev	Open	Tot Vol	Trades	BuyVol	SellVol	Estimate
HDR	0.0			0.700			0	5007512	2239650	0.705

	188 Bids			140 Asks			Last 20 Trades		
Count	Buyers	Volume	Price	Price	Volume	Sellers	Price	Volume	Time
1	1	3333	0.750	0.700	274123	20	0.700	2000	15-Apr-02
2	1	5410	0.740	0.710	253870	15	0.700	609	15-Apr-02
3	4	106491	0.720	0.720	277552	16	0.700	3130	15-Apr-02
4	7	157401	0.710	0.730	354542	14	0.700	4408	15-Apr-02
5	15	92524	0.700	0.740	189633	9	0.700	5592	15-Apr-02
6	8	144664	0.690	0.750	167150	11	0.700	8708	15-Apr-02
7	6	487434	0.680	0.760	93840	5	0.700	1292	15-Apr-02
8	10	184559	0.670	0.770	83000	4	0.700	3000	15-Apr-02
9	12	283090	0.660	0.780	43001	5	0.700	10708	15-Apr-02
10	14	163356	0.650	0.790	23000	4	0.700	14292	15-Apr-02
11	6	133500	0.640	0.800	107327	8	0.700	46261	15-Apr-02
12	11	331500	0.630	0.820	10000	2	0.700	8000	15-Apr-02
13	11	204414	0.620	0.840	7570	1	0.700	5700	15-Apr-02
14	13	361997	0.610	0.850	23465	6	0.700	1000	15-Apr-02
15	16	1336198	0.600	0.880	100000	1	0.700	579	15-Apr-02
16	7	108855	0.590	0.890	10000	1	0.690	10000	15-Apr-02

This is a more attractive trading opportunity because of the high level of indicated trading activity. It is preferred to LUO.

The final option is BIR. The order line shows a potential gap pattern open on heavy buying volume. The eventual open is at $0.92 which is higher than yesterday's high of $0.90. The gap opening increases the probability of the stock trading upwards during the day.

We selected BIR based on heavy buying volume, a potential gap-open pattern, and good price leverage. The plan is an entry at $0.92, buying 22,000 shares with an exit $0.022 higher at $0.94. This delivers a $440 return, or a $660 return with an exit at $0.95.

MINUTE MANAGEMENT AIMS HIGH

The order line confirms a gap opening and in the moments before the stock starts trading we take action. These notes conclude the actual management of the BIR trade. We use the

ASX opening match process to buy the stock on the open. This is achieved by placing a buy order at the head of the buying line and $0.01 above the highest bid price. The objective is to achieve the estimated match price on the open which turns out to be $0.92 as planned.

We use a five-minute tick chart to monitor and manage the trade. As the five-minute chart indicates in Figure 10.8, the sell target is reached and exceeded on the first opening move before we have time to place a sell order. This confirms the crowd excitement and opens the opportunity to improve the returns from this trade. We place a stop loss order at $0.93 locking in a $220 profit. Based on this initial excitement, our objective is to monitor the strength of price activity.

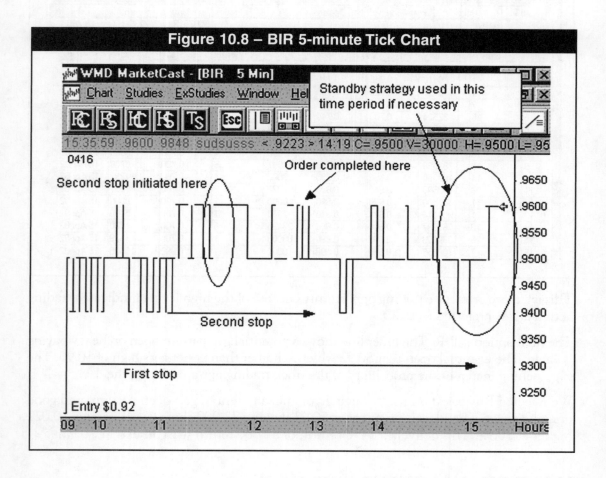

Figure 10.8 – BIR 5-minute Tick Chart

In these situations I place a sell order above the market in anticipation of a continued upward move. This intra-day method relies on constant screen monitoring so our objective is to move this sell order up or down during the day in an attempt to capture the best part of the daily price move. This is the reverse of lifting the stop loss during the day. As the trade moves into success we tighten the trailing stop loss conditions to protect the profit, and we set new profit targets based on the potential for further action during the day. Trailing stops are used to lock in profit while stop loss points are used to protect capital.

The sell is placed at $0.96. It is not first in line. This order is nibbled at in the morning session. A few trades take place at $0.96.

Once trading moves consistently above $0.94, a second trailing stop is put in place at $0.94, locking in a $440 profit. It is lifted because of the sustained sales at $0.96. Trading action has now consolidated in this range, and our order moves very close to the front of the order line at $0.96. We expect the order to be executed around the middle of the day. However trading activity may pause at this level, so we need a stand-by exit strategy.

The stand-by strategy is reserved for the last hour of trading. If buying pressure has further weakened we shift the sell order lower to meet the current bid at $0.95. An exit at this level returns a profit of $660.

The stand-by strategy is not implemented as our order moves to the front of the line and is executed around the middle of the trading day. This exit at $0.96 returns a 4.35% profit and adds an $880 profit. These are not large returns and many traders find the effort required to identify and manage these trades is not justified. Day trading thrives on small, regular returns.

The identification and selection processes discussed in these two chapters are based on trading notes made at the time of this case study trade. They reflect my application of these techniques in a real-life trade. The chapter is designed to provide a realistic account of what is involved in applying these short-term tactics in nervous market conditions.

For this real trade we used the Deel measures of volatility to identify an intra-day trade. The same measures are applied to identify trades which may last three to five days. It is good practice to treat planned intra-day trades as true day trades, buying and selling within a single market trading session. When day trades turn into overnight, or three-day trades, the risk profile changes. Sometimes this adds to profits, but there is always a temptation to let a losing intra-day trade ride overnight, hoping for recovery.

Volatility captures the range of price movements. Momentum captures the acceleration of price movements. A trend defines the continuation of momentum. Two- and three-day momentum-driven trades attract our attention during a scan of daily charts. These are the stocks where prices have zoomed upwards from $0.03 to trade at $0.14 a few days later. They provide several different types of short-term trading approaches which we examine in the next chapter.

≡SHARP SHOOTING NOTES

→ Rank candidates for volume, trend and leverage.

→ Select stocks with established uptrends.

→ Select stocks with deep order lines.

→ Manage the trade with a three- or five-minute tick chart.

→ Place sell orders above the market to reserve your place in the order line.

→ Adjust trailing stop orders during the day to lock in profits.

→ Prepare a standby sell strategy in case prices do not reach your targets.

Chapter 11

RALLY

INVITES

Momentum trading is one of the foundations of short-term trading approaches. It offers a variety of short-term three- to five-day trading techniques. These include those based initially on early or rapid access to breaking news. Many of the techniques discussed in the chapters dealing with surprise and leaked news are also applied to short-term momentum trades.

Some tactics rely on the quick identification of momentum activity. These fast-moving rockets lift in several stages and offer a variety of entry points. There is time, at the end of the first day of the rally, to jump on board. Some traders search the market for rally-driven stocks in the last hour of trading. They buy towards the end of the day and join a price move which has the potential to extend over several days.

Others run an end-of-day search for stocks showing an unusually large price range for the day. This is generally a default search on most trading software. It ranks stocks by the percentage increase of today's closing price compared to yesterday's. Those with the largest increases are potential rally candidates. The objective is to buy on day two of the rally and ride the momentum over the next three or more days.

There is an important final group of momentum trading strategies which make capital out of missed opportunities. How many times have you seen an excellent rally about two days after the rally has completed its run? Sometimes it seems we are always too late in discovering this fast-moving opportunity. A final group of short-term trading tactics watches for specific price behaviours following the collapse of the rally. These include trading bullish flag patterns, and a group of finger or rebound trading strategies. We look at these in detail in Chapter 13.

Remember the important difference between volatility and momentum. Volatility describes how much we expect a stock price to move on any given day. Momentum ties price movements together, and helps measure the acceleration of price over several days. Superficially, most rallies look similar, but they have different rates of acceleration. The rate depends on the character of the stock, its pricing, the degree of enthusiasm in the sector and other factors. We do not need to make a detailed analysis of the character of each rally, but we do need to understand how broad factors may affect performance.

A rally in a gold stock during a tech boom is of less interest than a rally in an internet-related stock. This helps the trader choose between opportunities. The trader is not required to undertake stock-specific analysis. Understanding the context of the rally is sufficient and we start this chapter with an outline of these distinctions before turning to the methods used to manage a rally trade.

RECOGNISING A RALLY

A rally is ultimately a failure to set a sustainable uptrend and so is best suited for short-term trading. A rally is most often a short-term substantial change and upwards reversal of price direction. This includes a change from a sideways pattern to a good up move. It includes the change from a downtrend to a potential new uptrend. In each case, the promise of the upwards price move is quickly filled and the up move collapses. A rally incorporates the concepts of speed, recovery and collapse.

Many new uptrends start with a rally. Very few extended uptrends develop from extended rallies. Instead there is a pattern of rally and retreat to establish the initial conditions necessary for a new sustainable uptrend.

The CML chart in Figure 11.1 provides a good example of this difference. The first feature is the way the initial downtrend shown as A, was broken by a

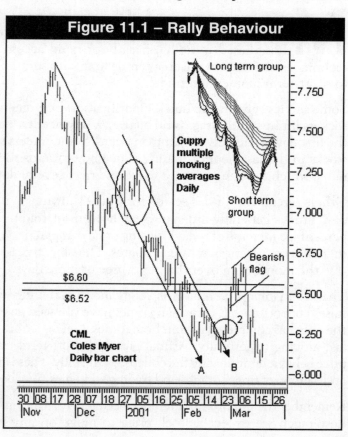

Figure 11.1 – Rally Behaviour

Long term group

Guppy multiple moving averages Daily

Short term group

Bearish flag

$6.60

$6.52

CML
Coles Myer
Daily bar chart

1

2

A   B

-7.750

-7.500

-7.250

-7.000

-6.750

-6.500

-6.250

-6.000

30 |08 |17 |28 |07 |18 |27 |05 |16 |25 |05 |14 |23 |06 |15 |26
|Nov |Dec |2001 |Feb |Mar |

short-term rally in area 1. At the time this rally had the potential to become a trend break and many people bought CML on this basis. Instead prices declined, using trend line A as a support level. This is often a signal of an impending trend reversal as the trend line shifts from playing a resistance role to a support role.

With CML this downtrend developed in parallel to the original trend line. Traders watch the new trend line B for any indication of a new uptrend break. This comes when CML moves above the trend line in area 2. This rapid rise brought many new people into CML in anticipation of a new trend.

Instead it has all the characteristics of a rally. These include:

➜ The very rapid rise over just a few days. This type of fast rise is unsustainable. We expect a pullback and then a re-establishment of the new trend.

➜ The development of an up sloping bearish flag. This bearish signal gives ample warning to those who had bought around $6.28 that an exit at $6.60 is a good idea.

➜ The resistance band between $6.52 and $6.60 is based on spike lows and resistance levels in 1998 and 1999. We would normally expect prices to pause in this area. When this pause is associated with a bearish flag pattern then another sell signal is generated.

➜ The price breakout is identified early as a rally by using the Guppy Multiple Moving Averages. When the breakout begins, the long-term group of averages is well separated. The rally is driven by short-term traders and has little probability of being able to reverse the solid downtrend established by the long-term investors. This confirms the breakout is best treated as a rally rather than as a trend break.

By understanding these factors, the trader is able to make a better decision about the nature of the trading opportunity. These are quick profits, usually taken over a three- to five-day period.

Database searches for rallies use volume and price as an entry criterion. Samples are included at the end of the chapter. The exit is signalled by a drop in volume on a lower close than the previous day. Where pattern-based profit targets are not set, the trade is closed when indicator exit conditions are met.

UNDERSTANDING RALLIES

The lure of the rally is always present. They represent a good opportunity to make good money often in a very short timeframe. This desire to make quick profits is dangerous. Rallies are traded successfully as part of a clear and disciplined trading strategy where quick cash is the last consideration. Rallies provide good trading opportunities for the skilled and disciplined short-term trader. They provide an easy way to lose money for traders who are hungry for profits.

Rallies come in four main types. They are:

1.   Rallies in a rising trend.

2.   Rallies within a generally falling trend.

3.   Rallies in range bound or choppy markets trading in a sideways pattern.

4.   Breakout rallies at the end of a downtrend reversal pattern.

Prior to entering any rally trade we need to recognise the type of rally as each calls for a different trading strategy. The rally we all lust after is the bull market rally shown in Figure 11.2.

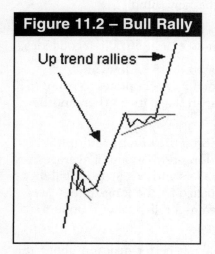

Figure 11.2 – Bull Rally

Up trend rallies →

The first type of rally takes place within the context of a rising trend. The direction of the trend is clear and the stock often makes new historical highs. These rallies are often based on bullish chart patterns, such as bullish downwards sloping flags, and upwards sloping triangles. The more frenzied the bull market, the more frequently these bullish rally patterns appear. In some speculative stocks, one pattern follows another very rapidly.

These rally patterns are traded by setting targets based on the chart pattern projections. These are minimum targets. The stop loss conditions are triggered by any break below the bullish chart pattern. Profits are taken as soon as the momentum, as shown by volume of trading, begins to slow.

The second type of rally takes place within the context of a downtrend as shown in Figure 11.3. These rallies trap many investors, particularly when they appear in blue chip stocks. The price for a previously high-priced blue chip begins to fall. Eventually it reaches a point where many investors believe it is a bargain. They step into the market and buy it. Their buying creates a temporary rally as with CML. Soon the downtrend reasserts itself and price falls further. The downtrend is characterised by many false rallies. In blue chip stocks these tend to be several days of steady upwards price action rather than just a few days of extremely fast moving prices.

The context of these rallies is identified using a Guppy Multiple Moving Average indicator. This allows the trader to place a probability value on the chances of the rally becoming a new uptrend. These rallies are traded with clearly-defined target exit conditions based on the way price penetrates the long-term group of averages on a Guppy Multiple Moving Average. Other trades are based on resistance levels. All are managed with tight protect profit conditions.

The third type of rally is confined to range-bound markets, as shown in Figure 11.4. The XAO chart extract is an example of this behaviour. This is channel trading where prices, or index values, bounce back and forth between clearly defined support and resistance levels. These sideways markets provide trading opportunities if the distance between the support and resistance level is wide enough. The rallies in Figure 11.4 are shown by the thick lines on the chart.

Here we use techniques for trading choppy markets. This includes the use of oscillator style indicators like Stochastic, and MACD_Histogram to confirm the potential turning points at the bottom and the top of the range. Often in these markets the levels are not accurately defined by support and resistance lines even though the range-bound activity is self evident. The support and resistance levels are sometimes more accurately defined as a range of support and a range of resistance.

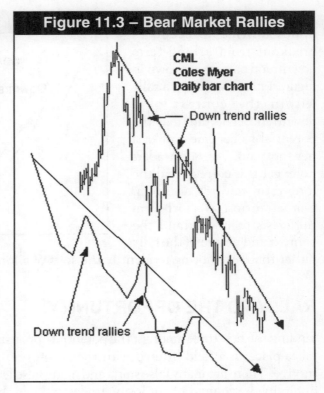

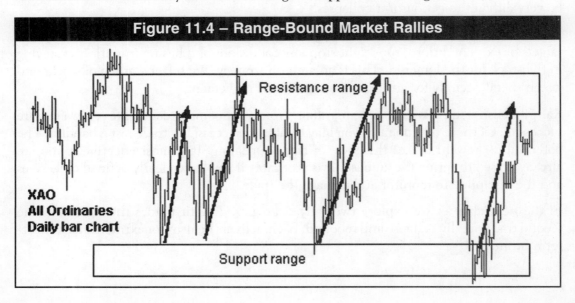

The fourth type of rally opportunities precede a breakout from a long-term downtrend pattern as shown in Figure 11.5. This is not a rally within the context of a downtrend. The rally has the potential to become part of a new uptrend. Position traders note: get this correct, and the long-term rewards are high. Our intention as short-term traders is to understand the context and nature of the rally rather than attempting to identify the start of a long-term trend.

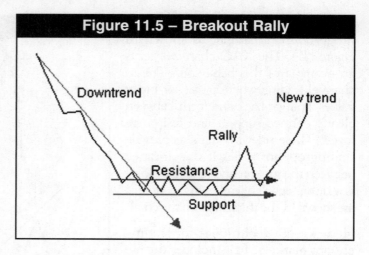

Figure 11.5 – Breakout Rally

RALLY TO THE OPPORTUNITY

Finding the best trade amongst the potential opportunities is difficult. This ambush hunting takes place in a field littered with the corpses of failed rallies. Only a few recover and survive. There are many false starts and many false leads in this environment. Good trading discipline is required to cut losing trades and false breaks very quickly. There is an added execution danger because trading volumes may be low. It is easy to join a rally, but it may be very difficult to get out if it collapses.

Rally trading recognises a short-term opportunity. As a result the trader sets realistic profit targets or exit conditions, runs tight stop loss conditions and has no intention of staying in the stock for the long run. This is an ambush strategy. We select a group of stocks and watch them carefully for any sign of our preferred movement.

Rally ambush trading is a hit and miss affair. From a list of many candidates only a few are successful. Of those that do rally, you may be able to successfully trade just a handful. The potential for reward makes this style of trade appealing. It is most effective if you are already poised to spring the ambush. It is profitable if you have clearly defined objectives and the discipline to monitor and manage the trade.

In the next chapter we explore two rally strategies. The first rides the tiger, and the second trades a rally collapse and rebound. Each delivers healthy, or extraordinary, short-term profits.

Rally Search Formulas

The MetaStock search is simply chosen from the Function menu when making a New exploration:

➜ RallyWithVol( )

Alternatively stocks are ranked by percentage gain over one to three days. Using MetaStock Explorer we screen to find securities where the price has increased 5% and the volume is 50% above the 10-day moving average. The parameters are adjusted to suit your needs. The formula is:

ColA   CLOSE

ColB   REF(CLOSE,–1)

ColC   ROC(CLOSE, 1,PERCENT)

ColD   VOLUME

ColE   MOV (VOLUME,10, EXPONENTIAL)

ColF   ((VOLUME –MOV(VOLUME,10,EXPONENTIAL))/
          MOV(VOLUME,10,EXPONENTIAL))*100

Filter   WHEN (COLC>=5) AND WHEN(COLD> =COLE*1.5)

The Ezy Chart search formula for rally stocks is:

➜ The High price of Today is equal to the Closing price of today; and

➜ The Volume of Today is greater than the Volume of yesterday.

≡TARGET NOTES

➜ Rallies are trend failures and are traded as short-term opportunities.

➜ The best rally opportunities occur in bullish markets.

➜ Trading rallies in established downtrends calls for good trading skills.

➜ Rallies have defined targets or exit conditions and are managed with a tight stop loss.

➜ The failure rate is high.

Chapter 12

STARTLED
RABBITS

For a while I lived on the edge of the Little Desert in Victoria. The sandy country was a paradise for rabbits. In the days before the calicivirus cut rabbit numbers, shooting rabbits was a popular sport and a community service. I hunted rabbits with a single-shot .22 calibre rifle. Success did not depend on speed. It rested on careful stalking and good reflexes. Moving carefully along hedgerows, or moving amongst fallen timber, the objective was to spot the rabbit before it became a white-tailed blur. There was a brief opportunity to snap off a shot as the rabbit started to bolt. The shot gunner throws a spread of shot at a moving target with a high probability of scoring a hit. Few traders have the capital to apply the same techniques in the market. The rifleman must be more exact in his aiming point. As traders we have limited capital, so it pays to be exact in the choice of trading opportunity.

Short-term trading requires careful planning ahead of speedy execution. Wild snapshots at rapidly disappearing targets are unlikely to be successful. Snapshots based on careful planning hit the target. We examine this type of approach in the first case study below which returns over 1,000% in three days.

In heavy scrub there were always a few rabbits which hopped to the next bit of cover, paused, and looked back to see if danger was still present. Some rallies behave in the same way, and in the next chapter we look at a rebound strategy based around price behaviour after the initial rally has faltered.

If you happen to hold a stock that rallies dramatically from a low bottom you are handed an excellent trade. For traders who do not own the stock, the first inkling they have of a rally taking place is when it shows up on an exploration search. The most common of these are price and volume searches, or just price searches looking for the best percentage gains for the day.

These searches identify price rallies as they happen. This is often too late for us to take advantage of them. Trading in anticipation of rallies carries three types of risk. The first is the obvious risk of failure. Some stocks look like they are going to rally but make a false start. Instead of running quickly upwards after the breakout, they dramatically collapse. It makes it very difficult for traders to capture any profit from the move.

The second risk of failure also comes from an unexpected drop below the closest support level. Instead of a rally, we get a rout. This is particularly true of stocks that have paused in a downtrend rather than with those building consolidation patterns at the bottom of a downtrend. It is difficult to tell the difference in real time as the MYO chart in Figure 12.1 illustrates.

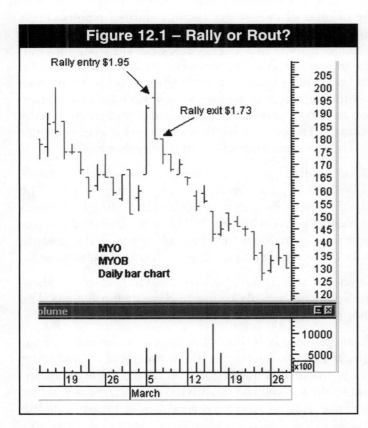

Figure 12.1 – Rally or Rout?

Both of these situations mean we enter the trade too late, after we hear about the rally. By the time it is reported on the news or shows up on a database exploration, most of the move is over. We buy MYO at $1.95. It is a disappointment to see it close lower on the day, and the next day, if we have enough discipline, we get out of the trade at $1.73. This is an 11% loss. If we do not have the discipline, then the trade takes us even lower, all the way to $1.13 and a 42% loss before it shows any sign of a new rally.

The third type of risk is the way trading capital is locked up. In this case the stock does nothing. Instead of breaking out it drifts sideways, locked in price paralysis. You do not lose money but nor do you make it and your capital is tied up preventing you from chasing other profitable trades. There is a temptation to hold on and hope it breaks into a rally.

Rally trading is aggressive trading where the trader is trading against the prevailing trend. He expects a downtrend to turn into an uptrend. Rally trading depends on timing. Enter late and we miss most of the large rewards and snatch just a few crumbs before the rally collapses. With three- to five-day rallies, traders need good skills to take advantage of these opportunities.

STARTLED RABBITS

Before the road south from Darwin was sealed it was a long three-day drive to reach Adelaide. Tired after twelve hours behind the wheel and at three in the morning I pulled off the dirt highway for a sleep under the stars. I rigged a mosquito net above my swag on the ground and quickly slipped into a deep sleep. Unbeknown to me, I had camped alongside a long bend in the Alice Springs to Adelaide railway line. An hour later I woke in fright with a train headlight blazing through the darkness and apparently heading directly at me. I leapt out of the swag and provided a few comical moments for the dog as I stumbled through the bush fighting fear and a tangled mosquito net.

Sleepy stocks react the same way to unusual events and become startled rabbits. Their explosive action is a perfect rally trading opportunity. On their charts, prices move sideways for an extended period with no volume. It looks like a sleepy stock but the stock flies into action on very low volume, and the impact of a small number of trades is magnified. Where there are reluctant sellers it means buyers must bid very much higher to get stock and this creates rapid price movements. Low trading turnover means the only way for a new buyer to get stock is to bid higher. Low prices and no volume do not always indicate disinterest in the stock. It sometimes indicates existing shareholders are happy with the stock so they are not prepared to sell at the current bid. They are only enticed to sell with higher bids.

Simple trading techniques yield solid results for short-term traders. These include simple searches based on traditional relationships, such as price and volume activity. The advantages gained by complex database searches, and sophisticated trading techniques are often not very great. They are most effective when applied to derivative products like warrants, options and futures, where small gains are turned into substantial dollar rewards. In trading ordinary, everyday stocks, these more complex approaches are of less benefit.

Every few days we run a price and volume search across the database to find stocks where the price has increased 5% and the volume is 50% above the 10-day moving average. The parameters are adjusted to suit your needs and preferences.

This is not a very complex or sophisticated search. It simply finds stocks where both volume and price have increased. We are interested in changes in the 10-day average of volume as this helps identify rally behaviour. There is no magic combination for perfect results. If the parameters are too loose – a small rise in price and volume – you end up with too many candidates. If they are too tight – screening for a big increase in price – too many good candidates are excluded.

RALLIES BY VOLUME

Once the list of candidates is created, we turn to other analysis methods to determine which are the most suitable for trading. In this example we consider a sleepy stock appearing on a price and volume search. It is an extreme, but real, example and we use it to highlight the factors behind a successful rally-style trade.

We consider two issues in this process. The first is the problem of trading volume, or liquidity. The second is the reliability of this volume-based selection process.

Some traders who use a price and volume search add a filter to weed out stocks trading less than, for instance, 50,000 shares. Other traders filter candidates by using an average 10- or 20-day volume figure. Their objective is to ensure the stocks have consistent trading volume. This is a sound approach but it also weeds out some of the stocks which have the potential to provide the best opportunity.

The relationship between liquidity, volume, and trading opportunity is a complex one. We all want to avoid stocks where little trading is taking place because this makes it very difficult to buy stock, and often seems to make it even more difficult to sell stock just when we want to. However, we need to examine the reasons for this low trading liquidity.

One reason may be genuine lack of interest. Nothing particularly exciting is happening, so those who hold the stock are not really interested in selling. Those who potentially want the stock, are not very interested because there are better opportunities in the market. With MNR, for example, there are around 2,000 shareholders, and only a few of them are interested in trading in the period shown in the chart extract in Figure 12.2.

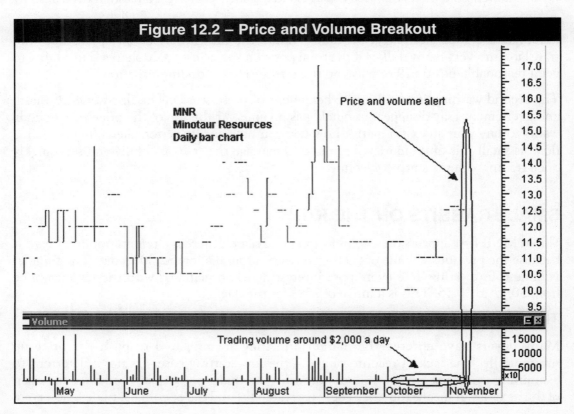

Figure 12.2 – Price and Volume Breakout

This is a sleepy stock because nothing is happening. The lack of liquidity reflects a lack of interest but this may change quickly. When we look at a chart like MNR we should not immediately dismiss it because trading volumes have been low.

Another reason for low trading volumes is that shares are simply unavailable for trading because most of them are held by the top 20 shareholders. This is not the case with MNR. Here, the top 20 hold around 30% of the available shares. The 'free float' is 70% of the available shares. This is important because it tells us there are a lot of shares available for trading when something does happen. The 2,000 shareholders have most of the shares and if they decide to act they quickly restore liquidity to the market. Under the right conditions, this provides an opportunity to accumulate a larger parcel of shares than recent trading volume would suggest is prudent. This is an important consideration once the price starts to run up.

Low volume also occurs when most of the shares, up to 60% and sometimes more, are held by the top 20 shareholders. This information is found in share registry records. For mining companies I use the *Register of Australian Mining* as a source. This much smaller number of available shares paradoxically adds to the potential for significant price rises when the sleepy stock wakes up. With only a few shares available, demand rapidly outstrips supply. This is an ideal situation for a meteoric price rise as excited traders chase just a handful of shares.

This situation comes with two important warnings. First, it may not be possible to accumulate a good size parcel of shares. While the return may be 30%, this does not translate into very many dollars if the total position size is just 5,000 shares. The ability to get a reasonable position size may cap the returns in this trading situation.

The second warning is found in the behaviour of these stocks. The flood of enthusiasm and excitement may disappear as quickly as it came. At the top of the price rise, nobody wants to buy your stock no matter how few you have available for sale. When the 'free float' is small it is often more appropriate to manage the trade carefully and sell quickly once trading volume starts to decline.

SMALL RABBITS ON THE RUN

When MNR first appears on a volume and price search there is a temptation to discard it because the previous volume of trading averages around a low $2,000 a day. The surge in volume is interesting. It is even more interesting when matched with the surge in price from $0.12 to $0.15. This is a move of 25% for the day.

This is an important alert despite the previous low volume.

Many buyers have entered the market and they are prepared to push the price up substantially. The lack of recent volume – the low starting base – is not a deterrent to examining this stock further. It does not mean the trader places a buy order for the open of the next day. It means the stock goes on a watch list and the opening of trade is observed.

If buying pressure continues on the back of a 25% rise in the previous day, then it may be worth buying into the stock as a rally opportunity.

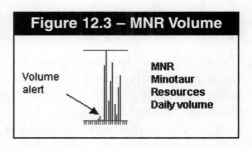

Figure 12.3 – MNR Volume

It is difficult to adjust the scaling on this chart display in Figure 12.3. The initial price volume breakout looks insignificant when compared with subsequent volume activity. The breakout is confirmed the next day and continues over the following week. With increased liquidity we easily fill a $20,000 order. This underlines the importance of recognising the change in volume behaviour rather than dropping the stock from a watch list because of a past history of low volume behaviour. The massive and continued trading volume alerts traders to significant price activity in this stock. Although traders may have dismissed it in an initial scan, the stock appears on our routine database explorations over several days, and provides a number of trading opportunities. The full trend development after the initial price and volume alert is shown in Figure 12.4.

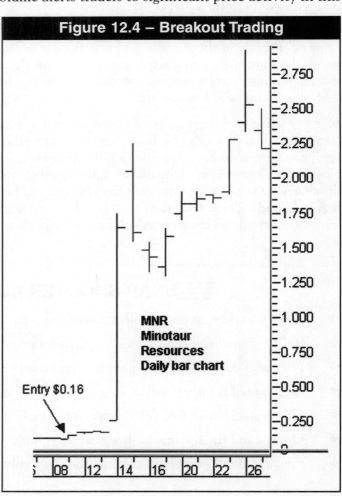

Figure 12.4 – Breakout Trading

This opportunity is large enough to deliver the bulk of trading profits for a yearly period. This trade returns 1,731% from an entry at $0.16 based on the initial breakout price volume signal, and an exit on the high of $2.93. Using a $20,000 position this buys 125,000 shares at $0.16 and creates $346,250 in profits.

Even an exit at $2.21, on the first high, still returns a whopping $256,000 profit on a $20,000 trade.

This is an extraordinary short-term trade. They do exist and these excellent opportunities are found using simple methods. You do not need a $7,000 black box trading program to find them. You need skill to trade them.

The second point, in this extreme example, is to remind readers no single trading approach yields consistently excellent returns. Most times these short-term trades are bread and butter trades. They return 10% to 30% per trade. This is nothing very exciting, and although they add steadily to trading capital, it takes consistent management every day, or every week, to ensure the trades meet all our management conditions.

Some of these trades fail. Then they must be stopped out and small losses taken. The selection method used does not guarantee success. A more complex selection method does not dramatically improve the chances of success. Success comes from the way the trader handles those trades returning a profit and from the way he cuts losses when the trades do not perform as expected.

A very small number of these trades perform spectacularly, as with the MNR example. Capture just one of these a year and manage it successfully, and it is good compensation for all the hard work and discipline applied to all the rest of the 'also ran' trades. These spectacular trades are a bonus delivered to traders with the discipline to manage all their trades, including the losers.

Many of these trades get away. We spot them too late, or lack the courage to trade the astounding increase in price believing it is impossible to sustain. In smaller rallies we apply the same reasoning, fearful the price we see today is close to the ultimate high of the move. Not all traders are temperamentally suited to trading short-term rallies. This often shows when they buy the rally near the very top and hold onto the stock as it retreats and then rebounds. These traders miss some important short-term trading opportunities that rely less on speed and more on judgement. Some of these are examined in the next chapter.

≡SNAP-SHOOTER NOTES

→ A good understanding of rally behaviour prepares traders for speedy execution.

→ Rally risk includes sudden price collapse or price paralysis.

→ Price and volume searches identify opportunities.

→ Entry speed is important.

→ Sleepy stocks with low volume accelerate rally speed and returns.

→ Understand the reasons for low trading volume.

→ Low free floats propel prices when turnover volume increases.

Chapter 13

PATTERNS
OF PROFITS

Rally trading calls for fast reflexes and constant attention. Many traders are better at finding rallies after they have happened than at identifying them as they develop. Rather than lamenting lost opportunities traders turn these into another set of opportunities designed to take advantage of the pause in momentum. Most rallies collapse, some fatally. Others collapse into a temporary retreat before regaining strength and moving upwards again. These are short-term three- to five-day opportunities based on chart patterns. The most reliable of these is the bullish flag, but other patterns such as upward sloping triangles also signal defined short-term targets.

The rabbit shooter prowls the scrub waiting for opportunity to present itself. When opportunity emerges he is primed to take action. Similarly, these post-rally trades involve a set-up period which may last for a week or more as price action regroups for the next charge. The trader watches the development, ready to take action as soon as any breakout develops.

Some price behaviour comes as a one-two punch. This means although we miss the first part of the behaviour, we successfully trade the second part. Rally trading, and trading the aftermath of rallies, provides three types of opportunities. Three primary patterns develop in these situations. They are:

1. Flags.

2. Rebound or finger trades.

3. Upward sloping triangles.

These three patterns form my core short-term trading strategies.

The failure rate in rally chasing is high, so many traders discard these stocks quickly. This is unfortunate because they provide trading opportunity. When rallies fail they often move into a profitable recovery pattern of behaviour. These opportunities are provided by the way the rally pulls back, or collapses. I keep all failed rallies on a watch list because of the potential they offer for further trading.

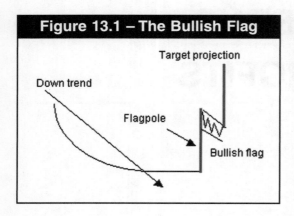

The most powerful and consistently reliable pattern is the bullish flag shown in Figure 13.1. I use this as one of my main short-term trading techniques. The flag forms when the initial enthusiasm for the stock slows down. There are few sellers as most new stockholders hang onto their recently acquired positions. Buyers collect stock from long-time stockholders who are selling into the unexpected strength, but who are frightened the rally has failed completely. Gradually prices move downwards, but maintain a steady trading band.

This is the key characteristic of this chart pattern. The flag pattern only occurs at the top of a flagpole. It is created by one to five days of extreme and continuous price action moving in the same direction. There are no significant retracements during the construction of the flag pole.

This price action appears on a price and volume breakout search, or just on a price search tagging extreme price ranges. Find these and you have a starting point for a flag trade.

A flag is not a triangle, or a pennant. Like most flags, this pattern has parallel sides. Identification starts as prices begin to pull back from the high created by the flagpole. We want two to three points to plot a tentative down-sloping trend line. This is the starting point for the pattern and it usually takes a minimum of three days to confirm.

Once the top straight-edge trend line is plotted we hunt for the potential parallel trend line to define the downside in this pattern. To do this we simply take the upper trend line and plot it as a parallel line using the most recent low in the emerging pattern. We do not have to wait for two or three lows to develop before we plot the trend line.

Instead we infer the position of the lower parallel trend line and plot it from a single low. We then look for future price action to confirm the initial placement. Why the rush? In a fast-moving bull market, this pattern may develop over three to five days. Sometimes there are only two lower points in the pattern, and if we wait for validation from a third we miss the opportunities for the bullish breakout. By plotting an inferred parallel trend line based on the confirmed upper trend line we give ourselves the advantage of early recognition of the pattern.

The pattern may take longer to develop. When it does, we have more points to confirm the placement of the upper and lower trend lines. Aggressive traders buy the stock as it approaches the value of the lower trend line. More conservative traders wait for proof of the pattern before buying. I tend to be aggressive, so I buy near the middle of the pattern spread when I am confident the pattern is for real.

The stop loss is placed one tick below the value of the lower trend line. This gives room for price to move within the bounds of the pattern development. If the pattern continues its downward trend, the stop is moved lower. We do not want to be stopped out of this trade prior to full pattern development. In moving the stop lower, it is important to ensure the amount at risk in this trade does not exceed 2% of total trading capital.

How far can we let the flag drop before the trade is abandoned? There are no hard and fast rules here. It is a judgement call based on the way support develops near the bottom of the flag and the structure of the order line. The examples discussed below show how this judgement is applied.

Other exit signals include a drop below the value of the lower trend line. In most cases I find this pattern develops fully over five to ten days. As we move beyond ten days the pattern loses its vitality. It develops a lower probability of success and, of course, as the top of the trend line continues to fall the potential returns are also diminished as the projected exit target also drops. The flag pattern comes in faster markets. This is not a slow pattern taking weeks to develop.

Setting profit targets applies the same price projection techniques we apply to triangles but with one important difference. This is a pause pattern. The market is redeveloping strength. To set the potential target we first measure the height of the flagpole. This is why the flagpole is such an integral part of a flag pattern. The flagpole starts with the day signalling the beginning of the fast rise. Usually this is very clear. The distance from the base of the flagpole to the top of the flag pole is calculated in cents.

This value is then projected upwards from the point of the breakout above the flag pattern. This sets the minimum target. In many cases this target is exceeded. When the breakout occurs it is often very rapid. It is not uncommon for prices to gap above the top of the flag trend line and this is a disadvantage for conservative traders. They end up chasing prices.

These are fast developing patterns so, in most cases, price moves rapidly towards the target projections in three to five days. This is not a slow trend. It is a continuation of the initial rally. Breakouts drifting sideways have lost momentum. I abandon these trades, taking a smaller profit because the probability of success is reduced to around 5%. The trades are still profitable but they have less chance of reaching the profit target.

TRADING THE FLAG

These are fast developing patterns so, in most cases, price moves rapidly towards the target projections. Aggressive traders enter in anticipation of the flag breakout developing. This is a sensible strategy in a bull market because breakouts from the flag are very rapid. In a nervous market breakouts tend to be a little slower, so there is less disadvantage from waiting for the breakout to take place. Conservative traders wait for pattern confirmation to occur before taking the trade. The two real trades below illustrate these approaches.

The Singapore listed stock, Singmas HK in Figure 13.2, shows a conservative entry into a flag trade after the breakout has taken place. This trade was identified in real time during a live interview on CNBC Asia.

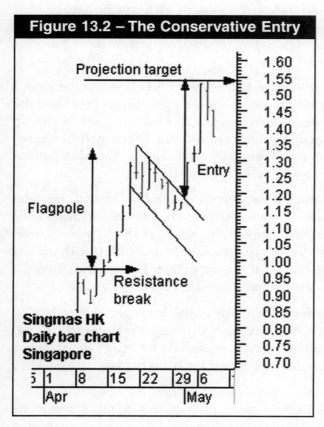

Figure 13.2 – The Conservative Entry

Conservative traders got a position at $1.32 on the day after the flag breakout. It takes four days for the breakout to achieve the projected targets. The conservative trader surrenders a significant part of the potential profit by delaying his entry into the chart pattern. The total price projection, based on the breakout point above the upper edge of the flag, provided a 29.46% return.

These conservative traders who entered the day after the flag breakout at $1.32 captured an exit at the target price of $1.54 two days later. This late entry into the pattern reduced the return to 15%.

The flag pattern captures the flow of greed and fear. The pattern of greed and fear is repeated in all markets and all countries. The flag pattern in American listed Simula in Figure 13.3 provides an 83% to 108% return in four days for aggressive traders. Prices hover near the upper edge of the flag. The bottom is defined by a parallel straight-edge trend line starting from the single low. As long as prices are contained within these two parallel edges, the flag pattern remains valid.

The aggressive trader enters in anticipation of the breakout at $2.40. Three or four days later he gets out at $4.40 and collects an 83% return. Holding the trade up to $5.00 adds a 108% profit to his account.

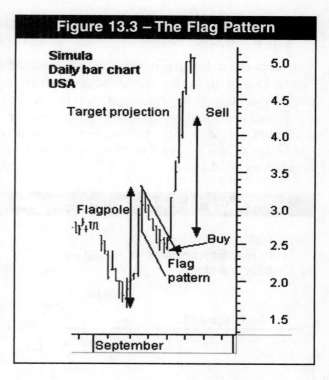

Figure 13.3 – The Flag Pattern

The consistent achievement of these price targets within three- to five-day timeframes makes these chart pattern techniques so useful in short-term trading.

In a bull market, the bullish flag targets are usually treated as a minimum target. In nervous markets we treat them as a maximum target so we trade the breakouts with a pre-set sell order in place. This is set just at, or slightly below the target level. Use the depth of market screens to help estimate the potential selling strength at these levels. If there are a lot of orders already in place then good traders place their order slightly lower. This gets them to the front of the order line and gives a better chance of completing the trade.

CATCHING THE REBOUND

The second pattern developing from rally failure is a finger or rebound trade. This chart pattern starts with a price spike, usually on substantial volume, and lasts a few days. Prices show massive ranges, accompanied by substantial volume. This is not a price volume breakout in the normal sense because the price ranges are so great. Traders wait for the retracement. The pattern is completed by a dramatic fall, of usually no more than three to five days. Prices drop back to around the midpoint of the initial rally move. This does not create a flag, although the starting point is similar to a flagpole and is identified using the same database scanning techniques. This signals the finger trading strategy.

The flag trade offers targets higher than the top of the flagpole. The finger or rebound trade usually limits targets to the height of the flagpole. The real-time trade in this example is unusual because the prices gap through the target level. How prices behave once the target level is achieved is difficult to forecast. Many times prices retreat, drifting sideways or collapsing quickly. How they develop is not our concern. We use this pattern for a three- to seven-day short-term trading opportunity.

The important feature is the development of short-term support levels shown in Figure 13.4. This is not proven support in the normal technical analysis sense. It is anticipated support developing around the 30% to 50% retracement level. Some traders use Fibonnaci numbers to set these levels. We use a support level established by a minimum of two or three points. Sometimes it is signalled by a sell-off price dip on a single day which recovers to close near the open. These are all signs the rally sell-off may have ended.

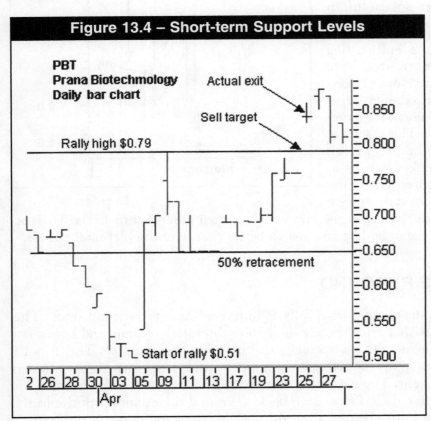

Figure 13.4 – Short-term Support Levels

With PBT, the rally starts at $0.51 and ends at $0.79. A 50% retracement sets the bottom level at $0.65 and support develops here. An entry at this level has an exit target at $0.79. With this particular trade the first exit opportunity is at $0.84 and returns 29%.

This is trading with significant risk. Get this trade wrong and you are caught as the price collapses quickly below this very temporary support. You need good stop loss discipline to succeed. This is why it is called a finger trade – if you get it wrong the market gives you the finger!

The objective with this pattern is to enter near the support level and to exit at the previous rally highs. The stop loss conditions are a collapse below the support level. In stocks with price leverage this offers a good opportunity for useful profits.

FOLLOW THE TRIANGLE

The third pattern I look for after the rally is an upward sloping triangle. This is a standard bullish pattern where short-term resistance is challenged by a short-term upward sloping trend line. The sloping trend line shows changing values over time, and the horizontal support and resistance lines show unchanging values over time. The most exciting feature on any chart is when the two forces represented by these two lines meet. Here we get a range of different prices and potential activities all based on triangle patterns. These chart patterns form the basis of price projection techniques. Get them right and we make money. Get them wrong and trading becomes guesswork.

The most useful feature of these patterns is the way price projections are calculated. This is done by measuring the base of the triangle and then projecting it upwards or downwards. This provides a very precise method of measuring risk and reward as shown in Figure 13.5.

The up-sloping triangle forms when a horizontal resistance line is intersected by a rising trend line. Price rises to the resistance level where sustained selling forces the price back. Buyers can bid less and still pick up stock. However, on each pullback the extent of the fall is reduced. Buyers have to bid slightly higher to get the stock. This creates the rising trend line as each new low is higher than the previous one. When there are no more sellers at the resistance level buyers have to bid higher to get stock.

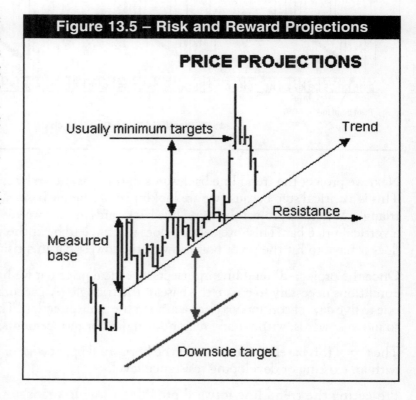

Figure 13.5 – Risk and Reward Projections

Often this means bidding substantially higher and the breakout takes place. This is a strong chart pattern and breakouts present short-term trading opportunities taking one to five days to reach their targets.

Setting the resistance level is an easy task but some traders find it difficult to identify the base of the triangle. This is set by price action and the sloping trend line. The cluster of lows in area B on Chart A in Figure 13.6 provide the potential to plot a trend line. We join this initially with the thin line using the two major lows. This provides the slope of the trend line. Remember this is a retrospective plot created at the time shown by the last bar on the chart.

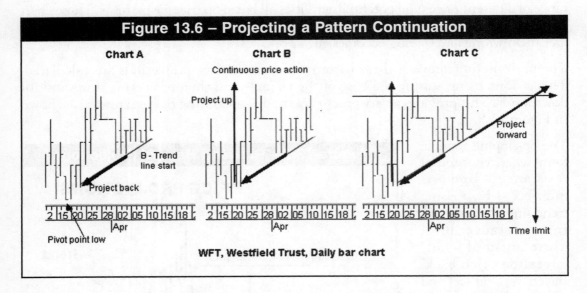

Figure 13.6 – Projecting a Pattern Continuation

WFT, Westfield Trust, Daily bar chart

Next we project the trend line backwards in time, as shown by the thick line in Chart A. This is a critical step because we are looking for a triangle base. Without a base there is no triangle. When we project the trend line backwards in time we keep going until it intersects a vertical price bar. This intersection does not have to be at the very base of the bar. Nor does it have to hit the pivot point low or the lowest bar in a rising trend.

Once the projected trend line intersects a vertical price bar we have the beginning of the conditions necessary to create the base of the triangle. An accurate triangle base calls for one to five days of continuous price action in the same direction. This means price continues to move upwards, without any major down days or retracements, as shown in Chart B.

The top of this baseline is used to set the horizontal upper edge of the triangle if it matches with an existing or developing resistance level.

Projecting the trend line forward provides a way to manage the trade as it develops. The intersection of the horizontal line and the trend line sets a time limit for pattern development shown in Chart C. We look for a breakout before the time limit is reached. We expect future price retreats to fall no further than the projected value of the trend line. This maintains the integrity of the developing triangle pattern. A close below this trend line generates an exit signal.

We finish this chapter with a real triangle trade in QTK shown in Figure 13.7. This is a short-term pattern and we use just two points, A and B, to set the short-term resistance level. In most cases two points are not enough to set a valid resistance level. We increase our confidence in this level with QTK because of the way the up-sloping trend line develops so strongly and clearly. The upwards sloping triangle is a clear development with three points used for plotting the line.

Aggressive traders enter after the second resistance point. The preferred entry is at, or

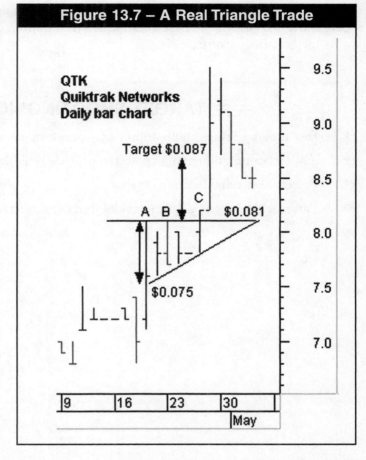

Figure 13.7 – A Real Triangle Trade

QTK
Quiktrak Networks
Daily bar chart

Target $0.087

A B   C $0.081

$0.075

near, the value of the up-sloping trend line. Conserv-ative traders wait until the upper resistance level is broken and then make an entry at point C. This is a valid strategy in a nervous market, as often the breakout from this pattern is initially weak. In a bull market the breakout is often very much stronger so the conservative trader puts himself at a disadvantage by waiting.

We use standard triangle projection techniques to set a price target at $0.087. With an entry from inside the triangle pattern at $0.078 this gives a minimum return of 11%. An exit on the close at $0.090 is a 15% return. These are not big returns in themselves but they are very useful returns for a one- to five-day trade.

The success rate in chasing the initial rally behaviour is not high unless you identify the rally just prior to the breakout. Add these missed rally trades to a watch list and the trader has the opportunity to pursue a series of follow-up trades. Just because we miss the first opportunity does not mean we should dismiss the stock. The recovery from a rally retreat is a worthwhile hunting ground for short-term traders. We examine some more variations of these techniques in Chapter 22 but before this we examine tools for boosting profits.

≡TARGET SHOOTING NOTES

→ Fast moving rallies create follow-up opportunities.

→ Flag, rebound and triangle patterns provide reliable short-term trades.

→ Patterns set reliable price targets.

→ Patterns take many days to develop but breakouts hit targets in three to five days.

PART III

PRODUCING
PROFIT

Chapter 14

GETAWAY

CARS

An expensive sports car sitting in your driveway is a symbol of success and status. It shows what money can buy even though state-imposed speed limits prevent you from exploring more than a fraction of its performance potential. You bought the vehicle for all sorts of reasons and drive it within the conditions imposed by the city, traffic lights and speed limits. Underneath the bonnet or nestled behind the front seat is a powerful engine and an excellent drive chain that, if unleashed, could take you to your destination very much faster. Unfortunately circumstances conspire to prevent you from using the potential power.

Who wins in this deal between you, the manufacturer and the car salesman? In financial terms it is the manufacturer. He collects a substantial profit from the car sale and is able to offer an extended warranty because this is literally the sports car owned by a little, old executive who never drove over 120 kilometres an hour without getting a speeding fine. The car salesman takes his commission even if you total the car in a crash just a kilometre from the show room floor.

The expensive sports car sitting in your driveway is just the powerful getaway vehicle a steal-to-order thief is looking for. He has customers who need a high-powered vehicle to make a fast getaway after robbing a bank. The thief examines your car as a potential candidate for a fast getaway vehicle. You might consider his assessment improper, but his customers want to fully exploit the power and performance of your vehicle.

Welcome to the world of warrants. These high-power trading instruments deliver substantial profits to the warrant issuers, a steady commission flow to the brokerages who handle the sales and, when used by investors in the way most commonly advised, deliver limited performance from a much larger potential.

Short-term and day traders do not drive warrants this way. Warrants have a large range of proper uses. These are explored in books written by Chris Temby and Chris Tate, and in the many warrant seminars run by those who issue the warrants and who want you to buy them. Proper uses do not interest us here. We are interested in improper uses that open up full-throttle warrant trading.

Short-term traders are not thieves although some people outside the market put traders in the same moral category as thieves, bankers and tax officers. Traders are called on to crack the market safe. Nobody in the market willingly gives us money. We collect it as payment for our analysis and trading skill. It is earned, often at great expense.

Before the accelerator pedal goes to the floor we need a *short* revision course in the true sense of the word. We must look behind the popular sales image of warrants and understand the structure of the market before exploiting it more effectively. This is not a warrant primer. We assume you are familiar with the basic concepts so we are not going to spend a lot of time explaining them. Our focus is on the subtleties of the application of trading techniques in this market area.

We buy warrants for their performance created by leverage. Other traders purchase options or futures contracts for the same leverage advantages. The techniques discussed in this section are also applicable to the options market and broadly applicable to futures trading. We do not trade these markets because we are uncomfortable with the risk profile and the execution risk involved. Readers who wish to extend the information below to options markets will find it useful to combine this information with advanced options books by Guy Bower and Nick Katiforis. Those reaching for the futures markets have a wider choice, starting with Jack Schwager's comprehensive books on futures trading.

LEVERS FOR PROFIT

Leverage has a number of different meanings depending on which side of the financial world you are talking to. Leverage is gained when you have a mechanical advantage. You lift very large objects using a lever and a fulcrum. A small weight is able to lift a very heavy weight.

Financial leverage works in the same way. The first form is based on derivative instruments, like options, warrants and futures contracts. For a small amount of cash – good faith money or option premium – you control a large block of shares. There are other more specific forms of financial leverage involving margin trading and futures margins.

Our interest is in just one form of leverage common to all derivatives and to many speculative stocks – price leverage. This second form of leverage is based on low price and relies on common misconceptions about value. It does not seem to matter if we pay four cents or five cents for an item. The difference in price is minor and haggling is not a serious issue. This gentle acceptance changes as the price rises. When an advertisement quotes a product's price at $4 but we find the price marked at $5, when we get to the store we take exception. We are not prepared to pay $5 when the advertisement quotes $4.

The percentage difference is the same but the psychological difference is very large. Our resistance to meeting the same percentage increases in price grows as the dollar cost increases. This has a significant impact in the market. It means low prices move upwards more easily while high prices move slowly. This gives low prices a leverage advantage.

We use price leverage to our advantage in trading warrants and other low-priced speculative stocks. It is a key concept in delivering better short-term profits.

Psychological leverage is the third important form of leverage. When just a few dollars are at stake we treat the activity as a game. A hand of cards at $1.00 a hand is recreation. A hand of cards at $1,000 is serious business.

When we trade the market and commit thousands of dollars we cross the threshold from casual indifference to serious concentration as the cost of entry is leveraged upwards. The threshold level is different for all traders but the impact is the same. Once trading becomes serious we may suffer from trading paralysis as our reluctance to take a loss increases significantly. This is a serious drawback for those who take on short-term trading opportunities.

ARTIFICIAL MARKETS

A derivative is a financial instrument whose value is 'derived' from another asset. Warrants and options are the most familiar products but derivatives also include instalment receipts and futures contracts. A derivative's value depends upon the underlying value of the assets, usually a single share. Pricing the derivative depends upon the current value of the asset, its volatility and the strike or exercise price of the derivative. It also depends on the date of warrant expiry. As these relationships change the market value of the derivative changes in a process summarised as time decay. The Black-Scholes method is most commonly used to calculate fair option pricing given implied market volatility.

Never forget warrants are a created, artificial market. Some derivatives markets contain a third party as a necessary part of the transaction between buyer and seller. This is the market maker. Like you, he trades to make money. Unlike you, he is a full-time professional backed by lots of money. Where possible you want to avoid trading against him because odds are he wins and you lose. Trade *with* him and you make money if your trading skills are good enough to follow his action.

Warrants are issued by a third-party financial institution like ANZ or SG Australia. Do not confuse these with warrants in the US which are a debt instrument issued by the parent company. In return for the right to issue warrants over selected companies, the warrant issuer is required to make a market in each warrant. This simply means when the public does not want to buy or sell the warrant – when there are no orders from the public

– the warrant issuer must quote buy and sell prices at which they are prepared to do business. We examine these important implications in detail below.

The hallmark of an artificial or created market is when trading is based on prices quoted by a market maker rather than on orders received from buyers and sellers who make a voluntary decision to participate in the market. We work with an order-driven market in shares in Australia. The range of buy and sell – of bid and ask – figures is set by the orders delivered to the brokers. When you ring your broker, your order is placed in line on the Australian Stock Exchange SEATS system with every other order for the stock. We see the full depth of market. The market of many individual buyers and sellers – you and me – decides what prices are offered and the spread between the bid and the ask. The differences are summarised in Figure 14.1.

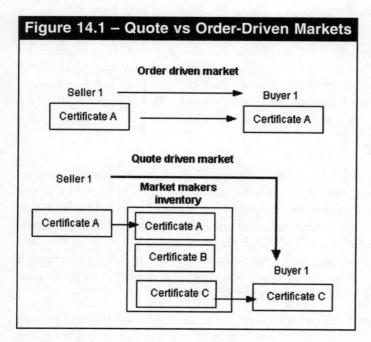

Figure 14.1 – Quote vs Order-Driven Markets

In a quote-driven market, the range of buy and sell – of bid and ask – figures is set by a third party. This is a registered market maker – called a registered trader in the options market. He decides the prices at which *he* is prepared to buy and sell, and as a professional trader, he expects to make money out of this. The spread between the bid and ask is sometimes very large. In a busy market the spreads are narrower, but rarely so narrow the professional market maker fails to make a profit.

Warrants have an important advantage over other Australian derivatives. Most brokerages offer access to warrant trading and the bid and ask prices are shown on the standard SEATS screen just like ordinary shares. Once the relevant risk acknowledgement documents are signed, it is just as easy to trade a Westpac warrant as to trade Westpac shares. This trading ease attracts a larger crowd than the specialist traders who are active in the options market, or in futures trading. Many of this warrant crowd are attracted by the low prices and the high percentage gains. This is price leverage in action.

When crowds get excited they make mistakes. Market theory suggests the market always efficiently matches the buy and sell orders and any mismatches – any inefficiencies – are quickly spotted by traders and ironed out. This is very true in a quote-driven market where the professional traders play full-time. It is less true with an order-driven market which more accurately reflects the opinion of all market participants, from the professionals to the mums and dads. This crowd mismatch accentuates short-term trading opportunities.

If the public is not interested in a particular warrant, the market maker is obligated to post a quoted buy and sell price on the SEATS screens. These are not random prices. They are carefully calculated, generally using some form of option pricing model, most often based on the Black-Scholes model, to establish a fair value price.

Remember the way you feel about your sports car and the way the thief thinks about it? Here is the core of the important difference between the intention of the market maker and the public buyer.

When Bill and Mary from down the street decide to buy a warrant for the first time what do they consider? They are unlikely to delve into the depth of an Excel spreadsheet to calculate the Black-Scholes fair value warrant price and compare it with the current quoted price. Even if they stumbled across the market maker's warrant matrix they would not know what to do with it or how to use it. Concepts of time decay, delta and other measures of volatility are broadly acknowledged but not really understood at even a basic level.

They consider just one thing: How much could they make, and how much more could this be if they buy the cheapest warrant?

Here is an important fork in the road. As traders we could outsmart the crowd with our superior knowledge of fair value and pricing matrixes, or we can better understand the psychology driving the crowd.

The techniques discussed in previous chapters all rely on understanding crowd behaviour. Effective short-term warrant trading is no different. If we understand the impact of this process we take the first step to better short-term warrant trading. If we accept the model of an orderly market defined by market makers who know the fair value then we miss an important opportunity to trade warrants to their full potential. Understanding where we stand in relation to actual and theoretical warrant pricing means our search for the best warrant opportunity is more realistic, practical and profitable.

WARRANT PRICING

The warrant market trades in two importantly different ways. The first is as a free market where competing buy and sell orders from the market crowd are used to establish the last traded price. The second way is as a managed market, where the buy and sell orders are created initially by the company issuing the warrant – the market makers.

Although we believe we buy and sell with those who hold other warrants, in reality we buy and sell within the parameters set by the warrant issuer. The warrant issuers sell volatility. Traders buy volatility. Those who sell volatility – the market makers – actively manage their volatility risk.

A warrant is a financial product created by a third party – the warrant issuer. As with any product sold to the public the manufacturer makes a decision about the selling price. Pitch too high and the product does not move. Pitch too low and profit margins are eroded. Setting the right price has a significant impact on the success of the product. The market makers – the institutional warrant issuers – face the same problem with each new warrant series. They solve it by applying some variation of an options pricing model usually derived from the Black-Scholes methods.

The objective is to factor in all the measures of volatility and sensitivity to price movements to reach an optimal 'fair value' figure to show what the warrant is worth. Each of these factors is given a Greek name, such as Delta, Theta, Beta, Gamma, etc. This optimal figure is adjusted up or down to show indicative warrant pricing for any future movements in the price of the parent stock. The result is a warrant pricing matrix, shown in Figure 14.2. These are obtained from the warrant issuer or from some brokers including AOT Online and Hubb Data.

Figure 14.2 – Warrant Pricing Matrix

UBS Warburg - warrant pricing matrix

Spread is always $0.01

ASX Code	AMCWSD	AmCall
Expiry	21-Feb-02	adj.Delta .17
Strike Price	$6.75	3:1

Price	Bid	Offer
$6.48	$0.110	$0.120
$6.50	$0.110	$0.120
$6.52	$0.115	$0.125
$6.54	$0.120	$0.130
$6.56	$0.120	$0.130
$6.58	$0.125	$0.135
$6.60	$0.130	$0.140
$6.62	$0.130	$0.140
$6.64	$0.135	$0.145

Spread is always $0.02

ASX Code	LLCWSD	AmCall
Expiry	20-Dec-01	adj.Delta .10
Strike Price	$12.00	4:1

Price	Bid	Offer
$10.95	$0.080	$0.100
$11.00	$0.080	$0.100
$11.05	$0.085	$0.105
$11.10	$0.090	$0.110
$11.15	$0.095	$0.115
$11.20	$0.100	$0.120
$11.25	$0.105	$0.125
$11.30	$0.110	$0.130
$11.35	$0.115	$0.135

These combined factors produce a single 'fair value' figure for the warrant for every anticipated price level in the parent stock. The market maker needs to make money at each of these levels, so he sets a buy price below the optimal figure and a sell price above the optimal figure. This is the 'spread' and may be measured as tightly as two ticks or be very much larger, reflecting the market maker's view of liquidity in the warrant.

In a perfect world managed by the market maker, warrant trading activity would closely match the indicative prices shown in the warrant pricing matrix. This is the key reference point. The warrant is an artificial product. In the absence of true market trading feedback, the market maker proscribes the range of trading alternatives based on a theoretical model. Generally, the market maker attempts to keep traded prices within these parameters. This theoretical structure of prices is designed to make money for the market maker. This world is very similar to options trading in the way pricing is calculated and the market managed. Opportunities exist to trade against the market maker when market inefficiency carries prices too far away from the theoretical fair value price. These strategies are well documented in options trading literature. Some traders also apply these to warrant trading.

RUNNING FROM THEORY

Warrants are not designed for us as traders to make money. Like any product, they are intended to make money for their producers. Any money we make is incidental to the primary intention of the warrant issuer. Just like a casino, the operator gives the punters some wins but, on balance, the bulk of the cash passed over the gambling tables stays with the casino. The warrant issuer has different objectives from those of us who trade the warrants.

In a freely traded market it is difficult to maintain this link between the price of the parent stock, the theoretical fair value price of the warrant and the actual traded price of the warrant. It is difficult because the broader crowd trading warrants is not usually aware of the detail of warrant pricing. These traders do not run a search to find warrants trading beyond fair value. Instead this crowd is attracted to the leverage and the activity of others. This leads to increased volatility and the market maker may be active in this area in an attempt to dampen volatility by actively participating in buying and selling.

In a free market the last traded price of a stock, or warrant, or other derivative, reflects the feeling of the crowd. The last traded price is an emotional figure. It is not a carefully crafted figure based on theoretical modelling. When emotions enter trading there is a greater opportunity for error. In technical terms this is market inefficiency. It is created when the market does not respond in a rational manner to all the known facts about the stock being traded. In a warrant it means the market does not conform to the theoretical pricing matrix.

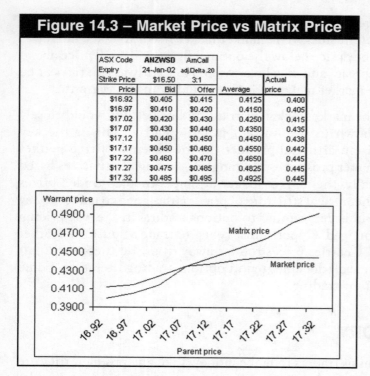

Figure 14.3 – Market Price vs Matrix Price

ASX Code	**ANZWSD**	AmCall		
Expiry	24-Jan-02	adj.Delta .20		
Strike Price	$16.50	3:1		
Price	Bid	Offer	Average	Actual price
$16.92	$0.405	$0.415	0.4125	0.400
$16.97	$0.410	$0.420	0.4150	0.405
$17.02	$0.420	$0.430	0.4250	0.415
$17.07	$0.430	$0.440	0.4350	0.435
$17.12	$0.440	$0.450	0.4450	0.438
$17.17	$0.450	$0.460	0.4550	0.442
$17.22	$0.460	$0.470	0.4650	0.445
$17.27	$0.475	$0.485	0.4825	0.445
$17.32	$0.485	$0.495	0.4925	0.445

Prices simply run away from the theory as shown in Figure 14.3.

Traders are always alert for run-away prices where crowd emotions are high. These emotions create trend breaks, rallies, and momentum trading opportunities. This is where we trade in the stock market and under certain circumstances, we transfer these trading skills to the warrant market.

Emotional trading – this unexpected volatility – is a blip in the life of many warrants. Blips appear more frequently in warrants with three or more months to run before they expire. If the crowd moves pricing well out of the range set by theoretical modelling, the market maker does not have to worry a great deal. There is plenty of time for the crowd to lose its excitement, and for pricing to settle back into its theoretical constraints.

This is not the case when the warrant is short-dated and due to expire in just a few weeks or days. The warrant issuer's profit in this activity comes from carefully defined price ranges. The market maker makes money when pricing conforms to the warrant matrix. The market makers may become active traders in the closing stages of the life of a warrant to buy back the warrant if prices move too far away from the matrix. This decision is tempered by the profit record of the warrant series over its lifetime.

Remember, market makers are selling risk and volatility. They manage this risk by spreading it across futures, traded options and by trading the warrants from other issuers. But ultimately they must manage the risk of their own warrant issues, to ensure their products make reasonable returns for them. Their objective is to make money from the premium income of the warrants and from the way the warrants are exercised. Their preference is to manage the market to achieve these ends. They trade the market to lock in a profitable outcome. There are times when our profitable outcomes in our personal warrant trade are at odds with the profitable outcomes sought by the warrant issuer.

When this happens the warrant issuer – the market maker – becomes active in the market by offering to buy back warrants at attractive prices. They do this when markets become extreme – when prices stray too far away from the theoretical fair value prices as calculated by, for instance, the Black-Scholes model.

The result is interesting, as shown in the diagram in Figure 14.4. If we enter the market at point A we are trading with a crowd just showing enough emotion to start to move prices away from the theoretical fair value price. As volatility increases – as the market crowd becomes more emotional – prices move further away from the fair value. The crowd takes over. Volatility increases. The price of the warrant changes substantially. We take advantage of this change only if there is sufficient trading volume for us to sell effectively. When prices move too far away from fair value the market makers enter the market. Their trading sustains volume as they outbid their crowd competitors. When they buy back warrants they detract from the overall liquidity of the market. It is a little like taking sticks out of the fire as a way of cooling it down.

From our perspective as traders this is very useful. The only way the market maker achieves his objective is to buy at prevailing market prices. If we have warrants to sell then we have customers who want to buy them. As the warrant premiums increase, the market may be influenced by market maker intervention. This keeps volume high and enables us to execute our trading strategy.

As the 'fuel load' is removed, or as the crowd excitement dies away, warrant prices return more closely to their theoretical fair value level. The

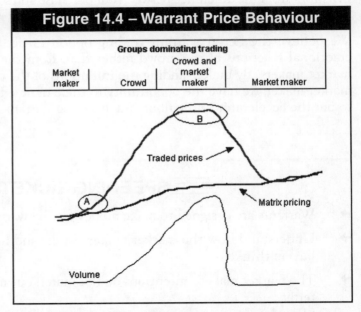

volume often dries up. The crowd leaves and the market makers lower their level of active trading. Calm returns to the market, and if we still hold the warrant, the profit leaks away because we are confined to selling at somewhere near the theoretical fair value.

CONVERGING INTENTIONS

Warrants provide many opportunities for trading. We either trade with the activity of the market makers, or we trade against it. Both these strategies require the trader to understand the warrant pricing matrix and to rely on the power and willingness of the market maker to manage the market. Errors are few and far between. An error is when the market price moves too far away from the theoretical price. For most traders this style of warrant trading carries a high risk of failure. Going head to head with market professionals is not a good survival strategy for the part-time trader.

The second group of warrant trading opportunities arises when the broader market crowd gets emotional and drives warrant prices well away from their theoretical values. The first clue this is happening is changes in volume behaviour. Emotional crowds make mistakes. They are carried away with greed and we intend to trade the impacts of this crowd emotion. Our trading is facilitated by the activity of market makers as they eventually attempt to control their risk by dampening the volatility of the crowd. Here is our selling signal, again assisted by good volume. By selling, usually unknowingly, to a market maker we trade with them to achieve their objectives. They buy our warrant to suit their purposes – to manage the risk to the warrant issuer. We sell our warrant to suit our purposes – to lock in a profit from the difference between our purchase and sell price. Our different intentions converge at a single traded price.

We believe the better warrant trading opportunities come from understanding the emotional reactions of the crowd rather than from the theoretical calculations of the market makers. By understanding the intentions of the crowd, and the objectives of the market maker, we have the opportunity to trade more effectively. Here is an opportunity to put the accelerator to the floor and drive the warrant at full speed.

SPEEDING TICKETS

➜ Warrants are designed to make money for the warrant issuer.

➜ Understand how the market maker thinks and how the crowd of warrant buyers think.

➜ The market maker's intentions do not match our intentions so we trade on our terms.

➜ Emotion-driven crowds overwhelm market maker pricing theory.

➜ Recognise the market maker's imperatives and use them to manage trade exits.

Chapter 15

SPREADING

PROFITS

Warrants provide a multitude of short-term and day trading opportunities. Some offer high returns, while others offer lower rates of return – around 7% to 15% for the day or overnight, as we illustrate with the inside spread strategy below. As with all good returns, there is an increased level of risk. The two most significant risk factors are instrument risk and execution risk.

Instrument risk is created by the nature of the warrant series. Every warrant series has a start date, and more importantly, an end or expiry date. After the expiry date the warrant stops trading. Those still holding warrants have the opportunity to exercise or convert them to the underlying shares if it is profitable to do so. If it is not profitable, then the trader carries the entire loss of his original purchase value. This makes sense only if the warrant was used as a type of insurance. Here the total cost of the warrant position is treated as an insurance premium. These hedging strategies are discussed more fully in books dealing with options strategies. When we apply these strategies our intention is to make money rather than to surrender the 'insurance premium' to the market.

As one warrant series ends another warrant series has already started in the same stock. These changeover periods use specific analysis techniques to identify opportunity. We look at the processes below.

Execution risk is directly related to volume. It describes the fatal slip between theory and reality. Time spent on in-depth analysis of theoretical pricing models is often time wasted in the warrant market. It is often impossible to trade the best theoretical warrant because trading volume is low or the market is created entirely by market maker activity.

Generally we take a short cut in analysis. We let other more informed and experienced traders lead the way. I enjoy good spicy Nonya Straits Chinese cooking which is very difficult to find in southern Australian capitals. I locate the best Asian restaurants by peering through the window and looking for a crowd of Singaporeans or Malaysians. Their patronage is more likely based on experience and proper analysis. Rather than undertake my own research, I use the fruits of their research. In the warrant market I look for evidence a crowd has gathered. The warrant they choose offers the advantage of good trading volume which makes short-term trading achievable.

These major considerations come together in selecting the best warrant to trade to achieve short-term trading objectives.

WARRANT SELECTION

Warrants give traders a convenient way to trade from the long side or the short side of the market. Exploring the relationship between volume and the expiration date of the warrant series provides a way to play with the market makers who are responsible for maintaining minimum liquidity in each warrant series. The market makers' orders are sometimes the only orders on the screen, often in multiples of 50,000 lots.

Warrants are issued in dated series. Each series has a common expiry date. The calculation of a warrant's value changes as time passes. Initially the price paid for the warrant in the market includes a strong component of hope. As the warrant nears the end of its listing period, traders have a better idea of what the market price might be for the parent share. There is less room for hope when calculating the market price of the warrant and this affects the way the warrant price behaves. This is the time decay effect.

A warrant series may include three to six separate warrants, all expiring on the same date. The warrants offer traders a variety of conversion ratios and strike prices. The conversion ratio defines the number of shares represented by each warrant. Some specify one warrant is equal to one share – 1:1. Others may convert ten warrants into a single share – 10:1.

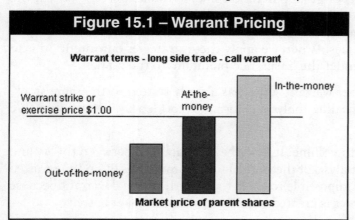

Figure 15.1 – Warrant Pricing

Warrant terms - long side trade - call warrant

Warrant strike or exercise price $1.00

At-the-money

In-the-money

Out-of-the-money

Market price of parent shares

The strike or exercise price is the price at which the warrant is converted into shares. A call warrant trades from the long side and is the equivalent to buying low and selling high. A warrant is at-the-money when the warrant strike price is equal to the current share price of the parent stock as illustrated in Figure 15.1. It is out-of-the-money when the current share price is below the warrant strike price. It is in-the-money when the current share price is above the warrant strike price.

When traders decide which warrant series, and which warrant in each series to buy, they bring together these three features. Some warrant traders include other factors such as the delta, gamma, and fair pricing calculations. In all cases the overall impact is the same. The trader uses his analysis skills to make a decision about the best warrant for his trading objectives. When many traders make a similar decision we see patterns of volume behaviour over the life of the warrant.

The diagram in Figure 15.2 shows two extremes of volume behaviour over the life of the warrant. Warrant A is the type of warrant traders avoid. Nobody is interested in it. Perhaps its strike price is too far away from the current share price. Perhaps the exercise ratio is too large when compared to other warrants in the same series with similar exercise prices. The exact reasons are unimportant because they all translate into a single pattern of volume behaviour.

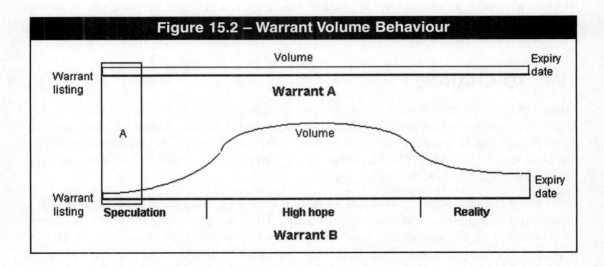

Figure 15.2 – Warrant Volume Behaviour

Volume is flat lined. Each day the market maker posts a bid and an ask, often in lots of 50,000. Nobody wants to trade. Day after day nothing really happens. The bid and ask prices rise and fall in unison with the parent price, but most traders ignore this warrant series.

Warrant B shows the type of volume action traders look for. This is an active warrant. Traders have decided the strike price is right, the conversion ratio is correct, and the relationship between the warrant and the parent stock provides a good opportunity to enjoy leveraged gains. The distinguishing feature is the bulge in volume.

When a warrant is first listed it attracts a few speculative traders. They take an early position in anticipation of trend developments. They move while the warrant is out-of-the-money. As the parent stock moves in a way consistent with this trend, more traders are attracted to the warrant. They have high hopes the trend will continue and they will benefit from this price action. This bulge in volume activity develops as the warrant moves towards an at-the-money relationship. High volume trading persists as the warrant starts to move into-the-money.

Typically volume declines as the warrant moves closer to expiry date. Here reality plays a bigger role in decision making. Traders have a better idea of what the price of the parent stock is likely to be when the warrant expires. There is less room for traders to hope the parent price may rise enough to make their warrant profitable. The trading volume declines as traders take profits and others buy the warrant for its conversion profits when they exercise the warrant and purchase the underlying shares.

The volume in area A is interesting. When the warrant is first listed it is often difficult to tell the difference between the volume action in Warrant A and the action in Warrant B. Traders who take a position in the warrant soon after it is listed run the risk of being caught out. They end up in the situation shown by Warrant A when they actually planned for a Warrant B style development.

TIME TO CHANGE

Some trading opportunities are complicated by the end of one warrant series and the beginning of the next series. Consider an example, call it WBC. The stock has started a new rising trend. We see an opportunity developing on 20 May. The first series of WBC warrants ends on 28 May. The second series of warrants ends on 27 July and is listed on 16 May. Which series offers the best trade?

If we select the first series of warrants we have a very short time to take advantage of the developing trading situation as shown in Figure 15.3. The best choice is the second series of warrants with the longer life span. They remain active and listed as the bulk of the expected WBC uptrend develops. Selecting the second warrant series involves a higher level of risk because it is difficult to tell in advance which of the second series of warrants is most favoured by other traders.

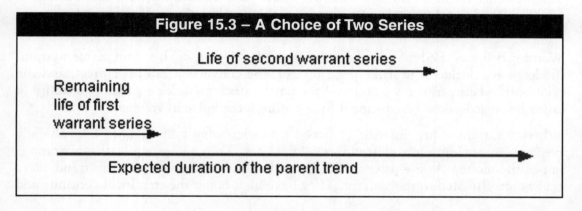

Figure 15.3 – A Choice of Two Series

Life of second warrant series

Remaining
life of first
warrant series

Expected duration of the parent trend

The problem is shown in the earlier diagram of typical volume behaviour. Initially, as shown by the boxed area A in Figure 15.2, it is difficult to separate success or failure in the warrant series based on volume behaviour.

There is an important overlap period between each new series of warrants. The next series of warrants is issued before the first series of warrants expires. At any time there are at least two series of warrants trading – a near-dated series and a far-dated series. The overlap period is shown in the box marked as area B in Figure 15.4.

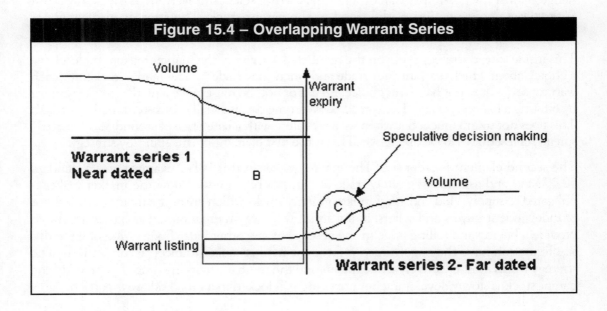

Figure 15.4 – Overlapping Warrant Series

In this trade we move in anticipation of the way other warrant traders will shift from warrant series 1 to warrant series 2. Consider the pool of active warrant traders who are trading WBC in anticipation of an uptrend. They already hold call warrants – shown as series 1. As the uptrend develops these traders are not interested in series-2 warrants when they are first listed because they have profitable positions in the near dated series – series 1.

When the series 1 warrants reach their expiry date many of these traders want to continue trading the WBC uptrend. Now their choices are limited to the series 2 warrants. Many of the traders migrate, or roll over, quickly to the next warrant series to further increase their profits. This interest shows up as an increase in volume. The volume curve begins to resemble the typical curve shown as Warrant B in Figure 15.2.

The initial bulge in volume is created by speculative trading. The bulge confirms we have made the right decision in selecting this warrant as the most appropriate warrant to trade the developing trend. In most circumstances we prefer to move with established warrant volume. In this rollover situation the trader moves in anticipation of warrant volume.

INSIDE THE MARKET MAKER

Does this mean we are at the mercy of the market maker and the market? This is always the case, but we use this change-over period, in area B, to take small profits from market maker activity. This helps to build a flow of profits from the position which is used as a hedge against the possibility that other traders do not select this warrant as the best warrant for trading a continuation of the trend in the parent stock. The strategy also generates profits when the parent stocks slips into a slow-moving or sideways pattern.

This inside spread strategy relies on the mandated activity of the market maker. Traders have a choice about which warrant they trade and when they trade it. The market maker for each warrant series does not have this choice. Like it or not, he must make a market in the warrant by offering a bid and an ask. The spread between the two is usually consistent, perhaps $0.01. This does not sound much, but when we are dealing with a base price of around $0.13, a $0.01 spread represents a 7.69% difference. This is the first element of this stand-by strategy.

The second element is order size. The market maker in this WBC example uses a standard 50,000 bid and ask size. We safely trade at this size because we know the market maker is obligated to supply a bid and ask. Unlike ordinary stocks which are at the mercy of the whims of independent buyers and sellers, in a warrant we have an organisation obligated to always provide a buying and selling price in the absence of any other bids. Traders who observe this size limitation have the opportunity to force the market maker to meet his obligations. The strategy works most effectively while traders and the trend are marking time. The trend in the parent stock is slowly developing but prices are still locked in a broad sideways pattern.

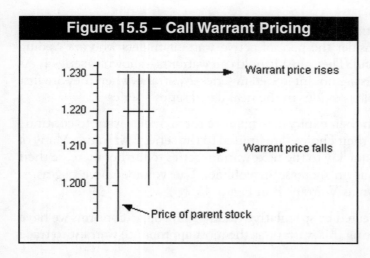

Figure 15.5 – Call Warrant Pricing

As prices for the parent stock tick upwards the market maker's bid price rises. As prices for the parent stock tick downwards, the market maker's ask price falls, reflecting the decreasing value of the call. This relationship is shown in Figure 15.5. The bid and ask do not represent prices actually traded. In a sideways market there may be several days where there are no trades at all. The bid and the ask represent the prices at which the market maker is prepared to do business.

If we want to do business with the market maker we should take into account two factors. First, the trading size is determined by the market maker. If he moves in 50,000 lots, then we move in a single lot of 50,000. As soon as we buy or sell 50,000 by hitting his bid or ask, a new bid or ask order appears from the market maker. Its size is the same as the previous trade – 50,000. It may be tempting to take additional trades, each of a 50,000 lot size but when it comes time to close the position it may be more difficult to exit. The market maker may still work in a 50,000 lot size, but the spread moves away from you. Instead of a bid at $0.14 the next bid shifts downwards to $0.13. With only you and the market maker active, this is a short cut to warrant disaster.

The second feature of the inside spread strategy is the way we open the trade by meeting the ask and close the trade by taking the bid. This is the reverse of our normal strategy when we wait for the market to come to ask. We buy on the bid and sell on the ask. The depth of market screen extract in Figure 15.6 shows how the market maker's bid and ask change during the day in response to the up and down movement in parent prices as they are trapped in the sideways trading pattern.

The day starts with a market maker's posted bid at $0.12. Later in the day the market maker posts an ask at $0.15. This is where we rub out hands together in glee. A buy at $0.12 and an exit at $0.15 delivers a 25% profit for the day. It is not possible to obtain this result using the structure of orders shown in this order screen.

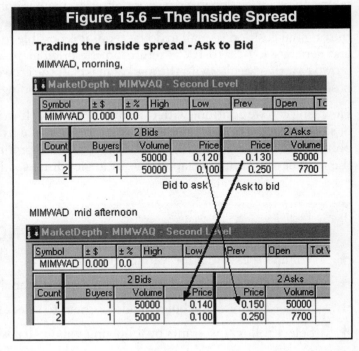

We cannot get these posted bid and ask prices from the market maker. We have to work the inside spread. This means meeting the ask in the morning at $0.13. The only person active in this market is the market maker so we trade on his conditions and buy stock from him at his posted price. Later in the day, as shown by the thick black line, we close the trade, meeting his bid. Again, he is the only other player, so we have to accept his bid price at $0.14. Instead of a 25% return for the day we take home a 7.69% return.

When the parent price is temporarily locked in a sideways or slow moving market where the movement is sufficiently wide to initiate changes in the market maker's bid and ask spread we have the opportunity to take these small trades on an intra-day basis. The same technique can be extended into a two- to three-day trade, buying stock today at the bid and selling it again several days later at the ask.

When the market maker dominates the market we have no choice but to trade on the inside spread – the difference between the ask and the bid. This is the reverse to the way we normally approach the market.

The most important restriction on this type of trading is the size. We trade just one of the market maker's lots. In this example this restricts trade size to $6,500. The exit collects $7,000 and delivers a $500 profit for the day. These are scalper's returns. Picking up 7.69% for the day is good trading, but when dollar profits are limited to $500 the result is too small for some traders.

We started this chapter with a choice between old and new warrant series. Trading the recently listed series entails a risk because we may select a series where volume remains low. The inside spread strategy provides some additional protection against the risk involved in taking an early position in a new warrant series that has not yet attracted many other traders. These trades, which munch away at the market maker, deliver small but steady returns. As the original position is small in dollar terms it is possible to execute a handful of these trades and generate a 70% to 100% return on the original position size. While waiting for the crowd to arrive we play with the market maker. If the crowd does not arrive we sell the open position and use the profits from the inside spread trading to compensate for any loss.

How long can we continue with this trading strategy? It works most effectively in a sideways or slow market. The market maker is required to make a constant market. Traders use this obligation to generate small, steady and consistent profits from the inside spread. When the market accelerates we apply the strategies discussed in following chapters.

≡SHARPSHOOTER'S NOTES

→ Volume is essential for warrant trading.

→ Volume changes show how other traders have analysed the market.

→ Understand volume bulges and use them to select the best warrant opportunities.

→ Select rollover warrants by following volume leads.

→ Inside spread trading delivers profits in sideways or slow moving markets.

→ Use the market maker's order sizes to safely trade the spread.

→ Inside spread trading buys the ask and sells the bid.

Chapter 16

CALLING

QUICK PROFITS

Trade the trend or fade it? The standard answers apply to long-term traders who join existing trends or trade breakouts to new uptrends. Our timeframe is shorter, so the answers differ in important ways. We trade the trend with rallies and short-lived bullish price patterns. When we fade the trade – trade against the trend in anticipation of a change – our objective is to capture the benefits of a bounce. Warrant leverage offers the opportunity to use volatility and price leverage to expand profits dramatically in short-term timeframes.

In this chapter we look closely at the analysis and implementation of two trades. The first shows how call warrants are used to fade the trend. The trade captures the rebound after an extreme bout of market depression and returns 47% for an intra-day trade. The trade highlights the issues involved in using call warrants to fade the trend.

The second example is selected from the same period and returns 78%. It shows how a short-term trade is added to a fast-moving new uptrend. Here we trade with the trend but with the intention of capturing the early extremes of enthusiasm. A long-term trader applies the same techniques and captures much greater profits by staying with the trade as the trend unfolds over weeks or months. The short-term trader chooses to ignore these longer-term opportunities and this is consistent with the short-term focus.

These two examples are personal trades. They have very good short-term returns based on price leverage, derivative leverage and market inefficiencies created by crowd behaviour. This is the mix vital for successful short-term trades. This chapter examines the detail of trade selection, planning, implementation management and exit. Snapshot trading compresses action but it is based on careful and time-consuming planning and analysis.

The trades were made in the aftermath of the terrorist attacks of 11 September 2001 in the United States. They were short-term trades because this tactic suited the market conditions at the time. I have talked to many people since that event. Some proudly told of how they bought shares near the September lows and held them all the way through to the new trend peak in February 2002. I congratulate them on their profits but remind them this was a gamble that paid off.

In the aftermath of 11 September several features were clear. First, any further attacks on the US would drive the market down dramatically. Many people used put warrants and other derivatives to short the market. Second, any attack was likely to occur overnight while the Australian market was closed. This added extreme risk to traders who held overnight positions. In the event of a new attack, prices were likely to gap down dramatically, locking in substantial losses even for those who acted quickly to get out.

Holding an overnight position, particularly in a derivative trade, entailed additional risk in this nervous period. I believed prudent risk control meant taking intra-day trades. I was not prepared to gamble against the possibility of further terrorist attacks. In this case the gamblers won. Apply the same strategy in the future and they may lose. When I apply the same strategy in the future I will be reasonably confident of winning because the risk is managed carefully.

We look at call warrant strategies below. The call warrant makes money as the share price rises. A call warrant is the right to buy shares at lower than current market price. A call warrant exercisable at $10.00, and which cost $0.50 to buy, does not make money until the share price is at $10.51 – warrant price plus exercise price is greater than the current stock price. We start the trade with an analysis of the relationship between crowd behaviour and pricing. We look for market inefficiency because this offers the best opportunities.

FADING THE TREND

This trading strategy uses a fall in prices of the parent stock as this deflates the value of the call warrant. The warrant value then increases dramatically as the parent stock price begins to rise. The relationship between the warrant price and the parent price is shown in Figure 16.1.

Theory tells us the call warrant price closely tracks moves in the parent stock. As prices fall, the call warrant price falls at the same rate. When the parent price recovers, the warrant price also moves up in lockstep. The main difference is the parent price may be counted in moves of $0.01 while the warrant price is counted in moves of $0.001. The moves are duplicated but on a different price scaling and so deliver a leverage advantage.

This theoretical pricing model is well understood by the warrant issuers. They try to keep traded warrant prices as close to the theoretical warrant prices as possible. Some warrant issuers produce an indicative pricing matrix which shows the prices they expect to see for the warrant matched with the corresponding price of the parent share. There is some room for profit with this level of market efficiency. There is more room for profit when the market is inefficient.

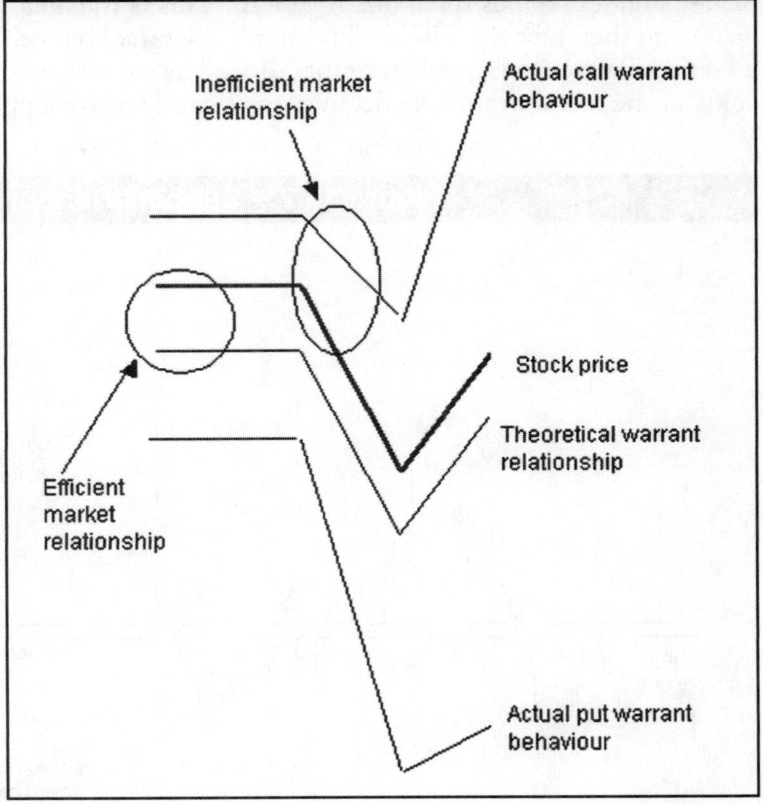

Call warrants show market inefficiency. When the parent price falls, the price of the call warrant falls more slowly than the theoretical warrant price relationship suggests it should. When the price of the parent stock rises, the call warrant price rises more rapidly. We want to take advantage of this market inefficiency.

The greatest inefficiency is with put warrants. This relationship, shown in

Figure 16.1 – A Parent Stock's Effect on Price

Figure 16.1, captures the positive change in warrant value. When the price of the parent share falls, the increase in put warrant value is not as great as the theory suggests. When the parent price rallies, the decrease in warrant value is greater than expected. This makes put warrant trading more difficult and we discuss this in the next chapter.

We take advantage of the call warrant market inefficiency by first locating a substantially oversold parent stock with an available call warrant. We use the banking sector in this example. Strong uptrends have come to a sudden end, sending prices into freefall towards old support levels. Our analysis starts with the daily or weekly bar chart. We look for two features.

➜ Prices moving towards support levels. This may include a pile driver pattern where prices dip dramatically towards support.

➜ Prices rebounding from the support level. This bounce initiates the market inefficiency in the warrant recovery.

The NAB chart in Figure 16.2 shows these characteristics with a good support level at $23.48 and a previous spike dip at $23.70. This is the area where we look for prices to pause and then recover. The weekly chart shows the bounce. We want to see evidence of a bounce before we buy call warrants. If we buy in anticipation of the bounce then the value of the call warrant may decline significantly if the support level fails to hold.

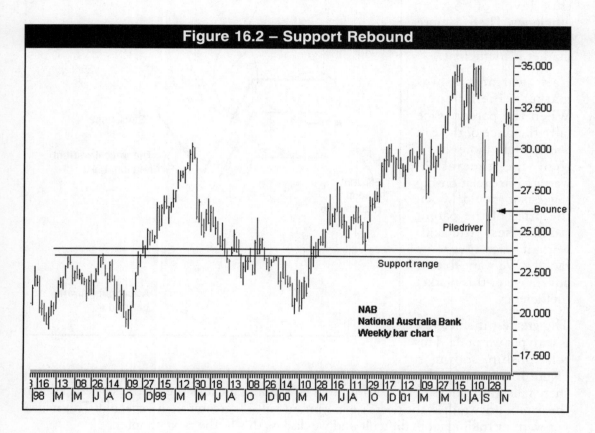

Figure 16.2 – Support Rebound

As position traders we might debate the potential for a longer-term trend reversal from this support level. As short-term traders we expect a short-lived rally, so our trading is based on this. We use a Guppy Multiple Moving Average with NAB to confirm the downtrend is well established. There is a low probability the first rally is the start of the new uptrend.

This means this rebound trade has limited objectives. This analysis suggests the best trade is a short-term warrant trade lasting just a few days.

How do we select the better warrant? The theory covered in books on warrant trading takes us deep into the world of derivative mathematics. These theoretical calculations are difficult and, quite often, irrelevant to market action. We get the answers most easily from the market professionals who are active in the warrant market. They show us the answers with their trading activity so we focus on the warrants with the highest current volume. I find this is a reliable and effective shortcut.

With 24 available NAB call warrants, this shortcut narrows the search down to three or four. We look for consistent recent trading volume. This does not mean consistent trading volume throughout the life of the warrant. The NABWGE chart in Figure 16.3 shows the preferred relationship with around one million warrants traded each day. It also delivers other important messages.

As the NAB price suddenly falls there is less public interest in call warrants. There are few buyers. Most of the inexperienced traders are looking at put warrants and are trying to join the crowd. Why then do we see steady buying of these call warrants as the price falls? This steady buying points to the activity of smart traders who are accumulating call warrants in anticipation of a bounce recovery in NAB. This is not just a one shot volume event. It is steady and consistent accumulation.

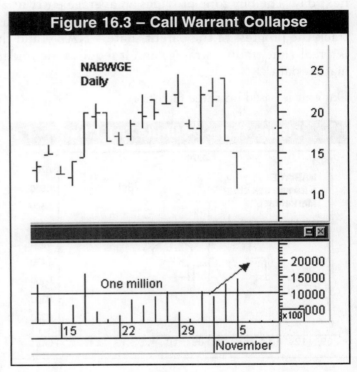

Figure 16.3 – Call Warrant Collapse

We are not quite as aggressive as this. We want to wait for the bounce to be confirmed. However, the evidence of steady accumulation supports our analysis and our strategy.

The next deciding factor in warrant selection is the level of leverage available. When we have a choice it makes more sense to buy the warrant with the best price leverage. NABWGE trading at $0.05 is more attractive than a similar warrant trading at $0.10 or $0.14 because the price leverage delivers better returns. When the NAB rally starts we expect the crowd to switch their attention to NAB call warrants. Many of these traders look for low-priced warrants so we expect greater activity in these issues.

When NAB rallies over two days NABWGE records the highest volume of the NAB warrants and the best returns. The other NAB warrant series retains good volume but on a smaller number of trades and with less total return. We cannot realise our trading strategy if trades are limited. We get this information from the course of sales details. A warrant with a 20% return for the day is not a practical trade if there are only five trades for the day. It is just too difficult to buy and sell the warrant.

The NABWGE warrant shows high volume and a substantial number of trades. This makes it a good candidate.

The intra-day chart on the right hand side of Figure 16.4 shows trading action for the next day. The buy zone provides an average entry at $0.047. The number of warrants traded at lower prices were very small parcels. We use the MarketCast live feed to track the progress of the parent share – NAB – and the warrant during the day. This is a real-time trading strategy and it requires the trader to have ongoing access to live market data.

Our exit is based on three factors:

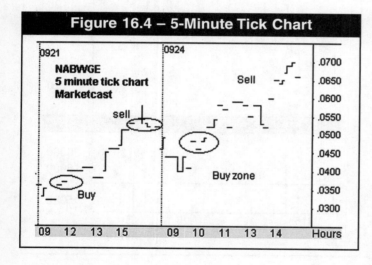

Figure 16.4 – 5-Minute Tick Chart

→ This is a short-term trade designed to take advantage of a short rally.

→ There is strong resistance at $0.070, shown by a large number of sell orders.

→ We want to avoid overnight risk created by a fall in the DOW.

Using these factors we place our sell order at $0.069. This is filled just prior to the close as NAB continues to tick upwards towards $26.00. The return on the trade is 46.81%. A similar trade was also possible on the previous day as shown in the left hand chart.

MANAGING THE EXIT

An intra-day trade calls for fine-tuning all exit conditions. We monitor a live screen and are alert for the smallest changes in buying or selling pressure. Profits depend on our reaction to developing trends. Trades based on fading the market, or participating in the very early stages of a rebound are fraught with danger. We stand in front of an ugly downtrend and use our trading skill to judge the moment of rebound.

A simpler and more traditional strategy trades with the trend. Here the objective is to identify an established uptrend. The analysis starts with the underlying, or parent, stock. The execution of the trade is completed in the derivative market. The objective is to maximise the trend returns by using the price leverage available in the call warrant.

In this section we consider the management of the exit from an established call warrant trade in ANZWZE. The purpose of this personal trade is to take advantage of the banking sector recovery rally. The objective is to generate leveraged returns using a warrant. This requires a small amount of cash upfront, $20,010, and delivers a good profit. This is a classic short-term warrant trading strategy.

Position traders use this to rebuild capital after market collapses. They use these short-term approaches to recapitalise their trading accounts. Traders trapped in open positions after 11 September used these types of trading opportunities to generate new capital.

We trade these warrant movements in much the same way as we trade any speculative share. The primary difference is the way warrant exits are triggered by movements in the parent share. Our key selection criterion is volume, and when it comes time to exit the trade, we plan for significant volume.

The first step in managing the trade applies analysis to the end-of-day chart for ANZ. We set the target in the area of the previous high at $17.48 as shown in Figure 16.5. As prices approach this level we move to protect open profits in the warrant position. As this trade develops, the pullback from point A is a concern. Using

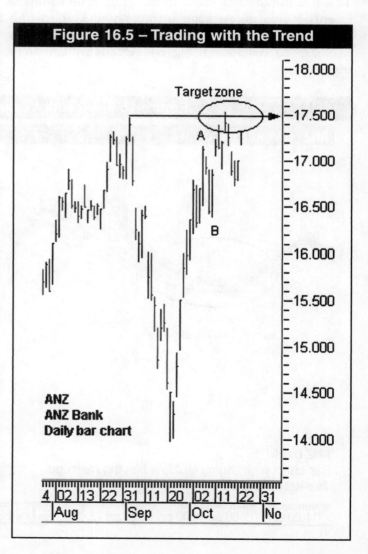

Figure 16.5 – Trading with the Trend

Target zone

A

B

ANZ
ANZ Bank
Daily bar chart

end-of-day charts we are prepared to exit once the low at point B is created. We do not act on this exit as prices rapidly recover on the next trading day. By watching the opening order sequence we remain confident ANZ prices will rebound. Had the opening order line suggested continued selling, we would have moved to sell the warrant trade to lock in profits.

On the day of the last bar shown on this chart we watch intra-day screens to see how trading develops as prices move towards our target of $17.48. The objective is firstly to determine if this old high is likely to cause a significant problem for the continuation of the trend. The second objective is to protect open profits at this level, and manage a trading exit.

This five-minute tick chart in Figure 16.6 uses MarketCast data and the GuppyTraders Essentials charting package. It shows how ANZ trading develops over the next few days. The collapse and contraction of the Guppy Multiple Moving Average in area A is an early sign of trend weakness. It suggests ANZ is unlikely to maintain upward momentum. This triggers our sell decision.

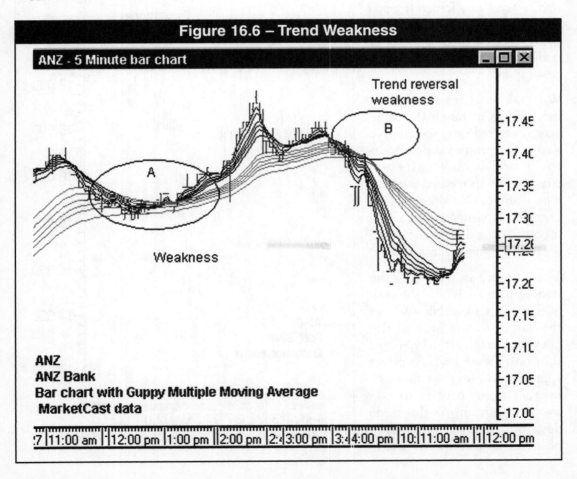

Figure 16.6 – Trend Weakness

This decision is further confirmed as the relationship in area B developed. This is a clear crossover signal of trend reversal. The slight developing recovery was most likely to be overwhelmed by further selling and confirmed the end of the trade. Our focus is on protecting, in this case, substantial profits. Our target near the previous high was optimistic. We should not compound this with greed. When watching the price development on the end-of-day and intra-day charts, our focus is on caution and profit protection. Once we see the development in area B we start managing our trading exit.

DIFFICULT EXITS

Getting out of the trade looks a simple exercise on the end-of-day chart. Enter at $0.29 and exit at $0.55. Real life is not as simple as this. The volume display in Figure 16.7 shows the reason – very low trading volume. The general volume trend of the preceding days is down. When we go to sell our 69,000 warrants it is difficult to find a buyer to trade with.

We start the exit by getting to the head of the sell line with a sell order at $0.55. We succeed in selling 5,000 but trading for the day is very slow. We need to facilitate the sale. The next buy order sits at $0.53 for much of the day. Nobody shows interest in our sell at $0.55.

Our problem is the balance between our need to exit the trade and the need to retain our position in the order line at higher prices. We want to attract buyers. When bites are slow on a fishing trip we throw small pieces of fish, or burley, into the water. This sacrifices some bait as a way of attracting more fish, one of which may take the bait on our hook. We do the same in this market.

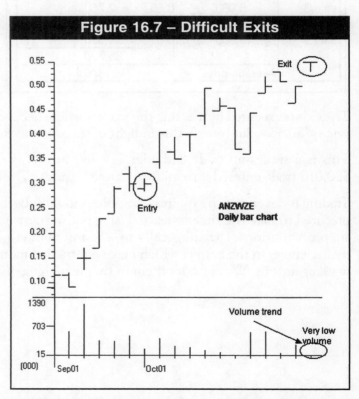

Figure 16.7 – Difficult Exits

It works like this. Our main order for 69,000 warrants sits at the front of the order line at $0.55. We can change the order volume without losing our position in the line. We do not change this order to $0.53 because we lose our position in the line and are unable to take advantage of any bigger fish attracted by the burley. Instead we meet the next buy order at $0.53 and sell 5,000 warrants. This is our burley. As soon as the order is filled, we adjust the existing sell order at $0.55 to 64,000 and retain our place in the order line at $0.55. Other traders are attracted by our burley and we sell another 5,000 warrants at $0.55. Using a mixture of set-price sell orders and at-market orders we dominate the trading for the day.

Just before the close, we meet the market at $0.53 and $0.51 rather than end up trapped with the remains of an unexecuted order. These five sales are shown in Figure 16.8.

The total return is $35,790, garnered by multiple exit sales. We manage this exit to take into account the decline in trading volume and the signs of trend failure in ANZ. The exit is triggered when ANZ approaches our target price. It is managed by watching for trend weakness confirmation developing on the intra-day chart. I find the Guppy Multiple Moving Average indicator a very useful way to monitor this trend weakness.

Figure 16.8 – Exit Sales

	vol	price	Return	
Sale 1	5,000	0.55	2,750	
sale 2	5,000	0.53	2,650	
sale 3	5,000	0.55	2,750	
sale 4	5,000	0.53	2,650	
sale 5	49,000	0.51	24,990	
			35,790	total
Average price		0.51870		

The exit is executed by meeting the market where necessary. We aim for our preferred exit price – $0.55 – but modify this in light of the way the trend weakness develops.

This is a successful trade and adds $15,780 in profits. This is a 78.86% return from a $20,010 trade entered into midway through the ANZ recovery rally.

Trading is never easy. It requires discipline and skill. Both are developed by anyone who is prepared to take the time to learn. Using put warrants to trade a falling market sounds a simple variation of trading calls in a rising market. There are important structural inefficiencies in the market which make put trading more hazardous. These inefficiencies work against us. We consider them in the next chapter.

☰ MARKSWOMAN'S NOTES

➜ Rebound trades fade the trend.

➜ Make good use of the lag between parent and warrant price moves.

➜ Analysis starts with end-of-day parent stock charts.

➜ Volume is the first selection filter.

➜ Leverage is the second selection filter.

➜ Trade with the trend using short-term trades.

➜ Analyse end-of-day charts for the trend but execute trade in the derivatives market.

➜ Order management is critical to success.

➜ Use live order screens.

➜ Use a burley sale to attract buyers in a slow-moving market.

Chapter 17

LAGS IN
THE FALL

Futures traders switch easily from trading the long side to trading the short side. Stock traders in the US have the same facility. Australian traders do not. There are ways of shorting ordinary Australian shares and some of them are included in *BearTrading*. However, in reality, most traders find it very difficult to find a brokerage which accepts short trades. Many will not allow you to short any listed share or to trade at less than a minimum $50,000 for each order. Many brokers tell you shorting is illegal in the Australian market. This is not true, but it is more difficult than many casual traders realise. Readers who want to explore trading strategies to short ordinary stock should start with Louise Bedford's book *Trading Secrets*.

Our interest is in using put warrants to benefit from any short-term or long-term downtrend. Essentially a put warrant rises in value as the price of the parent shares fall. This relationship delivers profit. The strategy ought to be as easy and as effective as trading call warrants in a rising trend. It is not. There are some very important differences in the way traders approach put warrants. The leverage impact is the same, the opportunity for short-term profits is good, but the range of choices – the mechanics of trading and trade execution – are much more difficult.

They are summed up in a two words: liquidity and lags.

Warrants are traded by all sorts of people, from professionals to mums and dads. The crowd is active in this area, which is one of the reasons we like these derivatives. The broader market crowd is not comfortable with the idea of selling something they do not already own, even if it is via a put warrant. They are slow to react to falling prices and slow to initiate put trades. This lag between trend action and price reaction in put warrants is enough to damage the profitability of many put warrant trades. When prices lift, people abandon the put warrant very quickly, making it difficult to close open positions. It can be a trap.

It is also very profitable as markets often fall more rapidly than they rise. The mechanics of working with put trades is different from call warrants so we include a thorough examination of them in this chapter. The differences may look minor at first, but the leveraged impact on profit, or loss, is major.

Theory takes a battering when it comes to using warrants to trade a developing or strong downtrend. As noted in the previous chapter, there are psychological friction points which slow the smooth transition from trading long to trading short.

In falling markets warrant trading has two appealing features. The first is the ability to easily short a stock using a put warrant. The second is the leveraged return which comes mainly from the way the warrant price is linked to movements in the parent share price. It also comes from the impact of price leverage generated when warrant prices start at just a few cents.

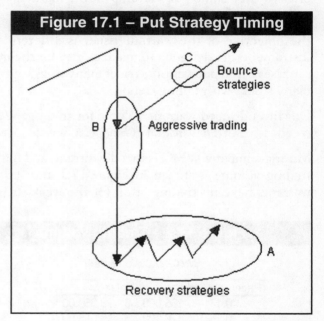

Figure 17.1 – Put Strategy Timing

The crowd believes the best way to make money in a falling market is by trading the short side. There is increased activity in trading puts, and a few lucky traders make money, but there are many traps. We look at a few of them here. These strategies are applied to area B on the diagram in Figure 17.1. These are not recovery strategies or bounce approaches. These are aggressive trading approaches designed to capture continued falls.

LIQUIDITY

We start with a list of all parent companies with associated put warrants – numbers vary between 20 and 30. This immediately narrows the field of choice. We narrow it even further by scanning for trading volume, the same step we use for culling call warrants. Some show no trading volume at all for the entire week and are immediately discarded.

We do not need to explore the reasons for this lack of volume. We may believe some stocks are good candidates for a price fall. Volume tells us if the market agrees with us. No trading for the week, or very low trading, tells us it is difficult to find warrants to buy, and it is also difficult later to find somebody to buy them from us. These may present good theoretical opportunities, but they are not practical opportunities. We eliminate these, leaving parent stocks with some useful trading volume.

This is a much shorter list and our next stop takes us to the bar chart. Although warrant trading is often seen as an area suitable for aggressive traders, we find it more useful to treat put warrants with a high level of conservatism. An aggressive trader acts in anticipation of a trend change. The conservative trader waits for some proof of a trend change. We want good proof that a downtrend has started.

This is the psychological friction point. Many traders are uncomfortable trading the short side of the market. They take a lot of convincing a stock is really falling and that a new downtrend has been established so they are slow to buy put warrants. On the other side of the equation, they are quick to take fright when the parent stock shows a few up ticks in price so they dump put warrants on the market.

The list of parent stocks with an established downtrend is often very small. Remember the objective of the warrant issuer is different from our objective as traders. These instruments are designed to make money for the market maker rather than for us. It is no surprise to find put warrants cover many stocks with rising trends and call warrants include many stocks with falling trends.

Downtrends need warrant volume for trading. We collect volume figures from the most recent issue of *The Australian Financial Review*.

Mining company WMC is in a downtrend and has 14 available put warrants. The weekly trading volume is shown in Figure 17.2 and has three significant features. First, some warrants have no trading at all for the week. It is very difficult to trade in this market unless you are prepared to meet the market.

Figure 17.2 – Trading Volume

WMC WXC Warrants

Price	Vol	Value	
0.17	165,000	$ 28,050.00	
0.15	120,100	$ 18,015.00	
0.022	320,000	$ 7,040.00	
0.043		$ -	Expire at end
0.017		$ -	of September
0.011	20,000	$ 220.00	
0.073		$ -	
0.04		$ -	
0.35		$ -	
0.285		$ -	
0.26	43,000	$ 11,180.00	
0.2		$ -	
0.097	27,300	$ 2,648.10	
0.11		$ -	

Second is the way the highest trading volume is found in the warrants which are closest to their expiry date. Trading short-dated warrants has advantages, but any sudden loss of confidence has a major impact on price as these warrants have very little time to absorb the shock and recover. Unless there are clearly excellent opportunities in these short-dated warrants, we are more interested in warrants with a longer time to expiry. We may need some time to unwind trading positions.

Third is the low value of trading for each day. It ranges between $228 and $28,050. The size of our order must be consistent with the liquidity of this market. We may be able to spend $20,000 to buy the warrant, but it may be more difficult to sell this amount. This is not acceptable as our intention is to trade the change of value in warrant pricing.

Consider a stock with a rising trend. Most people trade more naturally from the long side, buying low and selling higher. A price retreat in a rising trend causes little concern. These dips are treated as temporary and often signal an opportunity to add to the position in anticipation of a trend continuation.

The reverse of this price move is a temporary rally in a downtrend. It should provide the opportunity to add to short positions. Instead it tends to bring on panic. Many warrant traders view any rally as a signal for a rapid exit.

This psychological friction has several important trading impacts, shown in Figure 17.3.

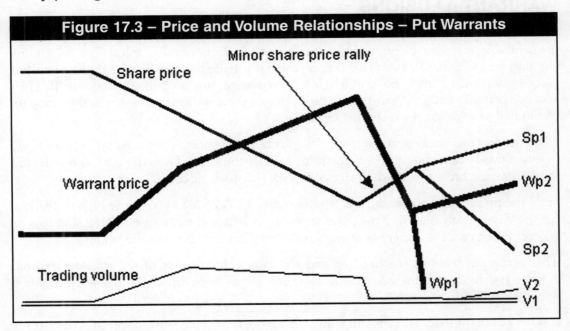

Figure 17.3 – Price and Volume Relationships – Put Warrants

The thin lines V1 and V2 are volume. The thick line labelled SP is the share price of the parent stock. The very thick WP line is the warrant price. The point SP 1 shows what happens when the rally continues and delivers a valid exit signal. Point SP 2 shows the result when the rally fails and the downtrend continues.

There are three features to note:

➡   Trading volume in put warrants does not increase until after the downtrend is established. This means it is difficult to take an early position in the warrant because there are few sellers. The sellers generally want a higher price and this leads to the second trading impact.

➜ Once the parent stock downtrend is well established there is a blip in trading volume. This is reflected in a substantial increase in the warrant price as excited traders chase the put warrant. They are prepared to pay a high price.

➜ As the parent stock price continues to fall, the warrant trading volume tapers off. There is not a sustained market in this instrument. The warrant price continues to rise, but on the back of a small number of trades. The rise in price is not evidence of frantic trading. It comes from a market with low trading liquidity. Only those really desperate to trade the put warrant pay the higher prices demanded by existing warrant holders.

WARRANT ILLUSIONS

This behaviour provides the illusion of put warrant trading profits. Good percentage returns are available, but they are often generated by just small amounts of capital. Typical trading size may be $4,000 to $5,000. This is acceptable if you are happy with this trading size. For some traders who want to trade in $30,000 lots or more, this trading size is too small. They end up spending $30,000, but the average price of their warrant increases as they mop up individual sales at successively higher prices.

Many traders are uncomfortable with the idea of going short. They join the rush to trade put warrants because many others are doing exactly the same. Their discomfort is reflected in the way they react when the price of the parent stock ticks up.

Here the price of the put warrant drops dramatically. A 25% loss from the high to the low for the day is not unusual. This price wipe-out is handled with an effective stop loss or protect profit order – if there is enough trading volume to execute the trade.

This is the put warrant trading trap and the most difficult part of put warrant trading. A price rise in the parent stock creates a much larger price dip in the put warrant *and* a massive decline in volume.

It is very difficult to lock in the full value of the theoretical put warrant profit. Put warrant buyers dry up and disappear as soon as prices in the parent stock start to rally as indicated by line SP1 in Figure 17.3. This is confirmed by the volume line V1 and the warrant price line WP1. It does not matter if the parent stock is still stuck in a strong downtrend, as defined by other objective technical indicators. The crowd does not notice this. The crowd who were attracted to the put warrant because the market is going down are trading on emotion. They see a rising parent stock price and they want out.

They offer the warrant at very low prices. Trouble is, there is no large crowd of buyers with the opposite view. For all intents and purposes the warrant simply stops trading. It returns to the same volume pattern that prevailed before the crowd started to look at the put warrant. You may be lucky enough to sell your put warrant, but it will be for a very low price.

The situation does not improve if the temporary rally develops into a full blown trend change as shown by the line SP1. The warrant price is dominated by the market maker because no-one wants to trade. The quoted price drops back to very low levels as shown by the line WP1.

The situation is not much better if the rally proves to be temporary, as shown by line SP2. Trading volume remains very low as shown by the line V2. After this rally fright it takes a much stronger downtrend to revitalise volume and lift it to the previous high levels. The same applies to price. The line WP2 in Figure 17.3 shows how the rise is crippled. These changes are less volatile than the previous reaction because the warrant is now closer to its expiry date. Time decay – the reduction in price as the warrant moves towards expiry – has

a negative impact on pricing. This impact is exaggerated in put warrants because the crowd is less skilled in trading this section of the market. If the parent stock price rises, there is no orderly retreat in warrant trading. Volume disappears overnight making it very difficult to get out of the position.

LAGS

The chart of the NAB put warrant NABWPS shown in Figure 17.4 presents some of this theory in action. Prior to the dramatic collapse of NAB there was little warrant trading volume. Trading volume spiked as NAB fell and warrant prices moved up rapidly, but this volume surge was temporary. As the NAB downtrend consolidated, the put warrant volume declined. This is a counter-intuitive relationship.

On the last day shown on the chart, NAB staged a strong rally

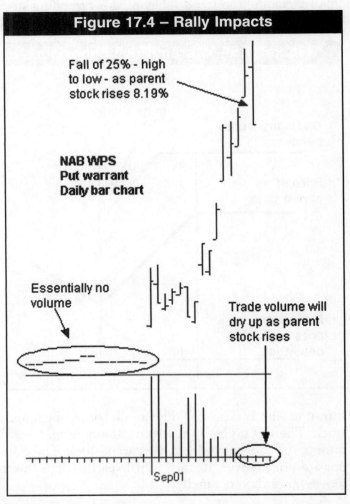

Figure 17.4 – Rally Impacts

Fall of 25% - high to low - as parent stock rises 8.19%

NAB WPS
Put warrant
Daily bar chart

Essentially no volume

Trade volume will dry up as parent stock rises

Sep01

within the context of a well-established downtrend. Prices rose by 8.19%. The put warrant price fell by 25% on very low volume. This is the same relationship examined in Figure 17.3. In contrast, one of the NAB call warrants rose by 81% on the back of the 8% NAB price rise.

Trading put warrants seems to be the sensible approach in a falling market. Profits are available to traders who move early in anticipation of the fall, or early as the downtrends are established. Rewards are not as great for traders who join the rush later. They buy put warrants from traders who have already locked in good profits. They are selling at a profit, and the new buyer hopes to make a profit. The 'greater fool' theory works in bear markets as well as bull markets.

As generally applies to the market, good profits come from going against the crowds. This involves fading the trend – buying downtrending stocks as they begin to turn up. This aggressive strategy uses the tendency of a crowd to participate more fully in events it understands. This is summarised in the relationship shown in the chart in Figure 17.5.

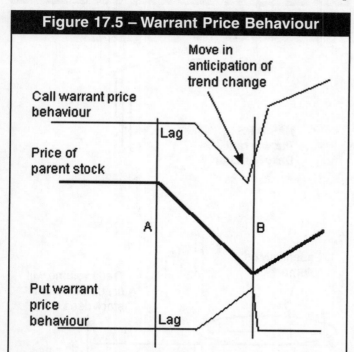

Figure 17.5 – Warrant Price Behaviour

It is all about reaction times. When there is a lag it makes it more difficult to trade. The first event is shown as line A. This is when the share price drops. The price of call warrants starts to drop soon after the trend change in the parent stock. The fall is steady, rather than dramatic.

Put warrants do not start to react until some time after the fall, when the trend has been proven. This delayed reaction leads to a substantial change in price once the warrant starts to react. We see some very fast moves which are exaggerated by low liquidity.

The second reaction point is shown as line B. This could be a rally, or the beginning of a new uptrend in the parent stock. There is no lag in reactions. If anything, the call warrant may begin its reaction prior to the confirmed rise in the parent stock. The call warrant is much more sensitive to upward price moves. It starts a little earlier than the trend in the parent stock – and it moves upwards very rapidly.

The put warrant moves at the same time as the rally. Prices drop very rapidly on just a few trades. There are many sellers, but few buyers. It is a buyer's market and they are not interested. Just like the sellers, the buyers are worried the uptrend will continue and destroy the value of the put warrant. They stay away and are not prepared to buy a put at almost any price.

The third feature is the future behaviour of price as the parent stock price increases. The call warrant continues to gain value. The put warrant simply stops trading, trapping traders in losing positions.

The call warrant consistently has more liquidity and reacts more swiftly to rises in the parent share's price. It reacts more slowly to falls in the parent price. This makes it an easier side of the market to trade in all market conditions. Although put warrants offer the illusion of excellent returns in a falling market they are not the best instrument for short-term trading. Our preference is to follow the tactics outlined in the previous chapters for trading call warrants when the market shows signs of recovery. These gaps in price offer specific trading opportunities and we examine these as the first of a group of specific trading techniques in Part IV.

SNIPER NOTES

➔   Puts have significant psychological friction points.

➔   Warrant price action lags behind downtrends in the parent stock price.

➔   The price linkage is distorted – put warrants overreact to any price rally in the parent stock.

➔   Put warrant profits often involve small size trades.

➔   Low exit volume severely limits position size.

Chapter 18

SLINGSHOT
TRADES

A stone hurled from a slingshot reaches its target more quickly and with more force than a stone thrown by hand. Slingshot trading uses price leverage to magnify the impact of small bursts of price activity. These blips may be unexpected and quite temporary price bubbles in an established trend. Other spurts in price are driven by earnings announcements and dividend dates. In Part II we considered some straightforward trading strategies based on stock price moves. Here we combine them with warrant power. These slingshot returns accelerate from a few percentage points to 40% or more.

Capture just the closing prices and there is always the room for exaggeration and dishonesty. Compare today's close with yesterday's and it appears that returns in excess of 100% are available. They are possible for those who already own the warrant but they are not achievable for traders who want to join developing price action. Their returns may be halved or quartered. Still, it's not a bad performance for a day's trading, but it is a long way from the mythology created by popular media.

One of the objectives of this book is to strip away the myths that have grown around day trading by examining the real difficulties in capturing profits.

A slingshot starts with a small missile, usually a pebble. Centrifugal force is applied by swinging the slingshot strap, and, in the case of David and Goliath, astounding results are achieved. There is a significant gap between myth and reality, although as we show below, reality still delivers a good result.

We start with the pebble. This is a small bump, perhaps an 8% kink in the price action of the stock. Our objective is to wrap this in a sling and hurl it towards more distant profit targets.

FINDING PEBBLES

The market provides the opportunity to put our trading theories into practice. Its feedback is often very rapid, and sometimes disappointing. Some popular approaches fail the practical tests although this does not appear to detract from the popularity of the approaches. One of the challenges of the market is to develop appropriate strategies for current market conditions and then recognise when those strategies are inappropriate in the particular trade you are contemplating.

In the earnings season traders focus on ways to turn earnings announcements into profits by using the price rises. Some stocks offer a direct trading opportunity. When ORG announced good news, its price gapped up from the previous day as shown in Figure 18.1. This price action sets the scene for a seductive lie.

How large is the price rise on this news announcement? Some measure the move from the close on the day prior to the news announcement, and compare this with the high for the day of the news announcement. This delivers an 8.8% return. This is the first seduction. New traders believe this type of return is possible from news announcements and when they do not achieve these returns, they blame their trading systems. They ignore the practicality of the market while chasing a theoretical return. This 8.8% return is a valid figure only if you already hold ORG at the previous day's close.

If you do not hold the stock the appropriate figure is 3.88%. This is calculated from the low price on the day of the announcement to the high for the day. Traders who act on the news release attempt to buy near the low and

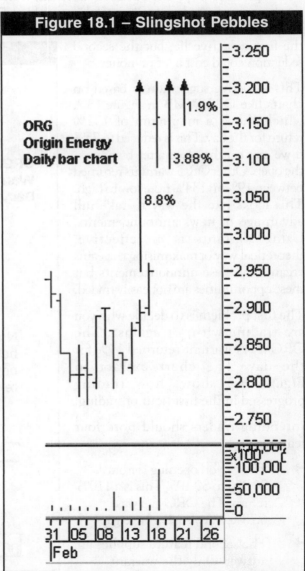

Figure 18.1 – Slingshot Pebbles

ORG
Origin Energy
Daily bar chart

sell near the high, or hold onto the stock as it continues to rise. The best they do is 3.88%. If they buy the open, the return is reduced to 1.9%.

This is the pebble we fit to our slingshot.

SELECT THE BEST SLING

The opportunity to profit from this news release is clearly shown by the ORG chart. Warrants are an obvious way to take advantage of this price blip. This introduces a more dangerous seduction.

The trader may waste a lot of time chasing the first seductive lie, but the second seduction could cost a lot of money.

This seductive suggestion is based on charts like ORGWMB in Figure 18.2, which shows a maximum of 137% return for the day. This is reduced to 75% if we exit on the close after buying on the open. Other ORG warrants returned between 19% and 34% from low to high. This looks like the way to take full advantage of news announcements. Using warrants is an effective, theoretical way of maximising the gains created by these announcements but these opportunities are not easily traded.

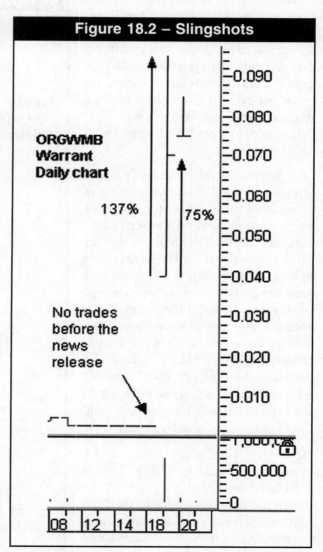

Figure 18.2 – Slingshots

The first problem is to decide who you are trading with, or against. The ORGWPA warrant returned 19% for the day. The chart extract in Figure 18.3 shows how trading progressed in the first hour of trading.

Intending traders should note four features:

→   The gap on opening is from $0.050 to $0.105. This is a 110% return. The ORG gap was 6.78%. Why such a large gap?

→   The second feature supplies an answer. Only the warrant

issuer, acting as market maker, is trading this warrant. Although this extract does not show the opening order lines we still see the common order size. The first trade is for 50,000. The next two trades also total 50,000. These consistent round-figure lots suggest the market maker is the person on the other side of the trade.

→ The current bid and ask line confirms market maker activity. When we see evenly matched order sizes on the buy and sell, we take this as evidence of market maker activity. This issuer sets the market in 50,000 trade lots and is the most active person in this warrant. If we trade this warrant we trade against professionals. There are few other traders interested. Professionals do not give much away, although they take a lot. They captured 110% on the opening gap, but surrendered only 19% for the day's warrant trading.

→ The time and course of trades data provide confirmation of limited public interest in this series. Three trades in just over an hour is not a fast market.

Figure 18.3 – ORGWPA Depth of Market Screen

Marketcast depth of market screen

MarketDepth - ORGWPA - Second Level

Symbol	± $	± %	High	Low	Prev	Open	TotVol	Trades	BuyVol	SellVol
ORGWPA	0.065	130.0	0.115	0.105	0.050	0.105	100000	4	50000	50000

	1 Bids			1 Asks			Last 20 Trades		
Count	Buyers	Volume	Price	Price	Volume	Sellers	Price	Volume	Time
1	1	50000	0.115	0.120	50000	1	0.115	25000	11:15
2							0.110	25000	11:00
3							0.105	50000	10:05

Market maker orders

The most active warrant is ORGWMB and, with its maximum 137% return, it looks as if it should have provided an opportunity to make a handsome profit from the ORG news release. To turn theory into practical warrant trading we check for an additional two features.

1. Where is the market maker and what is his trading size? The course of trades information suggests he prefers lots of 50,000. We infer this from the pattern of repeated even-sized trades. In the first ten minutes of trading there are three trades at this size. We need to watch these types of trades to determine how the market maker is reacting to the rise in ORG.

2. How interested is the public? These market maker trades are interspersed with outside traders selling 7,500, 4,000 and 20,000 shares. When the public joins there is a greater possibility of pricing inefficiencies. Crowds get excited and drive

prices up as they outbid each other to get a piece of the action. This is the activity we profit from. Professional traders do not get as excited, so if they dominate this market there is less opportunity for substantial profits.

At this early stage of analysis ORGWMB appears to provide a practical way to apply the theory of warrant-based news trading. Before combining the pebble and the sling into an effective slingshot trade we complete some additional calculations.

CHOOSING A PEBBLE

Small missiles accelerate more rapidly than larger ones. The pebble we fit to this slingshot trade must match the market conditions. We start with the amount – the pebble we would like to allocate to our slingshot trade. We routinely use a $20,000 position size so here is our first problem. To buy $20,000 of ORGWMB we have to buy all the way up to $0.047, based on the volume traded and shown in Figure 18.4. With this trading size it is not possible to establish the position at $0.04. Based on the actual course of sales our position costs an average of $0.052. This average is lifted because it includes trades at $0.076.

Figure 18.4 – Course of Trades ORGWMB

	COURSE OF TRADES ORGWMB			
	Price	Volume	$	
10.00	0.040	50,000	$2,000.00	
	0.040	7,500	$ 300.00	
	0.042	50,000	$2,100.00	
	0.042	4,000	$ 168.00	
	0.075	20,000	$1,500.00	
	0.076	50,000	$3,800.00	Trades to fill
	0.061	7,500	$ 457.50	a $10,000 buy order
	0.056	5,000	$ 280.00	
	0.056	10,000	$ 560.00	
	0.056	30,000	$1,680.00	
	0.055	25,000	$1,375.00	
	0.055	5,200	$ 286.00	
	0.056	30,000	$1,680.00	
	0.042	50,000	$2,100.00	
	0.047	35,000	$1,645.00	Trades to fill
	0.047	10,000	$ 470.00	a $20,000 buy order
	0.050	58,650	$2,932.50	
	0.055	10,000	$ 550.00	

We might think we do better if we use a smaller position size of $10,000. In fact we do worse, paying a maximum of $0.055 based on the average cost of the position. We pay up to 90% more than the opening price of $0.04. This happens because we are chasing stock in the first few minutes of a buying frenzy which drives prices to a high of $0.076. Prices quickly fall after this.

This is a slap in the face from reality.

The slingshot propels returns to 137% but only if we use a smaller pebble. The size of the most effective trade is set by careful reference to the volume of trading and this is often initially established by the market maker. The trader who purchases 50,000 warrants at $0.04 on the open for a total of $2,000 collects a 137% profit for the day with an exit at $0.095. This is a $2,750 return for the day. This slingshot kills no Goliath but it brings home a steady meal.

For traders who want to work with $5,000 to $20,000 positions, even this warrant does not offer a reasonable opportunity to trade the price rise generated by the earnings blip in the parent stock. With only 72,500 warrants changing hands for around $0.08 we are hung out to dry. This is around $5,800 in total trading activity for the day.

We have a practical problem with this exit. The high of $0.095 is made late in the day's trading and only one trade takes place after this. The trader who waits for a pullback from this high before selling is able to get rid of warrants to the value of $4,130 – and even then he needs to be very lucky. For this example in Figure 18.5 we have counted back from the last traded price to establish the average price of the exit from $10,000 and $20,000 positions. To achieve this in reality requires incredible luck. However, even this exceptional exit delivers a poor result.

The trader with a $10,000 position size gets out at an average of $0.081, based on this course of trades for the day. Compare this with his average entry cost of $0.055. This is a 47% return. Paradoxically, the trader with the $20,000 position size does better on these course of trade figures with an average exit price of $0.078. His exit captures more of the higher priced trades. This is a 56% return on his average entry price of $0.050.

These are the best possible results from this trading opportunity. The slingshot falls short of the theoretical 137% return by more than half. The short-term trader does not need to kill Goliath. The slingshot is a hunting tool and, with careful management, trades returning 47% or 56% for the day are a welcome addition to any meal table.

Figure 18.5 – Course of Trades ORGWMB

COURSE OF TRADES ORGWMB

	Price	Volume	$	
	0.060	25,000	$1,500.00	
	0.051	100,000	$5,100.00	Trades to fill
	0.060	100,000	$6,000.00	a $20,000 sell order
	0.051	10,000	$ 510.00	
	0.055	4,000	$ 220.00	
	0.075	10,000	$ 750.00	
	0.075	10,000	$ 750.00	
	0.085	30,000	$2,550.00	Trades to fill
	0.085	10,000	$ 850.00	a $10,000 sell order
	0.085	1,000	$ 85.00	
	0.095	11,000	$1,045.00	
	0.095	10,000	$ 950.00	
	0.095	11,000	$1,045.00	
4:00	0.070	59,000	$4,130.00	

The trader who uses the smaller pebble, accepting the 50,000 opening trade at $0.04 does better than traders using a larger rock in a $10,000 or $20,000 trade. We have calculated the average exits using the actual course-of-trades data. In real life, a single buy order for $10,000 placed at $0.04 changes the dynamics of the crowd reaction. The real impact forces prices up more rapidly and lifts the average price paid. Slingshot returns are reduced, but still effective.

Using a derivative like warrants is a theoretically attractive way of trading news and earnings releases. It is only practically possible if there is sufficient depth and trading activity in the warrant. Even with high-volume warrants there may be problems in obtaining a sufficient number of warrants at a price suitable for obtaining a realistic profit from the trade. Getting into the trade can be difficult. Getting out of the trade is often much more difficult. Slingshot trades are most effective when they are small.

Modern cavalry tactics using armoured personnel carriers rely on precise insertion of troops into a battlefield and where necessary, fast extraction. Warrants and other derivative instruments give the trader the firepower required to make this rapid excursion very profitable. These price relationships give day traders the opportunity to tell hair raising war stories from the trading screen. The mundane battles of every day trading are less exciting. These include gaps, trading new high breakouts and doomed rebounds. They are the basic grunt work of short-term trading and the subject of the next part of the book.

SLINGSHOT HUNTING NOTES

➜ Slingshot trades use leverage to increase the impact of price blips.

➜ Returns measured from yesterday's close to today's high are misleading.

➜ Use volume to identify whom you trade with or against.

➜ Use course-of-trades data and order lines to select the appropriate pebble size.

➜ The slingshot is a hunting tool. Do not expect to kill Goliath every day.

PART IV

LETHAL

WEAPONS

Chapter 19

GAPPING THE OPPORTUNITY

Price gaps appear when the public wakes up to a price shock. The most profitable gaps are unpredictable and uncharacteristic. Unless you already hold the stock, it is difficult to capture the profits they offer. Chasing gap opens is a great way to throw away money. Traded in a more effective way, gap behaviour provides steady, high-probability two-day returns. We start with an examination of gaps on daily charts and the way they are verified using intra-day screening techniques. Later we explore gap trading strategies based on the continuation of crowd enthusiasm.

A gap occurs when today's open is higher than yesterday's high, or when the open is lower than yesterday's low. An upside gap – higher open – tells us buyers are impatient. They want this stock and they bid ahead of the market, sometimes by considerable amounts. The larger the gap the stronger the buying pressure. Gaps are only significant in stocks with steady volume. Gaps in low-volume stocks are unimportant because they are caused by lack of liquidity, not by an excess of enthusiasm or pessimism.

Gap days appear for one simple reason – there has been a dramatic change in market sentiment while the market is closed. This change in sentiment shows up as a significant change in the value of buying and selling as the market opens. This change is sometimes unexpected and moves outside the average volatility of the stock's previous prices.

This volatility is usually created by news events, either about the particular stock, or about the market in general. This volatility operates in three areas:

1. Overnight volatility
2. Weekend volatility
3. Continuous volatility.

Overnight volatility is created by the impact of news events. The market closes at 4 p.m. and we do not get to trade again until 10 a.m. Increasingly many companies are choosing to make their continuous disclosure announcements after the market closes and this makes it difficult for private traders to take defensive action.

Part of the reasoning for this practice of after-the-close announcements is to give traders time to consider their reactions prior to the open. Companies worry a profit downgrade announced while the market is open might lead to a dramatic collapse in the share price. In reality this delay just transfers the dramatic collapse to the next day. Overnight volatility is difficult to manage because news announcements are irregular and spasmodic.

Weekend volatility is, by definition, a regular cycle. The primary cause is the activity of overseas' markets which are still trading Friday night and Saturday morning, Australian time. A collapse in the NASDAQ on Friday, US time, has a significant impact on Australian tech stocks on Monday's open. In times of increased instability on world markets, many traders close doubtful positions on Friday to avoid the risk of volatility over the weekend. Some stocks have low weekend volatility.

Weekends sometimes lead to significant changes in the opinions held about a stock. Your own activity is a good guide to how this happens. Most part-time traders do the bulk of their analysis over the weekend. News about a particular stock has an impact, but we suspect the additional time available for analysis of stocks has a larger impact. This effect is magnified by US market changes.

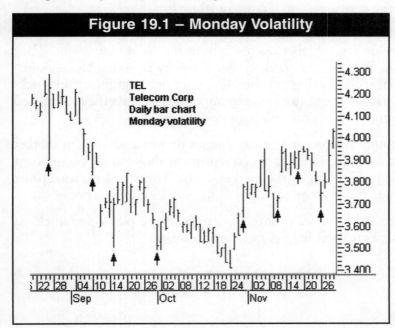

Figure 19.1 – Monday Volatility

TEL
Telecom Corp
Daily bar chart
Monday volatility

Weekend volatility is also defined as the relationship between Friday's price activity and Monday's activity. Many charting packages allow the user to highlight a selected day of the week. The TEL chart in Figure 19.1 highlights high volatility Monday trading with arrows. There is a 60% probability of a large range day on Monday in this stock.

This type of display shows you how reactive and sensitive the stock is to weekend volatility. A stock consistently moving in a large price range on Monday has a high weekend volatility risk. Traders in these stocks may consider closing their trades on Friday to protect open profits.

American trader, Robert Deel, has raised the issue of continuous volatility which is a developing feature of 24-hour markets. This sounds frightening but we believe it will diminish gap activity. A continuous 24-hour market moves essentially in three time blocks of six to eight hours each, as shown in Figure 19.2. Starting with our region, trading begins in New Zealand at around 8.30 a.m. our time. In Australia we open at 10 a.m. and close at 4 p.m. In this region trading continues to 6 p.m. our time via Asian exchanges in slightly different time zones. Trading then moves to Europe, effectively opening around 6 p.m. our time and closing around 2 a.m. The US markets fill the gap, opening just before the European close and closing just before the New Zealand open.

Each of these markets has its main trading activity within a six to eight hour block. In a 24-hour market Australians can trade the same stocks in Europe and in the US, but this activity is most likely to be via stop loss or take profit orders rather than direct, personal supervision. This is covered in *Trading Tactics* in greater detail. The key feature is the way the impact of an overnight, or out-of-market-hours, news event is reduced because there is no pent-up buying or selling

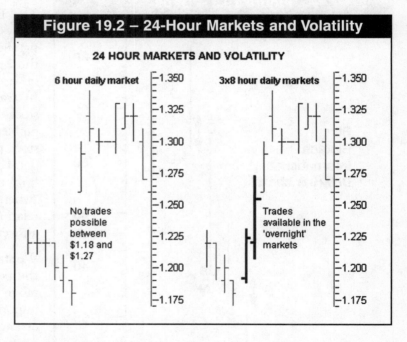

Figure 19.2 – 24-Hour Markets and Volatility

demand. The price gap in a six-hour daily market from $1.18 to $1.27 is filled by two additional overnight trading sessions shown by the thick bars. This demand is satisfied immediately as the next market opens and reduces the incidence and size of gap-trading events. It does not mean sudden rises disappear but there are many more price points at which trading occurs during the rise or fall. This increases the probability of a stop loss order being executed at, or near, the specified stop loss point.

This feature alone should allow traders to rest easy in the face of 24-hour market volatility. A central plank of charting and technical analysis approaches is the way market prices are primarily the product of crowd opinion – both informed and uninformed – about the future value of a stock. Crowds change opinions rapidly and this often leads to sometimes substantial and rapid changes in market prices. We rarely understand the specific reasons for this change in valuation, but we manage this volatility by understanding how it typically behaves.

GAPS IN THE CROWD

Just finding any gap is not enough. The most useful gaps appear in price action when today's open is higher than yesterday's high. We call this a classic gap. These are confirmed when the low for the day remains higher than the high of the previous day. This is an important distinction as some screening programs define a classic gap as when today's open is higher or lower than yesterday's close.

Figure 19.3 – Gaps

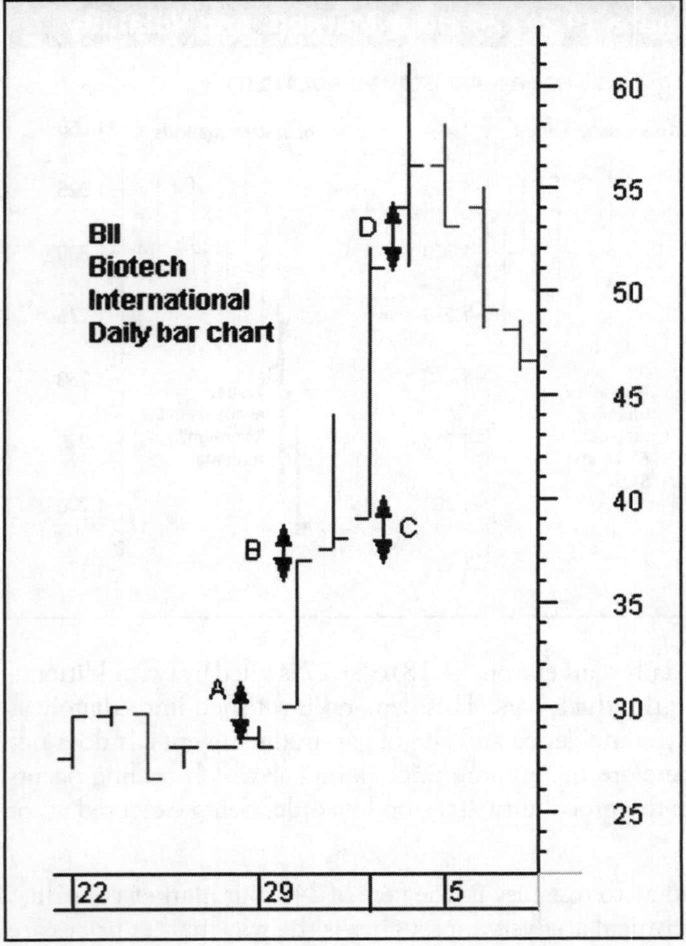

The BII chart in Figure 19.3 shows the difference between significant continuation gaps, and those gaps which suggest the end or weakening of an existing rally. In trading these fast-moving stocks the trader faces two main problems. For those who hold the stock the problem is when to get out. For those who would like to hold the stock, the question is "when is it too late to get in?" Gap relationships help provide some answers.

We start with the initial gaps at the beginning of the BII price move. The first gap at A is an important trading signal. It is a classic and useful gap where the open of today is higher than the high of the previous day. The relationship between the open of today and the close of yesterday is less important. This gap is also significant because of the increase in volume. This confirms a surge in buying activity. People who had only thought about buying BII a few days ago are now so desperate that they propel the opening price above yesterday's high and keep pushing the price up during the day. This is a powerful trading signal based on an increase in value, a higher close, and a classic opening gap.

The second gap, at B, is also a classic continuation signal. Many traders chase prices to get into BII. The price ends the day lower than the high but the bullish bias remains with a close above the day's open, and high trading volume. For end-of-day traders the gap at point B is a confirmation signal. If they want to participate in the BII rally then this signal confirms an entry.

The third day of the rally starts with an opening price relationship shown at point C. This appears as a gap on many market scans. The open is higher than yesterday's close, but not higher than yesterday's high. This is not a classic gap and we treat it with caution.

The price action remains bullish if two conditions are met. The first is when prices continue to climb above the open. The second requirement is for prices not to fall below yesterday's low. Such a fall is a bearish signal of rally weakness no matter what the volume of trading. A price slip on a high-volume day simply tells us many existing stockholders are very nervous about the prospect of the rally continuing. They are prepared to take a lower price just for the safety of being out of the trade. For traders thinking of selling, it is a warning to keep a close eye on the price action over the following days.

Like many fast-moving rallies, this is a two- to five-day rally in BII providing a short-term trading opportunity. The initial sign of weakness, given by the gap relationship at C, is confirmed by the gap relationship at D. This relationship is seen most clearly on the end-of-day screen so the trader is ready for action the next day. Sometimes the relationship develops clearly on an intra-day screen and this gives the trader an opportunity to take an exit at levels near the high of the day, but don't count on it.

Initially the gap at D looks bullish. The open is higher than the high of the previous day. These are the same conditions as the initial classic gaps at A and B. The danger signal comes in two parts. The first appears when the low of the day is below the high of the previous day. The second is the position of this bar in the rally. This is a fast rally with a potential 100% return over just a few days. Typically these rallies last for three to five days and then pull back. Our objective as traders is to ride the rally but not the pullback.

This combination of danger signals which starts with a failed gap on day four of this rally suggests it's time to start looking for the exit. In day five, if the opening price is near or above the previous day's high, we stay with the rally. Instead the open of the next day is at the same level as the previous close. This combination of a failed gap followed by a weak open confirms the exit. Smart traders exit around this level. Those who wait receive a confirmation signal as prices move below the opening price of the previous day.

Chasing gap openings is the most common, and least effective, way of trading gaps. Using gap behaviour provides more reliable opportunities. In this example an entry at $0.33 and an exit four days later at $0.55 provides a 66% return for this short-term trade. The trade management is based on two observations. First, classic gap activity shows a dramatic change in investor sentiment. Second, stocks with a high number of trades confirm a crowd has gathered and action is developing. By combining both these features we may identify a better trading opportunity built on riding the gap overnight.

≡ SNAPSHOOTER'S NOTES

➜ Gaps indicate significant changes in valuation.

➜ Gaps show overnight and weekend volatility.

➜ Continuous markets reduce the opportunity for gap trades.

➜ Look for classic gaps.

➜ The relationships between the gap open, the low for the day, and yesterday's high provide exit signals.

➜ Gap chasing calls for careful trade management.

Chapter 20

RUNNING WITH
THE GAP

The best gaps show excited crowds. They cannot wait to get their hands on stock and they just know it's going to dramatically increase in value. Their buying pressure helps make their idea a self-fulfilling prophecy. Often their emotional approach has fatal consequences when the buying pressure declines. With no new buyers, sellers desperately unload stock to lock in rapidly diminishing profits. Their fear and despair drive the market back. Buying these rises is often based on the so-called 'greater fool' theory. The buyer purchases stock at a high price and his success depends on a greater fool coming along to purchase the stock at an even higher price.

It is fashionable to sneer at those participating in these greater fool rallies. For day and short-term traders, the real fools are those who dismiss this price action as devoid of trading opportunity. These excited gaps provide an opportunity for a two day, or overnight gap trading strategy.

We start the chapter with the set up steps and search criteria for this two-day strategy. We end with real-time notes from a personal trade using this approach. It includes the assessment of the order screens, the management during each trading day, and the exit to lock in a 10.34% return from an overnight trade. This is a fishing story and we include it to show the practical detail of this strategy.

Unlike the fast-moving, leveraged warrant trades discussed in the last section, these types of returns are the bread and butter of short-term and day trading techniques. We use them to knock out consistent profits.

We want actively traded stocks with significant classic gaps. Additionally, when the gap appears, we want to see plenty of trading action. Some stocks show a lot of gap activity, but this is simply a move from one price level to the next. This may be a jump from $0.40 to $0.42 which shows up on the chart as a flat spot. This spot activity shows there is no trading range for the day. The open, high, low and close are exactly the same. Stocks with a history of this type of activity do not provide trading opportunities. With only a small number of trades all taking place at the one price level, there is limited opportunity to apply effective trading strategies.

We look for gaps driven by crowd enthusiasm and attracting many trades. Without trading liquidity, we cannot implement our trading strategy.

OVERNIGHT GAP TRADES

The overnight gap strategy shown in Figure 20.1 recognises we will not capture the benefits of a fast gap move on the first day the gap appears. The gap trade A, from the high of the previous day to the high of the gap trade, is available only to those who already hold the stock. It is not available to traders who chase the gap during the day. This opportunity is shown as line B. It is difficult to actually capture the full profit potential on the day of the gap. Typically there are few trades at the opening price, so the level of profit is substantially reduced.

The strategy based on running with the gap relies on a continuation of gap activity, or momentum on the day following the initial gap. This gives traders an opportunity to execute the trade shown as line C. The strategy aims to capture a mid-point entry on the day of the gap, and a mid-point exit on the day after the gap. This is shown as line D and it is an overnight trading strategy. It works most effectively when leverage is available. The sample gap trade discussed below returns 20% overnight.

The key to success in this strategy lies in the correct identification of the gap. Each of the bar chart configurations shown in Figure 20.2 are classed as gap trading activity, as shown by the arrows. Example A shows today's open higher than yesterday's close. This is typically the gap relationship identified by many charting program searches and by some live market scan searches. It does not set up a tradable gap. This is the relationship found by the standard MetaStock Gap Up exploration.

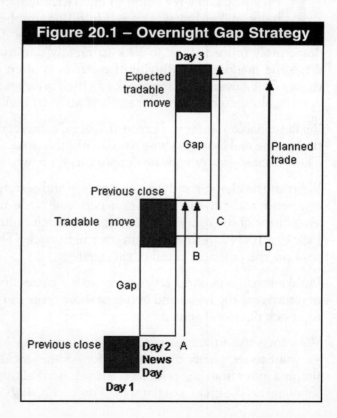

Figure 20.1 – Overnight Gap Strategy

Example B is also a common search criteria which shows today's open above yesterday's high. This is a better relationship, but it is not the type of gap we are looking for.

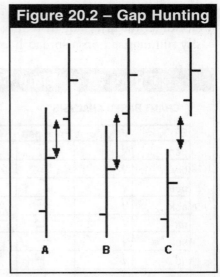

Figure 20.2 – Gap Hunting

We are interested in the gap shown in example C. The low of today is higher than the high of yesterday. This is where crowd enthusiasm goes into overdrive. This is a classic gap situation easily found using end-of-day data. We want to find the classic gap using an intra-day scan. We search for these gaps after the first 30 minutes of trading.

Opportunity screening starts with the scan facilities on the MarketCast or Hubb Data live feed. Other websites offer similar facilities. The scan does not start until 30 minutes after the open of trading, and it gives time for every stock to have traded. We start with all those stocks which have gapped on the open. The search compares the close of yesterday with the open of today. We want a true gap where the open of today is higher than the high of yesterday. This scan list is a starting point for further analysis.

Many of the gaps identified in this scan are small. On the day shown in Figure 20.3 they range from 1.53% to 50%. Our interest is in gaps greater than 3%. Eliminate those under 3% and we have 53 candidates. Next we eliminate all but the classic gaps. There is no easy way to do this.

Figure 20.3 – Market Gap Scan Results

Scan [Stocks] - Percent Gap Gainers - Showing Top 100 matches | Marketcast screen

Symbol	%Change	Last	Open	Previous	Low	High	Change	Gap	%Gap	Real Gap
EOX	50.000	0.003	0.003	0.002	0.003	0.003	0.001	0.001	50.000	
ECE	33.333	0.008	0.008	0.006	0.008	0.008	0.002	0.002	33.333	
SVP	33.333	0.040	0.040	0.030	0.040	0.040	0.010	0.010	33.333	
ISA	20.000	0.066	0.066	0.055	0.066	0.066	0.011	0.011	20.000	
JYC	15.385	0.300	0.294	0.260	0.290	0.300	0.040	0.034	13.077	
PEM	5.660	0.560	0.580	0.530	0.560	0.590	0.030	0.050	9.434	X
VOS	8.333	0.013	0.013	0.012	0.013	0.013	0.001	0.001	8.333	
PWT	7.692	0.140	0.140	0.130	0.135	0.140	0.010	0.010	7.692	
BRY	6.849	0.390	0.390	0.365	0.390	0.390	0.025	0.025	6.849	X
PCE	11.111	0.250	0.240	0.225	0.240	0.250	0.025	0.015	6.667	X
PMD	6.250	0.017	0.017	0.016	0.017	0.017	0.001	0.001	6.250	
ATC	6.061	0.350	0.350	0.330	0.350	0.350	0.020	0.020	6.061	
VXS	5.882	0.180	0.180	0.170	0.180	0.180	0.010	0.010	5.882	
TKG	5.882	0.018	0.018	0.017	0.018	0.018	0.001	0.001	5.882	
ABK	5.556	0.380	0.380	0.360	0.380	0.380	0.020	0.020	5.556	X
WEB	0.000	0.190	0.200	0.190	0.190	0.200	0.000	0.010	5.263	
CHF	5.263	0.800	0.800	0.760	0.800	0.800	0.040	0.040	5.263	
ASL	5.263	0.080	0.080	0.076	0.080	0.080	0.004	0.004	5.263	

We inspect the bar chart for each of the remaining 53 stocks on the list. This sounds like a monumental task, but in reality it is a fast process checking for a handful of features easily summarised on a spreadsheet as shown in Figure 20.4. Speed is not important but nor do we want to take too long to make this initial assessment. Of the 53 stocks, only eight meet our conditions on this day.

Figure 20.4 – Eight Candidates

CHART BASED ANALYSIS

STOCK	Volume	Price patt	Trend patt	MMA
pem	√	⌐	∧	√
bry	√	⊥	∧	
pce	√	⌐	∨	√
abk	√	⌐	∧	√
rbt	√	∟	⌐	
ssi	√	—	∕	√
rld	√	⊤	∨	
nam	√	∟	∧∕	

The next filter examines the volume of the previous day in particular, and over the previous week in general. We plan to trade crowd enthusiasm, so we expect to see some evidence of this on the day prior to the gap. The appropriate volume depends on our trading objectives. If we want to trade a $5,000 position size then we accept a lower volume than if we want to trade a $20,000 position. We need evidence that there is sufficient volume to support our planned trading size.

If this is supported by trading volumes during the week then it is an added advantage – a double tick on the spreadsheet notes. This is not a critical factor. Many of the best gap trades happen when volume floods the market. The previous week, or weeks, of trading activity may be very low. The stampede changes this which is why volume on the day prior to the gap open is more important than volume in the previous week.

In the next column we note the bar pattern. An excited crowd closes prices near the high of the day prior to the gap day. This is the most bullish pattern. A close above the open is the next most bullish. A close equal with the open is acceptable, but it must be supported by other bullish factors, including a very strong Guppy Multiple Moving Average – MMA – relationship. A close lower than the open is the least effective chart pattern as this is a crowd losing enthusiasm. It is unsuitable for our strategy based on continued enthusiasm.

The final note in this initial selection process is the trend pattern. This combines both Guppy MMA analysis and recent trend direction. The best pattern is a straight-edge trend line moving upwards. The next most bullish is a rising trend showing a small retracement. The current gap open signals a resumption of the uptrend. This may be extended to include a retracement followed by a sideways move and then a rebound from the consolidation pattern.

The least attractive opportunity is created by a breakout from a downtrend. Instead of a gap trade, this becomes a breakout trade using gap strategies. The danger in this type of trade is in a rally collapse from a resistance level, as the rally is overwhelmed by sellers. There is less probability of this in a rally starting in an established uptrend.

We want crowd enthusiasm and trend strength so the eight candidates are reduced to six as shown in Figure 20.5. Selecting the best rallies depends on three final filters applied to live depth-of-market order lines. The filters are:

→   More buyers than sellers.

→   Good trading volume on the buying side. We want to be able to place our order.

→   A reasonable spread between the bid and ask. If it is too wide we must wait for prices to pull back, or pay more than we should to get hold of stock.

Figure 20.5 – Better Gaps

LIVE ORDER LINE ANALYSIS

STOCK	Crt Vol	Activity	Price	Vol > yest
pem	B> S<	avtive	0.58	√
bry	B> S<	active	0.4	√
pce	gap large			
abk	Low vol	no trades		
rbt	Vol OK	few trades		
ssi	B> S<	low vol		

PEM and BRY meet all these conditions. The spread with PCE is too large. The buyer wants to pay $0.24 but the nearest seller is asking for $0.345. This spread eats away at the potential profits in this strategy, so we ignore it.

ABK has very low trading volume so our order would dominate the market. SSI has more buyers than sellers, but the order line has low volume.

We look at this screen up to 50 minutes after the open of trade. Our strategy is based on continued crowd enthusiasm, confirmed in two ways. First by a continued increase in prices, or at least, no slip back to the level of the previous day's high. Second there should be lots of activity in the stock. We want a large enthusiastic crowd fighting amongst themselves to get hold of stock. This is the penultimate filter. Those candidates with active trading go to the top of the list. RBT which met the order line conditions, fails this activity test. Fifty minutes after the open only a few trades have been completed. There is no crowd here.

The final filter is price. Our preference is to select the opportunity with the best price leverage. A $0.10 stock is preferred to a $0.50 stock or a $1.00 stock, all other factors being equal. Lower prices mean more opportunity for a substantial price rise today and tomorrow. It increases the percentage return from the trade.

We select PEM from this list because it has a stronger chart pattern than BRY.

LEVERAGING THE GAP

Management of the gap trade covers two days – the entry day and the exit day. The success of this strategy rests on entering the stock on day one with the objective of exiting the trade on day two. Rather than attempting to buy the bid, it is more effective to hit the ask. The order screen shows a bid at $0.57 and the ask at $0.58. Getting a position in these trades is more important than haggling about the entry price so we take the entry at $0.58 as shown in Figure 20.6.

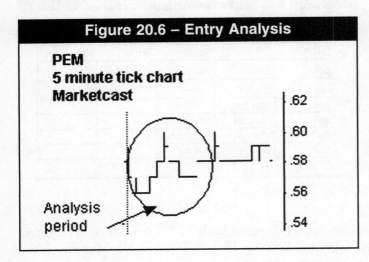

Figure 20.6 – Entry Analysis

PEM
5 minute tick chart
Marketcast

.62
.60
.58
.56
.54

Analysis period

In this trade we miss the low of the day set at $0.56 because we are still involved in analysing the potential trading candidates. This is significant if our focus is on trading the extremes of price action. It is less important in this strategy as our objective is to capture a portion of the price movement. We stress this because so many traders feel cheated if they miss the price extremes. This attitude blinds them to many other successful trading strategies.

Success depends upon running a tight stop loss. Using the low of the day we set a stop loss one tick below $0.56. A tick is the minimum price move permitted in the stock and with PEM, prices move up or down by $0.01 at a time. There are no half-cent bids. Our stop loss is set at $0.55. This is an automatic stop loss and has several advantages. First, the stop is executed automatically so you do not need to sit in front of the live screen all day. This automatic execution overcomes the temptation not to act. It is an artificial boost to discipline.

The second advantage is the speed of execution. Traders who use mental stop loss points have to watch the screen all day. Once the alert is sounded as a trade takes place at the stop loss price they must contact their broker. The time between the stop loss alert and order execution may be a minute or more. Prices may have slipped several ticks below the planned exit point, creating an unexpected large loss.

In the afternoon a new flood of buyers come into the market. They temporarily lift prices to $0.62. Some traders start to take profits at this level, and their selling drops prices back to a close at $0.60. Our objective is to remain in the trade, so we do not chase this rise as a selling opportunity. However, the rise provides the opportunity to lift the stop loss, shifting the trade to a breakeven opportunity. This is shown on the end-of-day chart in Figure 20.7.

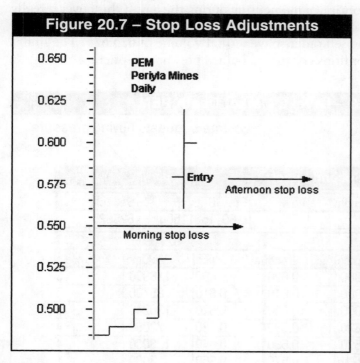

Figure 20.7 – Stop Loss Adjustments

The initial, or morning, stop loss on day one is placed one tick below the low for the period. The afternoon stop loss is placed after prices start to pull back from the high. The objective is to protect our capital. Lifting the stop loss means the worst outcome is now a breakeven trade – unless prices gap down past the stop on the next day's trading. However, with a gap open today and a higher close on increased volume this is an unlikely outcome.

In a position trade it is sufficient to set a stop loss at the end of each trading day. On an intra-day, or short-term trade, there are significant advantages in shifting a stop loss several times during the day. The first shift protects our capital. Later shifts start to lock in profits, and this is the first step on the second day of the trade. Stop loss points are only lifted upwards. They are never lowered.

DAY TWO MEANS PROFITS

This is a two-day trading strategy and day two is about profits. There is no intention to extend this trade into a third day. Prior to the open we focus on the order lines for evidence that the buying pressure is continuing.

We start with the estimated match price prior to the open. This is calculated by the ASX and is the average of the highest buy and the lowest sell order. Most live data screens provide this figure. In the order line up shown in Figure 20.8 the match price is set at $0.61 and represents a gap above the previous day's close. It is not a real gap above yesterday's high, but it suggests the upwards move is likely to continue.

Next we consider the balance between buyers and sellers. These figures take into account all the orders in the order line. This includes some very old buy orders which have little chance of execution at $0.42 and lower. However, the balance is tilted very heavily towards buyers with buying volume of 1,581,150. This includes an undisclosed buyer sitting at $0.57. It is unlikely prices will fall to this level, but the presence of this large buy order provides additional support for continued momentum during the day. If this buyer is really interested he may well decide to chase prices higher. If the undisclosed order is on the sell side it sends a bearish signal. The sell orders have a total volume of 625,625. The line is shorter than the buy line and confirms continued bullish pressure on prices.

Figure 20.8 – Level 2 Market Depth PEM

Volume suggests buying pressure

MarketDepth - PEM - Second Level

Symbol	± $	± %	High	Low	Prev	BuyVol	SellVol
PEM	0.000	0.0			0.60	1581150u	625625

	42 Bids			32 Asks		
Count	Buyers	Volume	Price	Price	Volume	Sellers
1	1	150000	0.620	0.600	116800	3
2	2	15000	0.610	0.610	85700	5
3	3	100000	0.600	0.620	130240	5
4	5	338630	0.590	0.630	72000	4
5	4	356500	0.580	0.640	129000	4
6	6	125271u	0.570	0.650	3000	1

Figure 20.9 – Day Two Prices

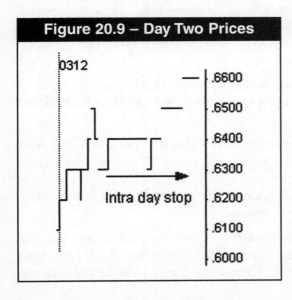

0312

— .6600
— .6500
.6400
.6300
Intra day stop .6200
.6100
.6000

The match price confirms a continuation of the rise so we lift the stop loss to the same level as yesterday's close. At worst, if triggered, this locks in a 3.45% return. Day two concentrates on exit management. It calls for close monitoring of intra-day price activity. Early in the morning prices test $0.63 as a support level before moving on as shown in Figure 20.9. Our stop loss is lifted to $0.63, locking in a potential 8.62% return.

During the day prices hit $0.66 on low volume, and then pull back. In the late afternoon sellers flood the market with orders at $0.65 and $0.64 suggesting the momentum generated by the gap on the previous day is losing strength. Our objective is to do the best possible on the day, and in the face of this selling pressure we meet the bid at $0.64. This exit locks in a 10.34% return as shown on the end-of-day chart in Figure 20.10.

Prices climb back to $0.66, but they close on just a handful of trades. The volume traded is not enough to close our position. These overnight gap trades return significant short-term gains. They are more effective than day trading strategies which rely on buying near the low of the day and selling near the high of the day. These gap trades reduce overnight risk because they rely on a continuation of demonstrated momentum. When traded with the advantage of price leverage these trades return 5% to 15% in a 36-hour period. The strategy is straightforward but the execution requires well-developed trading discipline.

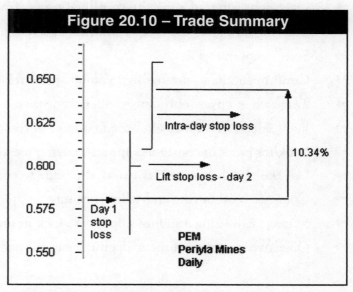

Prices gapping upwards offer comfort. Prices gapping down are a nightmare if we own the stock, and an opportunity for a rebound trade if we do not. We examine the last of these gap trading techniques in the next chapter.

Gap-Trading Exploration Search

This exploration finds stocks which have gapped upwards, with today's low higher than the previous high by at least 5%.

Col A: gap% $(((LOW–(Ref(HIGH,–1)))/(Ref(HIGH,–1)))*100)$

Col B: prev% $(((Ref(OPEN,–1)–(Ref(CLOSE,–1)))/(Ref(OPEN,–1)))*100)$

Filter   colA>**7** AND colB>**5** AND VOLUME>**10000**

Note: Change the figures in bold italics to suit your requirements. They currently filter for stocks with a gap for more than 7% and a range in the previous day of more than 5% and with volume greater than 10,000.

≡MARKSMAN'S NOTES

➔   Overnight gap trades use the continuation of crowd enthusiasm.

➔   Scan for gaps after the first 30 minutes of trading.

➔   Select gaps over 3%.

➔   Confirm candidates using high volume, price relationships and trend patterns.

➔   Trade when buyers outnumber sellers and where there is a reasonable spread.

➔   Final selection is made after the first hour of trading.

➔   Look for proof of continued upwards buying pressure.

➔   Use the match price of day two of the trade to confirm bullish continuation.

➔   Compare total buying and selling pressure.

➔   Manage exit using a sliding stop loss to lock in profits.

➔   Objective is to enter at the midpoint of day one and exit at the midpoint of day two.

Chapter 21

GAP

DEFENCE

S ome price shocks are nasty, driving prices down in freefall and slipping past stop loss points. If we own the stock this is a heart stopping chart display. As traders we often focus on bullish gaps where the opening price is higher than the previous day's high. These provide a number of trading opportunities. We are less inclined to effectively deal with the gap down in price. This is where today's opening price is lower – sometimes significantly lower – than the low of the previous day. It is more than just a sinking feeling. These gaps have the capacity to rip past our stop loss points.

In this chapter we consider a defensive reaction to downward gap behaviour. These gaps are a threat to short-term trading strategies so we must know how to manage an exit with grace, dignity and skill. These tactics might not deliver short-term trading profits, but they limit the damage caused to trading capital.

For traders working with end-of-day data these bearish gaps are a fact of life. There is little they can do until the next day's trade. We recognise these occasional disasters are part of the trading process. They are difficult to forecast in advance and they are often related to surprise announcements such as earnings downgrades. Rather than attempt to predict these gaps, we focus on ways to manage our reactions to them. The end-of-day trader should simply take an exit on the next day at the most favourable prices available. The trader with access to real-time screens has a wider range of management responses.

Panic is not one of them. Amateur and inexperienced traders tend to panic. They see the gap and they sell into it with total desperation in an attempt to get out before price falls even further. "Just get me out," they tell their broker, or they send sell orders to market set several cents below the last trade just to make sure they get an exit. The public, including the institutions, tends to overreact to bad news.

As traders we want to avoid participating in this panic and develop methods to either ignore the gap and stay with a trade as it recovers, or to manage a better exit from the gap. In developing these strategies we use the behaviour of the market on the open. It takes around 30 minutes for the market to establish its direction for the day. Trades taken in the first 30 minutes of market open, or in the first 15 to 20 minutes of trading in a single stock, carry a higher level of risk as the direction of the day is not yet established.

Here is a typical frightened gap open on the All Ordinaries – XAO – shown as a three-minute tick chart in Figure 21.1. For the first nine minutes the market accelerated upwards on the back of a higher close on the DOW overnight. In the next 21 minutes the market pulled back and began to establish its direction for the remainder of the day. This overreaction on the open is typical and traders find ways to deal with gap down days in these patterns.

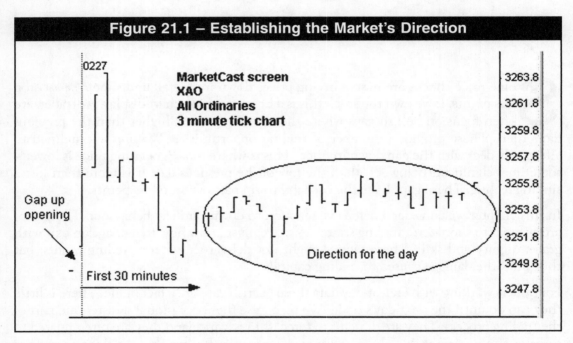

Figure 21.1 – Establishing the Market's Direction

MarketCast screen
XAO
All Ordinaries
3 minute tick chart

Gap up opening

First 30 minutes

Direction for the day

3263.8
3261.8
3259.8
3257.8
3255.8
3253.8
3251.8
3249.8
3247.8

0227

PROFESSIONAL HELP

There is something very satisfying about sitting down with a problem and nutting out a solution. It is also very time wasting because trading success is built upon the success of those who have gone before us. We do not need to repeat their every mistake for ourselves. We cannot afford to do this. Nor can we always take another trader's idea and apply it without modification to our own trading. Our market may be different. Certainly our appetite for risk, our trading ability, or discipline and experience, is different from the traders who successfully develop the initial idea.

This should not stop us from seeking professional help. I read books, talk to other traders and work with their ideas to improve my own trading. Earlier we applied some ideas developed by US trader Robert Deel. Later we examine some applications of techniques used by another US trader Tony Oz. When it comes to understanding how to survive and use down day gaps I turn to Oliver Velez, the founder of Pristine.com and the co-author of *Tools For The Master Day Trader*. His work sets the foundations for an adapted strategy we use to exit open positions in the face of difficulty and to take advantage of gap down days.

Velez sets out six rules for reacting to these gap down days. They are:

1.   Watch and wait.

2.   Mark the five-minute low.

3.   Sell half the position if prices go below the five-minute low.

4.   Mark the 30-minute low.

5.   Exit the remainder of the position if the price drops below the lower of the five- and 30-minute lows. We use the actual 30-minute low.

6.   Use a trailing stop loss for the rest of the day.

The first rule makes sense in any market because it prevents us from joining the market panic. The objective is to do nothing for the first five minutes of trading. It is a hard rule to stick with because the market may plunge dramatically, increasing your loss with every second. We should never sell shares when we are terrified, or when a market is panicked. It is not an appropriate state of mind for making good decisions.

Hindsight sometimes tells us we should have sold out in the first five minutes. If is difficult to know this for certain in advance. Waiting five minutes is not a guarantee of success, but it helps you to understand what is happening in the market so you make a more informed decision.

Rule two is to mark the five-minute low as shown in Figure 21.2. This is the lowest low for the five minute period. This is the most important price level for the next 25 minutes or so because it sets the short-term support level.

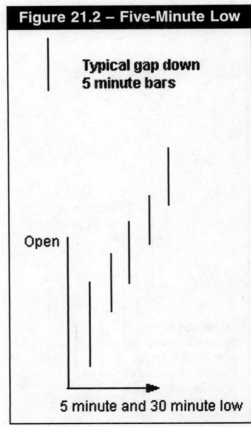

Figure 21.2 – Five-Minute Low

Typical gap down
5 minute bars

Open

5 minute and 30 minute low

Rule three tells the trader to sell half his position if price drops below the first five-minute low during the first 30 minutes of trading. We sell half the position under these conditions as protection against a continuation of the gap down as shown in Figure 21.3. We accept it may take 30 minutes for the market to set its direction for the day. However, between the first five minutes and the first 30 minutes the market may carry us a long way down. By taking a small loss on a close below the five-minute low we ease the burden of the potential loss and exercise some damage control. This sale is a protective action.

Rule four uses the observed behaviour of the market to capture the potential rebound on a real-time basis. We know the market typically sets the direction for the day after the first 30 minutes or so of trading. This makes the price extremes set during this period a particularly useful reference area. After 30 minutes of trading we mark the lowest point in the period.

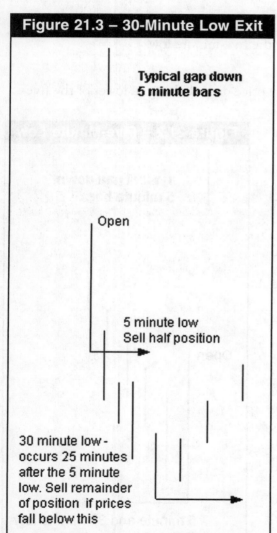

Figure 21.3 – 30-Minute Low Exit

Typical gap down
5 minute bars

Open

5 minute low
Sell half position

30 minute low -
occurs 25 minutes
after the 5 minute
low. Sell remainder
of position if prices
fall below this

This may be the five-minute, or 30-minute low. This is our primary stop loss condition and alert.

Rule five tells the trader to exit the entire position if there is a close below the 30-minute low point. This is the primary stop loss level based on the tendency of the market to react to extremes in the first 30 minutes of trading. If the stock does not trade below the 30-minute low and then moves to a new daily high we know the panic selling was an overreaction. Instead of exiting the trade at a panic disadvantage, we stay with the trade as it develops a new and stronger trend. The trend is stronger because the weak hands – the nervous stockholders – are shaken out in the first minutes of panic selling.

Here we note one important modification of the Velez approach. In plotting the five-minute and 30-minute low he uses the lowest of the two as the 30-minute low. We have found it is better to use the actual low of the 30-minute bar as the trigger level. In the example shown in Figure 21.4 this is higher than the five-minute low. We suspect this is because the Australian market is not as widely liquid as the US market and because we do not have market makers influencing the opening price.

Rule six defines a number of trailing stop strategies for use as the price rallies from the 30-minute lows. The suggestion is to use three timeframes, each a multiple of the first. We start with a five-minute bar, shift to a 15-minute bar and end with a 30-minute bar. After each period ends the trailing stop loss for the period is recalculated. A move below the closest stop loss is an exit signal. This is a

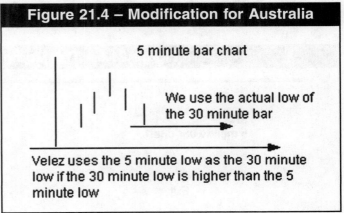

Figure 21.4 – Modification for Australia

5 minute bar chart

We use the actual low of the 30 minute bar

Velez uses the 5 minute low as the 30 minute low if the 30 minute low is higher than the 5 minute low

complex set of stop loss conditions and in some circumstances, as a stock trends sideways, the five-minute stop loss may equal the 15-minute stop loss as shown in Figure 21.5.

An alternative is to use a stop loss based on changes in the 30-minute low for the day. This approach may improve the outcome but it takes away the opportunity to reduce the loss.

These are bear gap rules developed by Oliver Velez and they are designed for the US market where much of the initial opening action is set by market makers. This is not the case in Australia so we have made modifications to the strategies for Australian markets where trading is a direct contest between buyers and sellers without the intervention of market makers.

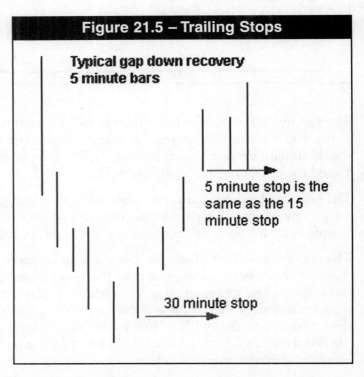

Figure 21.5 – Trailing Stops

Typical gap down recovery 5 minute bars

5 minute stop is the same as the 15 minute stop

30 minute stop

AVOIDING THE BLOODBATH

Some down gaps are a bloodbath and the Velez trading rules staunch some of the outflow of trading capital. This protective strategy is designed to improve the exit from losing trades. In Figure 21.6, SNX starts the day with an 8% gap down compared to the previous day's close.

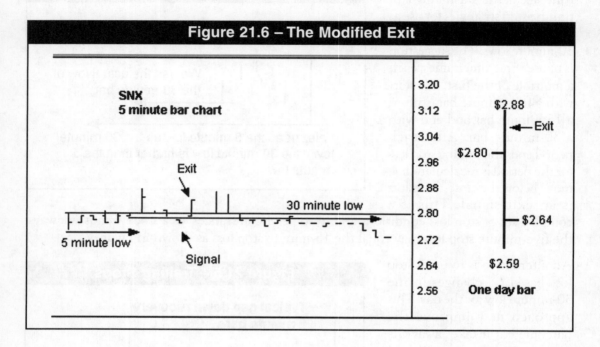

The first five-minute low is lower than the 30-minute low. Velez uses the five-minute low as the stop loss point. Adapting this rule for Australian markets means we use the low of the 30-minute bar as the stop loss point. This take us out of the trade at a higher level should the SNX price fall again during the day.

The exit signal is delivered as price dips below the 30-minute low line. We use the close of the first five-minute bar to make our decision, so our exit takes place during the next five minute bar. This takes us out of the trade at around $2.85.

The one-day bar chart illustrates how this exit captures a better price than available on the open. It is also a better price than those available later in the day when SNX closes much lower. This exit method will not get the trader out at the top price for the day, but it avoids an exit at the very low of the day. Waiting for the first five-minute low prevents the trader from accidentally adding to the initial overreaction and selling pressure. On a gap down day we do not have to take the worst price on offer. With disciplined planning we often obtain an improved exit.

The All Ordinaries chart in Figure 21.7 is another example of the protective advantages of this approach. The five-minute low is quickly exceeded and is a signal to sell half the open position. This is a nightmare gap so our first exit is somewhere in the third five-minute bar.

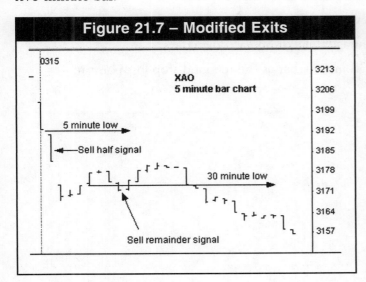

Figure 21.7 – Modified Exits

The actual low of the 30-minute bar is marked. This is higher than the lowest low for the 30 minute period. Index values fall below this 15 minutes later and we exit before the bloodbath has the opportunity to gain even more momentum. This modified Velez-style exit consistently protects capital more effectively than using the lowest low in the first 30 minutes of trading and avoids false exit signals.

In retrospect we know it was better to exit the entire XAO trade on the open. However, we cannot know this in advance. By taking a part-exit after the five-minute low is violated, we reduce our losses and still give ourselves the opportunity to participate in any recovery. If the down pressure continues, we sell the remainder of our stock. If the market continues to fall, the impact of the last sale of half the position is reduced because the size of the position is smaller.

LEARNING FROM EXPERIENCE

Our objective in this book is to include a selection of tactics we have applied to short-term trading. It is not an exhaustive list so we encourage readers to further explore the tactics discussed by Velez at Pristine.com and in his books. We aim for defence in this strategy. Velez plays a more aggressive game and many of his short-term strategies are applicable to our markets.

Back testing this defensive approach, with Australian modifications, shows we get a better exit using the actual low of the 30-minute bar. These trading rules don't turn a loss into a profit, but they help traders avoid hasty exit decisions based on panic. By understanding the behaviour of the crowd on these days, we give ourselves an advantage.

Sometimes markets bounce back from these downward gaps. Trading these rebounds provides another fruitful area for traders.

TARGET SHOOTING NOTES

➔ Manage gap down days to limit damage to capital.

➔ The Velez exit strategy prevents panic.

➔ Apply six Velez rules to manage the exit on gap down days.

➔ Use the actual low of the 30-minute bar as the rebound stop loss point in Australian markets.

Chapter 22

SNAPSHOT
TRADING

Traders are human. This gives an emotional behaviour to markets which is at odds with the classical economic model based on supposedly cool, rational economic decision making. Some academics are now exploring 'behavioural finance'. Traders have been exploring and exploiting this for decades. They understand a chart of price action shows a pulse line of emotion and emotional reactions to price behaviour.

Few readers will deny the racing heart, the increase in pulse rate and the clouding of rational judgement that comes when they discover one of their stocks has just gained 100%, or lost 70%. These are emotional figures. Better traders put these emotional reactions to one side and make a more rational judgement about appropriate action, but they cannot eliminate these emotions. The emotions we experience are largely duplicated by every other trader who purchases shares in the same company at around the same price. They have also just gained 100% or lost 70%.

By and large, these people have much the same emotional reactions as the untrained or inexperienced trader. By and large, these people do much the same as each other, selling if they have made 100%, and holding on tight if they have lost 70%. This is not a conspiracy. There is no communication between these geographically dispersed shareholders who are unlikely to physically meet or know each other.

They are part of a virtual crowd, connected by a bond of common human behaviour, and their decision to initially buy a single company at a common price level. Operating as individuals they may be able to put their emotions to one side but, as part of an unseen crowd, their emotions come to dominate their decisions as they see others buying or selling. These individuals act as a crowd, buying and selling in unison based on a common reaction to the same fears and enticements.

The smarter trader looks for these repeated emotional reactions. He finds them in a handful of clear and repeated price patterns on a bar or candlestick chart. The most obvious is a crowd driven by confidence in the future. It shows up as a rising trend and is easily defined by a classic straight-edge trend line. We know the crowd is turning ugly when prices drop below the trend line and smart traders and investors sell their stock to capture a profit before the trend changes.

As smart short-term traders we look for a different range of chart patterns and crowd behaviour. We use them to set defined price targets likely to be achieved within a three- to seven-day timeframe. The exact nature of the price projections, and their reliability, allows us to clearly establish the risk and reward ratio. We get to combine high probability trades with favourable risk/reward ratios in a simple solution for short-term success.

These are snapshot trades. They are not tourist photographs. Tourists take snapshot pictures. We take money from snapshot trades designed with lethal accuracy. The opportunity is defined with precision and the targets clearly exposed. Some of the most difficult conditions in competitive rifle shooting come on days with scudding clouds. The light changes and the black bullseye 500 meters downrange seems to change size. It is difficult to get a good sight picture. Expert marksmen do not chase the changing light. They wait for the break in the clouds when the sunburst highlights the target. Then they take a carefully prepared snapshot before the brief, favourable light conditions change. Pattern-based trades are the market equivalents.

Step out of training mode for a moment and cast your memory back to the early days when the market beckoned with untold riches and the reality of loss was concealed by your inexperience. One of the more exciting features of price action were those stocks that ran up dramatically over several days. Prices leapfrogged upwards, running from $0.05 to $0.15 or higher. It seemed impossible to catch these fast movers. If we succeeded, we usually got shares near the very top of the price move. The next day prices declined, and despite some minor intra-day up moves, prices continued to decline. We held onto losers.

A slightly more experienced crowd watches the same stock and the same action. When prices drop to a level they believe is reasonable in comparison to recent highs, they come back into the market as buyers. They believe they are picking up a bargain. These bargain hunters are the salvation of many a losing trade if the trader reins in his expectations.

Smarter traders do not bother chasing price as it races up the flagpole. They understand how the balance of probabilities is likely to change in the subsequent price action. Under certain conditions, examined below, when the bargain hunters come back into the market these traders join the buying.

We make our money by understanding how the crowd thinks and then outsmarting them. The bargain hunters buy stock because they believe price will go much higher than the most recent high. They believe the price retreat sets the conditions for a rebound. Quite simply, they buy a bargain in anticipation of making a lot of money. And sometimes they succeed.

The crowd who get their shares near the top of the price rise, and who ride the price all the way down to the current lows have a different view. They lose confidence and money. They want their money back. If prices rebound, this crowd turns into vicious sellers as prices reach up to the most recent high point. Their selling is sometimes enough to stop any further price rise completely. Sometimes it provides a blip of consolidation or resistance before price moves ahead buoyed by increased buying. It is difficult to tell the outcome in advance.

This is a consistent crowd reaction and in it lies the opportunity for a series of smart short-term trading tactics which deliver defined returns of 20% to 50% from three high-probability rebound chart patterns.

Bless the crowd for they hold your profits. We consider flag, finger and triangle patterns and each uses a different type of projection target. We include several examples to show how these short-term trades are recognised and traded.

FLAGS

One of the reasons I watch for chart patterns is because they provide such reliable and high-probability snapshot opportunities. Some of these trading opportunities exactly reach the projected targets. Others occasionally fall short by a tick. However, once the pattern develops and the breakout is confirmed, it is unusual for the projected target not to be reached, or exceeded. These trades are most profitable when there is a consistent pattern of behaviour in speculative and mid-cap stocks.

Many traders scan charts and find fast-moving stocks where the trend has accelerated upwards in a sharp, near-vertical climb. Most times when we see these it is too late. The trading opportunity, or the bulk of it, has disappeared. The near vertical climb creates the flagpole of trading opportunity. These opportunities are found in rising trends. They do not appear in the context of falling trends.

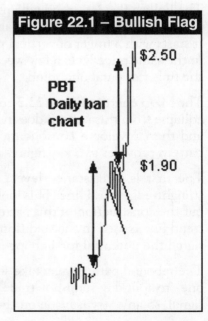

Figure 22.1 – Bullish Flag

PBT
Daily bar
chart

$2.50

$1.90

The flagpole is the starting point for these rebound trades and the PBT chart in Figure 22.1 shows the classic bullish flag discussed in more detail in Chapter 13. It starts with a six-day, consistent, vertical rise in prices. This flagpole is the alert signal. Rather than chase prices, traders build strategies around what happens after the vertical move is completed. With PBT the retracement, or price collapse develops into a four-day flag pattern.

It takes 10 days of patience for this snapshot opportunity to develop. The breakout is signalled by the close above

201

the upper, straight-edge trend line. An entry at the open the next day starts this trade at $1.90. The pattern projection target is at $2.50 and the trade returns 31% over five days.

The flagpole and flag pattern analysis always sets a projection target higher than the initial high of the flagpole. Price leverage is always an advantage but the consistently higher price targets make this an attractive snapshot trade in most stocks. A finger trade is more limited, setting a target equal to the high of the flagpole or finger.

PARABOLIC TRENDS AND FINGERS

The vertical flagpole is one type of starting point. Another is the parabolic trend. This is also a very fast, rising price action but it is not a sudden break upwards as with the flagpole start to the PBT trade. Instead prices start off in a slow trend. This trend accelerates over time. If we try to use a straight-edge trend line to define the trend we soon find the line is inaccurate. We have to use a new, and steeper trend line. This is the key, defining feature. The parabolic trend cannot be defined by a single straight-edge trend line.

The rising trend accelerates and this action is best captured by the construction of a parabolic curve. Mathematically this plots an exponential increase in values. For trading purposes it means the trend starts slowly and then accelerates into a near-vertical trend. The ability to plot a parabolic trend curve is included in the GuppyTraders Essentials charting pack. The end of the parabolic trend is sudden. Prices collapse quickly. How price behaves after the fall determines the rebound trading opportunity.

The bullish flag is a trend collapse and it is defined by two straight-edge trend lines. The finger trade contains more variables. The classic finger trade is a fast developing pattern. It starts with a finger of vertical price action and often ends with another finger reaching to the same price level a few weeks later. Traders watch for the price dip from the high of the finger or parabolic trend.

The MZG chart in Figure 22.2 combines a parabolic trend and a sharply rising finger. The collapse from this pattern does not set up a bullish flag. Instead prices open sharply lower, and then develop a consolidation pattern over the next few weeks. The consolidation pattern provides two key figures for the trader.

The first is a resistance level. With MZG this is defined by the downward sloping straight-edge trend line. This looks as if it could be used to define a down sloping triangle, but the construction of this pattern is incorrect. It has no well-defined support area. The trend line is used in the traditional way so traders look for a close above the trend line to signal the potential for a change in the direction of this short-term trend.

The rebound pattern may take some time to develop, but the rebound breakout is a fast, one- to four-day snapshot trade. A close above the initial trend line is an end-of-day signal, so an entry is made on the next day. For this example we take an entry at $0.052

which is possible at any time over the next five days. The window of opportunity is unusually wide in this trade.

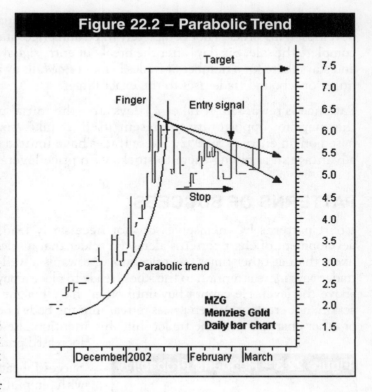

Figure 22.2 – Parabolic Trend

Some readers might argue the more accurate trend line is the upper line. On a retrospective chart they are correct. However, at the time of the initial break, the lower trend line is accurately placed, and it is the line traders use to make their decision. Rewriting history does not add to trading profits because traders must work with the information available at the time they make their decision.

Once the consolidation break is confirmed the next important figure is the stop loss. This must meet financial conditions – putting at risk less than 2% of our total trading capital – and chart-based conditions. On the day of the entry signal the lowest price in this pattern is $0.046. The stop loss is placed one tick below this at $0.045. A dip below this on an intra-day basis is an exit signal confirming the rebound has failed. This is set as an intra-day stop loss and is best executed electronically and automatically as discussed in Chapter 27.

This stop loss level is not the bottom of a downward sloping triangle because no valid triangle pattern exists on this chart. It is based on the absolute low attained during the consolidation period. The important features are the absolute low in the consolidation period, and the upwards price move breaking above a straight-edge trend line, or short-term resistance level.

In some price collapses from finger rises or parabolic trends it is not possible to define a consolidation period. The pattern of price behaviour is too messy and confused. These do not provide good finger trading opportunities.

The finger or rebound trade has a specific target based on the absolute high achieved by the previous trend rise. With MZG this is set at $0.074. As soon as the trade is opened, both a stop loss and a profit sell order are placed. As always, traders have a choice in using these targets. Some set sell orders exactly on the target level. Others place a sell order just below the target. Others prefer to watch price action, hoping the target will be exceeded.

My preference is to set the sell order exactly on the target and watch how price action develops. If my order is not completely filled and prices start to fall, I chase prices down to complete the sale. Six days after the breakout entry signal the MZG price opens at $0.074 and stays there for a number of trades before price falls away. Our sell order is filled as this finger or rebound trade rises to the exact target.

Patience is rewarded. It takes 23 days after the initial peak of the parabolic trend for the snapshot opportunity to present itself. It takes six days to deliver a 42% profit based on an entry at $0.052. These trades have limited targets so there is a significant advantage in applying them to stocks with price leverage.

PATTERNS OF SUCCESS

Chart patterns by themselves do not necessarily lead to consistent outcomes. The development of chart patterns alerts the trader that a selected range of outcomes is more likely than at other times. As price moves towards a well-established resistance level the trader pays more attention to the stock, ready to place a buy order if prices move a few ticks above the level. He cannot buy until others have bought because he wants to follow the action, not create it. When prices retreat into the body of the support and resistance band, or other chart pattern, the trader shifts his attention elsewhere. Chart patterns signal the increased probability of certain outcomes.

Figure 22.3 – Rebound Probability

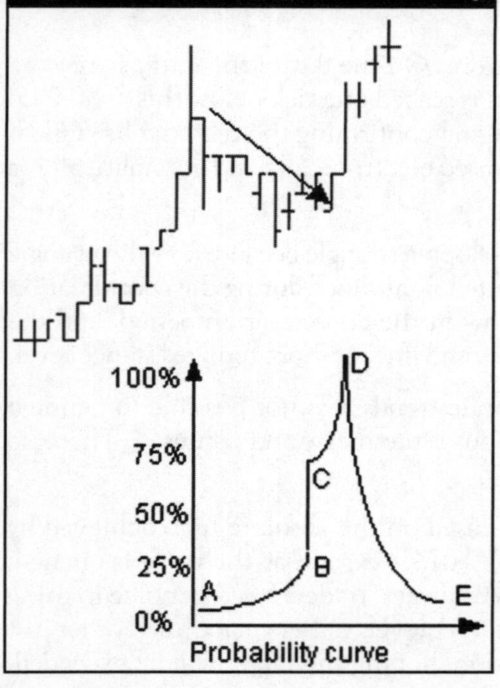

Successful pattern trading involves a flirtation with temptation. Traders who are just starting with this type of trading approach are most at risk. In the two examples shown below the breakouts quickly reach their pattern projection targets. The temptation is to treat this as a triumph of analysis and trading skill rather than just a probability outcome. The real temptation is to stay with the trade to maximise the results. Emboldened by success, traders look for indications the price rise will continue. Rather than take an 18% to 36% return, these traders want a little more. This desire fails to understand the way probability unfolds with the pattern development.

The rebound opportunity starts with a sharp price rise followed by a price decline. This is the starting point for a potential rebound trade. On a probability scale this starting point has a value of around 5%, shown at point A on the chart display in Figure 22.3. As prices

204

continue to drift downwards or sideways from the rally high, the probability of this developing into a rebound trade increases steadily. By the time we get to point B, the day before the rebound breakout from the downtrend, there is a 25% probability of this developing into a successful rebound trade.

Please note these probabilities are meant to be indicative estimates and are based on market observations. The probability does not increase with time. It increases steadily from low probability to high probability until the point of the rebound breakout.

When the breakout takes place, as shown by point C, the probability of success increases dramatically. The breakout takes this opportunity from a 25% probability to a 75% probability of success. As prices continue to rise the probability increases dramatically again, until the pattern projection targets are reached. At this point the probability of success is equal to 100%.

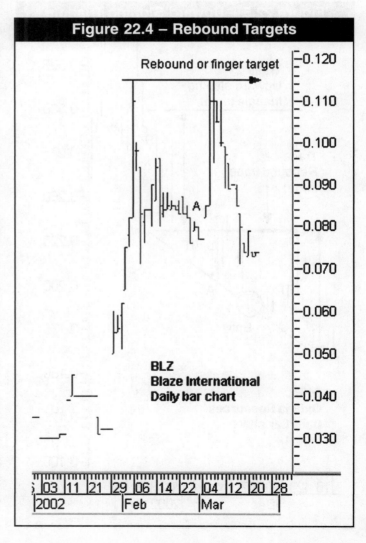

Figure 22.4 – Rebound Targets

Rebound or finger target

A

BLZ
Blaze International
Daily bar chart

2002   Feb   Mar

Holding onto the trade is not going to increase the probability of success as the objectives have already been reached. Just because the trade has reached these targets does not mean prices will automatically continue to rise. Instead the probability of continued price rises declines very rapidly, in this example to around 5%. Once the pattern targets have been achieved we cannot estimate what follows with any degree of confidence.

The BLZ rebound trade in Figure 22.4 takes four days to reach the projected target. Traders have two days at the target level to manage their exit. An entry at around $0.082 and an exit at $0.115 delivers a 40.24% return. What happens next?

The rebound pattern, by itself, provides no clues. In this example prices move into a steady decline, dropping even lower than our original entry point.

AFTER THE REBOUND

Rebound trades are sometimes part of a larger pattern development. The OXR chart in Figure 22.5 shows two trades. Trade 1 is the same type of rebound opportunity as BLZ, but a different pattern emerges once the initial rebound pattern is completed. This is a more complex pattern development, and sets up a new short-term trading opportunity shown as

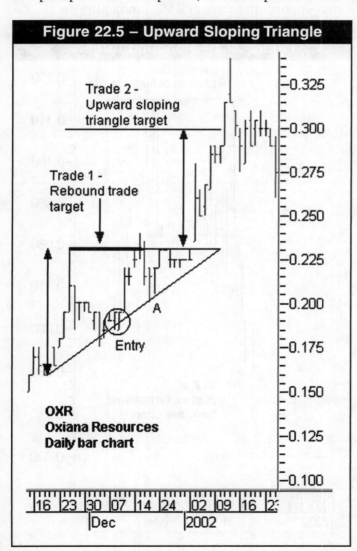

Figure 22.5 – Upward Sloping Triangle

Trade 2 - Upward sloping triangle target

Trade 1 - Rebound trade target

Entry

A

OXR
Oxiana Resources
Daily bar chart

Trade 2. Although it is unwise to rely on the initial rebound pattern continuing upwards, there are often additional snapshot opportunities in the days or weeks following a rebound trade. These stocks remain on my watch list.

The rebound trade target for trade one is shown as the thick line and is reached four days after the entry. Traders who placed a sell order at the target price were successful as prices stayed at, or above, this level for three days. An entry at $0.195 has a capped exit at $0.23 and delivers an 18% return.

The OXR collapse from the finger trade target becomes part of a larger triangle chart pattern offering another short-term trading opportunity. The price retreat from $0.23 confirms the placement of the uptrend line. This is combined with a new resistance level based on the rebound target to create an upward sloping triangle and sets up Trade 2.

The triangle uses two types of straight-edge lines. The first is a sloping trend line defining the way the crowd changes its idea of value over time. The second is the horizontal support or resistance line. These show unchanging values over time, where the crowd seems to place a set value on the stock, refusing to pay more for it. When these two emotional forces meet in an upward sloping triangle the pattern breakout provides a high-probability short-term trade.

The trend line starts at $0.16 and gives a triangle base $0.07 high. When projected upwards from the resistance level, as shown by the double-headed arrow, the triangle breakout target is $0.30. This is achieved on the day of the breakout and provides a 30% return for traders who bought at $0.23.

Even though OXR goes on to develop price behaviour and patterns leading to higher highs in Trade 2, this development is not dependent upon the initial rebound pattern in Trade 1. The balance of probabilities once the rebound pattern has fully developed remains the same. A new pattern or trend may develop, but immediately after the rebound pattern is completed, the probabilities shoot back down to 5% or less.

Pattern-based trading is snapshot target trading. The risk in any trade is easily assessed against a known level of reward. These patterns have a high probability of success. What happens after the pattern is completed is a more difficult question to answer. If we stay with the trade beyond the completion of its pattern, we turn a high-probability trade into guesswork. After the pattern has been completed the most effective course of action is to execute the trade as planned and then keep an eye on how prices subsequently develop.

OXR offers a much larger glittering prize than the 18% return captured in a single day. Initially the return looks fantastic, but as prices continue to rise in a new trend the short-term return starts to look tatty. We yearn for the missed profits and lament the foregone opportunity. This captures one of the most significant dilemmas of short-term trading.

The objective of snapshot trading means waiting to capture short-term opportunities with a high level of probability. Inevitably we miss out on much larger price moves because our attention is focused on short-term patterns. You must decide if this compromise is worthwhile. Capping greed and learning to ignore what happens in longer-term trends is an important behavioural skill required for successful short-term trading. In the next chapter we investigate the application of a short-term technique developed by US trader, Tony Oz. It delivers high probability trades while ignoring long-term trend developments. The profits are very small but they add up in a most satisfactory way.

≡ SNAPSHOT NOTES

➔   Wait for the right conditions to develop and then act.

➔   Do not chase price. Wait for rebound opportunities to develop.

➔   The three reliable rebound patterns are flags, fingers and triangles.

➔   Patterns set reliable price targets.

➔   Trade with patience and wait for the pattern set up conditions to develop.

➔   When targets are limited to recent highs, select trades with price leverage.

➔   These are short-term patterns so do not rely on a continuation of the uptrend.

➔   Short-term patterns may be part of a larger pattern so keep completed trades on a watch list.

Chapter 23

SMALL
CHANGE

Every day I go to the nearby shopping centre to buy the newspapers, shop for fresh coriander and chillies, and to collect the mail. When I return I have a pocket full of small change and it goes into a large decorative bowl to provide lunch money for my son. By the end of the year it provides enough for a very expensive meal. Little bit by little bit, the small change builds into a significant sum. Intra-day trading rests on the same principle.

The unifying factor in all intra-day approaches is the small dollar and percentage level of returns. These strategies are designed to scalp the market. Typically they shoot for returns of $300 to $2,000 a day, although some opportunities may offer a lot more. These returns cannot always be scaled upwards, as liquidity is a major consideration. The final filter in choosing any of these trading techniques is liquidity. Unless volume is consistent and deep enough, these strategies carry a much higher level of execution risk. It is difficult to buy the stock, and even more difficult to get out of the position.

Why bother with these particular approaches when dollar returns appear small? We are interested because small change adds up to a significant return on capital.

In Chapter 21 we called in help from other professional traders. We do the same in this chapter, turning to US trader Tony Oz. The techniques discussed below are based on one of the approaches used by Tony Oz in his book, *The Stock Trader* where he documents every personal trade over a four-week period. The notes include planning, management, and post-mortem analysis. His trading is all from the long side and restricted to Nasdaq stocks. A major component of his strategy is to buy new daily highs.

His return on $50,000 over a four week period is 32%. What makes this more astounding is the period covered includes the April 2000 tech crash. This is a robust trading approach with potential in other market conditions. We selected one aspect of his approach and built on it, making modifications where necessary to adjust for Australian markets.

Trade selection is based on a scan of end-of-day data. Do this during the evening, or in the hour before the market opens. The search identifies four to 25 trading candidates. These are further filtered against several criteria, including the reasonably expected return. Around six stocks make the final list. About half of these go on to become successful trades, meeting the trigger conditions during the day.

This looks a poor hit rate, but to stop here fails to understand the success of the Oz approach. Only stocks passing the trigger conditions are traded. The trader does not act in anticipation of a trigger. He acts only when the trigger is tripped and this increases the probability of success to around 90%.

There are four steps in getting from search to go in this strategy. They are:

1.   Scan the end-of-day database for stocks with price activity with the required potential.

2.   Examine the end-of-day chart to select those candidates with a higher probability of success.

3.   Set the trigger conditions, stop loss points and target exit price.

4.   Use a spreadsheet to calculate position size and returns. This is a reality check.

These steps are completed before the market opens. They take less than an hour and when completed the trader has a precise set of numbers used to track each of the potential trading candidates. We show how this is implemented and managed in real time in the next chapter. Here we take you through the four set-up steps.

THE SORTING HAT

New students at Hogwart's School of Witchcraft and Wizardry featured in the Harry Potter novels by J. K. Rowling are sorted into one of four school houses by a magic sorting hat. Modern software gives us the tools to apply the same magic to searches of very large databases in a few minutes. When the sorting hat comes to Harry Potter it cannot decide between Slytherin and Gryffindor. Harry is allocated to Gryffindor and his adventurous tests in each novel prove the choice was a good one. Our database search is our sorting hat, but each of the candidates returned must pass additional tests before they are confirmed as full members of our profitable trading circle.

Our objective is to locate stocks showing bullish strength and the potential to continue to break out to new highs on the next day of trading. We broaden the original Oz search parameters a little to suit Australian conditions. The exploration or search scans used to identify potential candidates are:

1.   Find all stocks. Exclude warrants. This trading method is only applied to ordinary shares.

2.   Find all stocks trading more than 500,000 shares today. This is down from the original 1,000,000 requirement used by Tony Oz which is too restrictive in Australian market conditions.

3.   Find all stocks with a volume spike of 10% or more compared to yesterday's volume.

4.   Find all stocks with three consecutive higher highs for the past three days.

We also include an additional scan to develop a second list of candidates. This scan includes the first three of the above steps, but replaces the final filter with this condition:

➔   Find all stocks with consecutively higher closes over the past three days.

These scans return between four to 25 candidates each day. The exploration formula for MetaStock is at the end of this chapter. This scan identifies trading candidates which have a good probability of delivering short-term intra-day profits. Some are duplicated, appearing on both lists. When these are screened out we are left with around 15 stocks. Stocks appearing on both lists – higher closes and higher highs – have a marginally increased probability of performing well. The scan also identifies stocks offering three- to five-day trading opportunities, but we ignore these in favour of the intra-day trades.

CHART SCREENING

Once the candidates are selected we turn to a bar chart to determine the general direction of price activity. We save a lot of time by moving straight to this chart analysis because it weeds out those candidates that meet the mathematical conditions but which are locked in price patterns which are unlikely to yield good trading opportunities.

The objective of chart screening is to improve our success rate. There are four broad patterns of daily chart activity. The first is the beginnings of a hook pattern shown in Figure 23.1. It comes when a stock has completed a long-term trend, suffered a significant pullback in prices, and is now developing a rally from the pullback. This looks like a small hook and is not related to the Ross Hook trading approach.

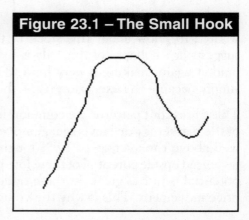

Figure 23.1 – The Small Hook

In a bullish market these rally recoveries offer good trading opportunities. In a bear market we weed out stocks with this pattern. They provide intra-day trading opportunities, but they also carry a high level of risk in a bear market because any change in sentiment quickly drives prices below our stop loss points.

Stocks in the second pattern, shown in Figure 23.2, are trapped in a sideways movement and are also filtered out. There may be good opportunities in stocks moving steadily between support and resistance levels but there are better opportunities available which have a higher probability of success. We screen out these sideways trending stocks unless there is strong evidence of a rebound from the support level along with steady and consistent volume.

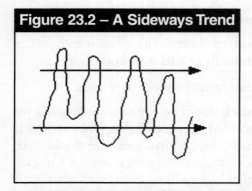

Figure 23.2 – A Sideways Trend

The third pattern comes from breakout stocks, shown in Figure 23.3. They always attract the trader's attention. The initial selection is based on the chart pattern and verified by the volume pattern. For a rally to succeed we look for increasing volume. If volume is falling away or not particularly high – even though it meets our 500,000 screening criterion – the stock is dropped from the opportunity list.

The AZR chart in Figure 23.4 shows the preferred volume relationship. The volume rise is sharp and distinct. This rally is well supported by lots of trading. The 500,000 volume filter is not just a one-day event. Additionally, the volume starts from an already high level so even if the rally collapses, we expect to find other traders to trade with.

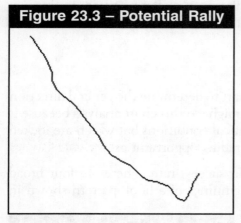

Figure 23.3 – Potential Rally

Compare AZR with DWY and we see why DWY is dropped from the list of opportunities. The volume increase is small. There is some market enthusiasm here, but this crowd is not particularly large. It is more difficult to trade in this shallow pool, even though the price rise may provide a larger percentage return. Additionally, the volume rise with DWY starts from a very low base. Nobody wanted to know about this stock in the past. Low volume has been the rule and this suggests any collapse of the rally is likely to see low volume very quickly dominate the market again, making it very hard to get out of the trade. We exclude stocks like this simply because the execution risk – the ability to execute trades – is seriously increased.

These breakout patterns are common in low-priced stocks. One of the appeals of this end of the market is price leverage. A move from $0.115 to $0.13 offers a 13% return which is well above the average of 1.8% for this style of trading. It is tempting to focus on the leveraged upside potential of these low-priced stocks, but remember the leveraged downside potential is just as great. In these trades we can lose 13% just as rapidly on an intra-day price movement. This is why the volume of trading is particularly important in applying short-term strategies to these lower-priced stocks. These breakout patterns also appear in some of the more highly priced stocks. Here the trader is not assisted by price leverage so returns are closer to the average 1.8%.

The final pattern we observe is created by stocks moving steadily upwards in well-established trends as shown in Figure 23.5. These fall into two categories. The first have long-term trends. Although our intention is to trade these on an intra-day basis, the general bullishness of this trend offers additional protection. Sudden reversals are unlikely. If we get the entry, or exit wrong, the damage to our trading position is likely to be minor. Unlike the breakout situation, the trader does not face the prospect of a sudden, heart-stopping collapse in prices.

Stocks in the second category are those which have developed new strong trends. These have moved beyond an initial breakout pattern and established a firm trend over eight to ten weeks. Applying intra-day trading approaches to this type of chart pattern shifts the balance to bullish outcomes. These established, and well-established, trends provide the lower-risk environments for the application of the Tony Oz trading techniques. By selecting just those stocks in these trends, or breakout conditions we reduce the initial list of candidates to a smaller, more manageable number.

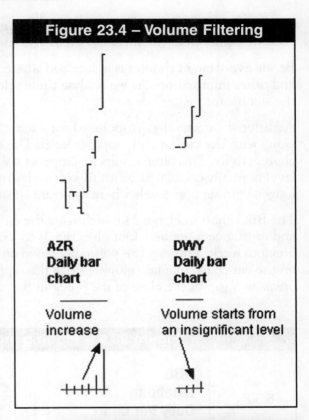

Figure 23.4 – Volume Filtering

AZR
Daily bar
chart

DWY
Daily bar
chart

Volume
increase

Volume starts from
an insignificant level

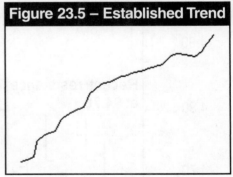

Figure 23.5 – Established Trend

SETTING THE TRIGGER

The old stand-by infantry weapon, the SMLE .303 rifle has a two stage trigger. The marksman takes up the first trigger pressure as soon as he sets his sights on his target. Then, breathing controlled, he applies just a touch more pressure to push through the second trigger barrier. This delivers accurate snapshots. The Oz approach uses two pressure points. We set the first pressure point using an end-of-day chart. The second, and lighter, pressure comes from the intra-day chart and snaps the trade into action.

Beside every target shooter is a note pad where he plots the fall of shot, wind conditions and other information. As we analyse these selected charts we use a spreadsheet to note the significant figures.

Additional information is included for each candidate. The high for the day is noted along with the closest daily support level. The support level is based on the recent daily chart activity. This often results in a support level substantially different from the support level normally calculated. With this intra-day trading technique it is inappropriate to use longer-term support levels where a current short-term support level is at a higher point.

The BBG chart in Figure 23.6 highlights the difference in the way this concept of support and resistance is applied. Our objective is to locate the closest support level set over the previous week. The stop loss points are based on well-established support levels identified on the bar chart. In a fast-moving stock the support level may be set just a tick below the breakaway gap or the close of the previous day.

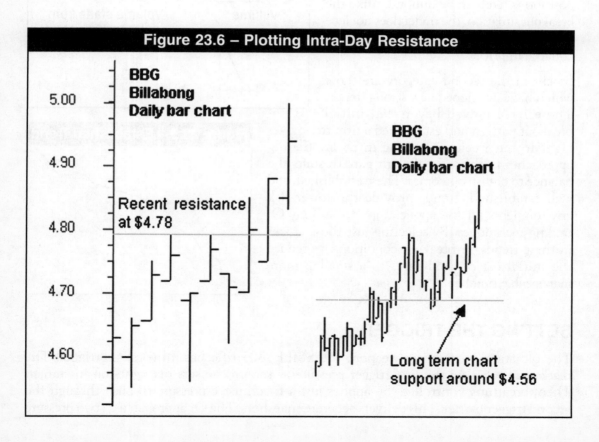

Figure 23.6 – Plotting Intra-Day Resistance

BBG
Billabong
Daily bar chart

Recent resistance at $4.78

BBG
Billabong
Daily bar chart

Long term chart support around $4.56

The long-term support based on a one-year chart, is around $4.56. On the daily chart, there is a short-term resistance and support level at $4.78. This is the most likely trigger point for any current daily action so it is used as the support level.

TRIGGERS BREED SUCCESS

Setting the stop loss figure is vital to the success of the strategy, so we fast-forward for a moment to show in more detail how the stop loss is set and applied. We use three examples, AZR, AIE and EQS as shown in Figure 23.7. Each has a trigger entry price simply set at the high of the previous day. Any trade above this price trips the entry trigger.

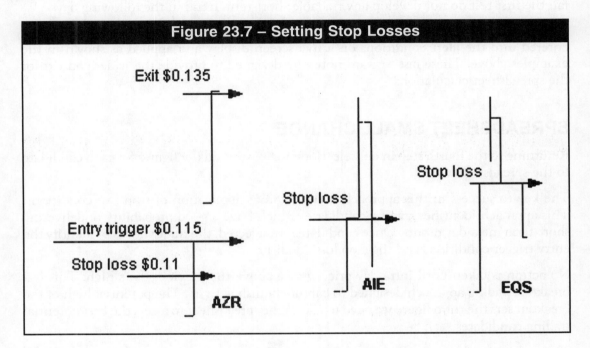

Figure 23.7 – Setting Stop Losses

The stop loss in the AZR sample is based on the price action of recent bars. With AIE the stop is placed at the bottom of the previous day's price action. This is part of a series of up days and the closest support level is too far below the current price action. This applies the same placement method used with BBG above to set support at $4.78. The EQS example places the support at the bottom of the previous day's price gap.

This series of chart extracts show how price action developed during the day and the role the stop loss played in success. The successful trade is AZR. The entry signal is given by the gap open above the entry trigger price of $0.115. There are several exit strategies but at best, this trade returns 12.5% for the day based on an entry point at $0.12.

The other two trades were failures. The AIE trade opened well but then dropped through the stop loss point. AIE did not move above the entry trigger level of $0.195 so no position was taken in this stock. The same situation applies with EQS. At the end of the day it closed on the stop loss level. The EQS chart shows a collapse of the short-term rally. Traders who bought on the stop loss level in anticipation of a rebound did not succeed.

We may be tempted to keep EQS on our watch list for a potential recovery away from this stop point. Some opportunities may develop in this way but they are not consistent with the approach used by Oz. When stocks fail to meet the buy criteria on the day, they are removed from the watch list for the next day. Each day we use the same exploration techniques to identify a new batch of potential candidates. Often those candidates which fail the first test do not develop any tradable short-term trend in the following days.

The breakout trigger price and the support level are critical for this strategy. Later they are entered into the alert conditions on a live screen display and applied as shown in the examples above. These fast-forward notes are designed to provide the wider context for the spreadsheet calculations.

SPREADSHEET SMALL CHANGE

Returning to the fourth step in our selection process, we add the figures for each candidate to the spreadsheet notes.

The key to success in this approach is the rigorous application of stop loss conditions. This approach identifies trading candidates which have a good probability of delivering short-term intra-day profits. Once candidates are selected, the trader needs to identify the entry trigger conditions and the stop loss conditions.

No action is taken until intra-day prices move above the previous day's high. This is a breakout trading approach designed to capture bullish activity. The potential high of the breakout sets the third figure we need to add to the spreadsheet to assess the best potential trading candidates.

The trade target figure is set in one of three ways. Some charts show nearby resistance levels and these are natural target points for any short-term rise. In other stocks we reach into our toolbox and select the volatility tools developed by Robert Deel and discussed in Chapter 10. We add the Average Dollar Price Volatility measure to the trigger price and set a return target. We could use the value of the 2xATR calculation projected above the breakout high. The objective is to set a reasonably achievable target for the next day's trading.

Estimating a reasonable target, is, at best, informed guesswork. We compare the figures and opportunities using the spreadsheet calculations which are designed to indicate the necessary position size required to achieve our projected return, based on our target level. This provides the third way to get these figures. We work backwards from our entry trigger figure and set the necessary exit figure based on our other preconditions. Then we decide if this is more or less likely to be achieved.

The spreadsheet is the real magic in this sorting hat. It captures the three base figures: trigger point, support level and profit target. Candidate selection depends on a final calculation to capture the value of our small change.

The key feature turning this approach into a success is not the percentage return on each trade, but the consistent size of the dollar return on the trade. In *The Stock Trader*, Tony Oz provides a breakdown of the returns achieved from his trades. Most returns fall between $200 and $400 per trade. We set a small change return target of $300 per trade and add $60 for brokerage. This means each trade has a target return of $360.

Using the return as a starting point rather than as an end point, we calculate the position size required for each trade to achieve this $360 return.

The spreadsheet* in Figure 23.8 shows the results of this calculation for a typical daily list of candidates. We use the notation '2' after the stock code to indicate it appears in both the modified Oz searches for higher highs and higher closes. The average percentage return on all winning trades for the period shown is 3% and the best is 14.29%. The sorting magic is found in the calculations so we look at the information contained in each column.

Figure 23.8 – Typical List of Candidates

Code	High/close Previous day buy signal	High for day	Profit/loss	% return	Support	Quantity required for $360 profit	Purchase cost	Sell return	Desired profit level including brokerage
amp2	20.5	20.65	0.150	0.73	19.7	2,400	$ 49,200.00	$ 49,560.00	$ 360.00
bbg	5	5.16	0.160	3.20	4.78	2,250	$ 11,250.00	$ 11,610.00	$ 360.00
csr2	5.26	5.38	0.120	2.28	5.1	3,000	$ 15,780.00	$ 16,140.00	$ 360.00
god	0.035	0.04	0.005	14.29	0.031	72,000	$ 2,520.00	$ 2,880.00	$ 360.00
hah	3.99	4.01	0.020	0.50	3.95	18,000	$ 71,820.00	$ 72,180.00	$ 360.00
sme	11.66	11.8	0.140	1.20	11.43	2,571	$ 29,982.86	$ 30,342.86	$ 360.00
wmc2	8.58	8.75	0.170	1.98	8.2	2,118	$ 18,169.41	$ 18,529.41	$ 360.00
wow	8.33	8.35	0.020	0.24	8.21	18,000	$ 149,940.00	$ 150,300.00	$ 360.00
Col 1	Col 2	Col 3	Col 4	Col 5	Col 6	Col 7	Col 8	Col 9	Col 10

➜ Column 1 is the stock code and lists all those that passed the initial database scan and chart analysis.

➜ Column 2 contains the trigger price. This is the buy signal. For ease of calculation we assume an entry at this price once the trigger is tripped.

* This spreadsheet is available as a free Excel template from www.guppytraders.com.

→ Column 3 is the estimated high for the day – our target exit price. This is set using a variety of methods but, on balance, a lower figure is more realistic. This figure is a vital component in calculating position size.

→ Column 4 is the potential dollar profit generated by the exit taken in column 2.

→ Column 5 is the profit expressed as a percentage return.

→ Column 6 includes the support, or stop loss figure.

→ Now we skip to column 10. This column could be headed GREED because it contains the return figure you expect from this trade. This is small change trading, so our return is $360 per trade including $60 brokerage. Our objective is to clear $300 a day from each of these trading opportunities. Enter this figure and the calculation magic begins.

→ Column 7 uses the return figure to calculate the position size required for the trade to generate the requested profit. If we use a minimum exit target figure we set up a lower-risk trade. If we make money on the minimum targets then any additional movement during the day adds a bonus to the trade.

If we set an optimistic target and price fails to move this high, we increase the risk in the trade because we might not reach breakeven. Our objective is to set reasonable targets to achieve a reasonable return for the day.

→ Column 8 shows the cost of buying the position, and column 9 the dollar return once the trade is closed.

Each of the candidates shown meets our selection criteria. Based on our analysis of support, trigger and exit price, some of these trades are now more attractive than others. We may be comfortable committing $11,250 to the BBG trade. We are unlikely to throw $149,940 at WOW for a $360 return.

This sorting hat further reduces the number of potential trading candidates we need to follow on the live screen when the market opens. The live trading screen opens the door to opportunities which, like those detailed by Oz, are capable of returning 32% on capital over four weeks by accumulating small change. It does not suit the preconceptions of the media when they talk of day trading. Day trading rarely delivers large returns. Big profits are built from many small profits, consistently gathered day after day.

This magic done, we turn to the magic of the market using live screens to trigger profitable trades.

Tony Oz Exploration For MetaStock

Col A:	vol	VOLUME >= 500,000
Col B:	vol%	ROC(VOLUME,1,percent)
Col C:	close	CLOSE
Col D: –	1day	Ref(CLOSE,–1)
Col E: –	2day	Ref(CLOSE,–2)
Filter		colA=1 AND When(colB>10) AND When(colC,>,colD) AND When(colD,>,colE)

≡ MARKSWOMAN'S NOTES

→ This is a modification of a single strategy used by Tony Oz in *The Stock Trader*.

→ Scan the end-of-day database for stocks with price activity meeting our required potential.

→ End-of-day charts are used to assess trends and resistance.

→ Select established uptrends and strong breakouts.

→ Use end-of-day charts to set accurate short-term stop loss points.

→ Entry trigger is a trade above yesterday's high.

→ Use spreadsheet calculations to finalise the sorting of candidates for position size and return.

→ Visit www.tonyoz.com for more information on advanced techniques.

Chapter 24

TRADING
SMALL CHANGE

Small change adds up. Every now and then a ten dollar note is thrown into the mix. From the daily spreadsheet record we select two examples to show how the calculation and selection steps from the last chapter are applied in real time for real trades. The first sample trade returns 10.5% for the day. The second collects 27.7%. Each uses the advantage of price leverage to boost returns.

The successful implementation of this strategy calls for close management. You need to stay in front of a live screen while the trades are open. Successful exits call for your judgement based on tick and five-minute screen charts showing every trade. It is not always an easy call and the examples show how this judgement is applied.

Day trading is not a mechanical skill. The approach used here sets up all the conditions. All we have to do is take the snapshot when the final trigger pressure is reached. The first trade above the trigger price sets us in action. How we flinch, and when, determines our success. Experience counts when the average return we aim for is $360.

Snapshot shooters first acquire a good sight picture of their aiming point. Then they wait for the best conditions. We acquire the sight picture using an alert function with our real-time data supplier. We cannot watch all our potential candidates so we let the computer do it for us.

This approach relies on having real-time, reliable, direct access to market activity for the entire day. We use the MarketCast data service for this because it is delivered via a TV signal which is more reliable than an internet connection. A traded price at or above the High Limit triggers an audible alert to buy as shown in Figure 24.1. Once an alert is generated we use the AOT Online internet trading platform to execute the trade.

Once the trade is opened it is managed with a tight stop loss. As soon as prices trade at, or below, the nominated Low Limit we are alerted by the computer announcing "Sell on stop loss". For this technique to work traders must be able to constantly monitor the market, have alerts sounded when conditions are met, and act quickly to execute buy or sell orders.

GONE TRADING

The next two sections come direct from our trading screens. These are trades we caught using the modified Tony Oz methods. They are trading stories and the objective in each is to show you how the decisions were made in real time. Our preference is for stocks trading around the $0.05 to $0.30 level because they offer the additional advantage of price leverage.

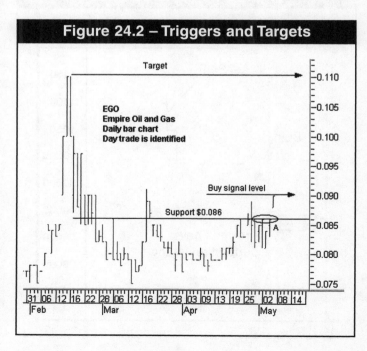

Figure 24.1 – MarketCast Watch Page

Buy alert   Sell alert

WatchPage - - vs Prev. Close

		Symb	Last Price	High Limit	Low Limit
▶	↔	AMP	20.480	20.65	20.16
	↔	AXA	2.850	2.82	2.72
	↔	CSR	5.280	5.38	5.18
	↑	GOD	0.039	.04	0.034
	↔	NRM	2.760	2.86	2.78
	↑	SRP	6.350	6.45	6.26
	↔	TCL	4.050	4.15	4.00
	↔	WOW	8.300	8.35	8.23
	↔	FBG	5.050	5.14	4.96

The first feature to set is the support level. The EGO calculations are based on the most recent resistance activity prior to the breakout. This is shown at $0.086 in the circle at area A in Figure 24.2. We plan for an intra-day trade, so we place much more weight on the recent resistance and support behaviour of price.

The second feature – the entry trigger level – is much easier to calculate. We buy as soon as there is a trade above the previous day's high of $0.09. The third feature sets a trading target based on the nearby logical chart point at $0.11.

This particular trading approach has some interesting and unique features. Most times we identify a list of trading candidates and then take a guess about which one will perform best. Of nine candidates, three may turn out winners, three losers, and three may trade sideways.

Figure 24.2 – Triggers and Targets

Target

EGO
Empire Oil and Gas
Daily bar chart
Day trade is identified

Buy signal level

Support $0.086

A

-0.110
-0.105
-0.100
-0.095
-0.090
-0.085
-0.080
-0.075

31 06 12 16 22 28 06 12 16 22 28 03 09 13 19 25 02 08 14
Feb   Mar   Apr   May

This day trading approach is different because the entry signal is only given by a trade above the entry price. No shot, or trade, is taken until the sight picture is perfect. All other trading candidates are ignored if they do not give an entry signal. Stocks moving sideways for the day do not take our money with them. Stocks trading below the support level do not concern us because they do not involve our trading capital. They are simply ignored.

We do not buy a stock with this approach until it proves it has the ability to be a winner by trading above the previous day's high. This greatly increases the probability of a successful trade because only winners are selected.

Remember there are two selection processes at work here. The first is a standard selection scan to find candidates with a high probability of providing the trading opportunity we are after. The second selection scan takes place on the day. An entry is only triggered if the stock trades as expected so the failure rate is very low. We do not try to identify winners in advance. We jump on winners once they get to the head of the pack.

MANAGING THE MINUTES

The EGO trade opens at $0.096 as shown in Figure 24.3 and generates an immediate entry signal. Our buy order goes in as an at-market order to meet the asking price. We get our

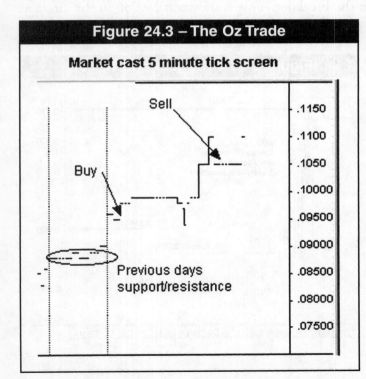

Figure 24.3 – The Oz Trade

entry at $0.095 in this example. Had prices continued to trend higher we may have paid $0.097. This trading strategy requires traders to chase prices.

We buy 215,000 EGO shares at $0.095 for a total of $20,425. With 3,899,318 shares traded for the day, our order is easily filled on both the buy and sell sides of this trade. This is why it is important to select stocks with a minimum turnover of 500,000 shares. We need a deep market for these trading strategies to succeed. As soon as our buy order is filled we place an immediate sell order at the resistance level of $0.11.

Selecting a proven winner is a good step but we need a stop loss

222

in case the winner stumbles. With EGO this remains at $0.086. The previous day's chart shows how trades clustered at this level. Any trade below this level takes us out of this trade.

As anticipated, EGO hits the target of $0.11 as shown in Figure 24.4. As the end of the day nears there are orders in front of us and buying pressure has slowed. This is an intra-day trade so we have no choice but to meet the bid and exit at $0.105. This returns 10.53% on the trade for the day.

Remember regret? It visits when we look at the intra-day return and compare it with the return available from other methods including two- and three-day trades. There is no room for regret here. This is an intra-day trade adding consistent small change returns.

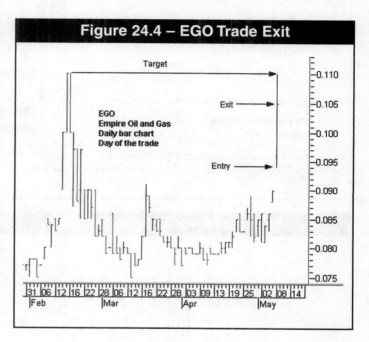

Figure 24.4 – EGO Trade Exit

BETTER BREAKS

These small change snapshot trades rest on pre-defined price conditions for every potential opportunity on the list. When the sight picture is correct, we take the shot.

Traditionally position traders trade the breakouts from long-term downtrends, but there are also good opportunities for day traders to ride the initial break. The increased trading activity makes these breakouts suitable for day trading. It is important to have enough volume and dollar depth to allow the trader to both buy and sell a reasonable number of shares. If we try to buy too many we have an impact on price, pushing it up. When it comes time to sell, on the same day, our large block of shares pushes the price downwards very quickly. If we take a smaller position the spreadsheet calculations tell us if we can reasonably anticipate collecting our preferred minimum return from the trade.

Generally we treat stocks locked in a long downtrend with caution. In a strong bull market there is the chance of a good, brief rally in those stocks on an attempted breakout. The ISC chart in Figure 24.5 shows the beginning of a breakout. The downtrend is well defined with a straight-edge trend line and the breakout is quite clear. The increasing volume is a confirming indicator in this type of trade situation. The detail is not very clear on this chart extract as we want to show the relationship between the downtrend and the breakout.

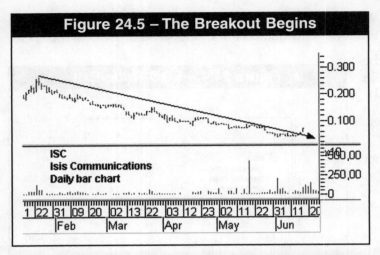

Figure 24.5 – The Breakout Begins

ISC
Isis Communications
Daily bar chart

The Oz approach uses set buy and sell trigger conditions so, even if we decide to add a downtrend stock, we do not trade it until it meets exact conditions on the day. The buy trigger is set using the current high value for the day at $0.07, shown in Figure 24.6. A trade above this level triggers the entry.

The support level used as a stop loss or sell trigger, is more difficult to set. A trade below this level signals an exit to take a small loss. We set support at $0.051 based on the high just above the more concentrated support at $0.05. This increases the probability we can get out, if necessary, at $0.05. It is a judgement call. Some traders may choose to use the high of the previous day at $0.056. We think this is too close to current action and is more likely to result in a whipsaw. These calculations are made for each of the candidates on the list of potential trades.

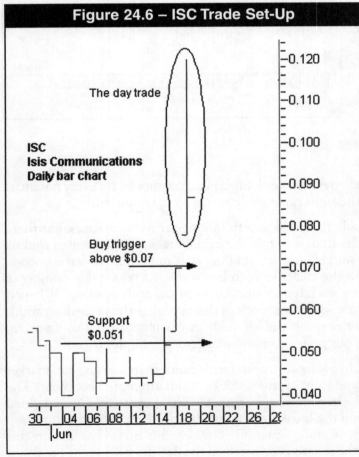

Figure 24.6 – ISC Trade Set-Up

The day trade

ISC
Isis Communications
Daily bar chart

Buy trigger
above $0.07

Support
$0.051

NO QUIBBLES

The chart in Figure 24.7 shows the immediate buy signal generated by the gap up on the open. Catching this, and managing the exit, calls for careful monitoring of the intra-day tick chart. There is no room for quibbling in implementing this strategy. Once buy conditions are met we meet the market using an at-market order. This is a snapshot taken without hesitation. In a fast-moving market it is pointless trying to meet the ask. By the time you click your buy order the ask you saw on the screen may have disappeared. It is more effective to place a buy order higher than the last traded price. This order takes precedence and is filled at the current ask.

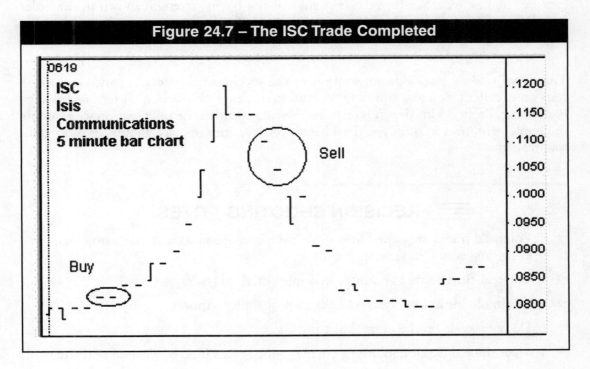

Figure 24.7 – The ISC Trade Completed

ISC opened at $0.078 and our entry is at $0.083, shown in the circled buy area. On the previous day around $60,000 worth of shares changed hands so we want to make sure our buy position size is not too large. We commit just under $10,000 to the trade. This is still relatively large compared to the previous day's trading, but once the Oz trading signals are delivered it is common for trading volume to increase on the day. This is likely to mean our $10,000 trade is relatively easy to sell when the time comes.

Once the trade is open we are committed. This requires a live screen and constant attention. The objective is to try to capture the top of the price move for the day. If you are shooting for a defined return then the exit is made once the price is achieved. If you are trying to ride the momentum you remain alert for downticks and a drop off in trading volume.

With ISC, the price goes through to $0.12, and then pulls back. The momentum stalls and the buy side of the order line weakens. We unload stock in two separate sales with an average price of $0.106. In this case the trade returns 27.71% for the day.

Some traders have a bad habit of thinking the low of the day is near the open and the high of the day is near the close. Once a day trade is open we need to be alert for any signal which suggests the buying momentum is weakening. The ISC trade weakens just before midday and then spends the rest of the day in a steady decline. We could run moving averages, channels or any of a wide variety of trailing stop loss techniques on the chart to capture the best exit. We find the best guide is the buying strength shown in the order line. When the price drops and buyers do not enter the market to take advantage of the new, lower price, it is a good indication the trend has weakened. In a day trade this indication is enough to start preparations for selling.

These two trading stories demonstrate how the success of this small change technique rests on excellent stop loss and order execution. It demands the best current technology has to offer. Profit taking depends on order execution and in the next section we examine the implementation features you need before you step into the day trading, or short-term trading game.

PRECISION SHOOTING NOTES

→   Potential trades are culled from end-of-day analysis and carry exact stop loss, entry trigger and target exit points.

→   Use real-time alerts to monitor multiple potential trades.

→   The trade initiation filters select high probability winners.

→   Do not haggle on the entry. Meet the ask.

→   Meet the bid if exit conditions are met but not executed by the end of the day.

→   Adjust position size to reflect minimum return or a sensible size given recent volume.

→   These are precision trades so ignore the larger trend picture and keep regret at bay.

PART V

PROFIT

TAKING

Chapter 25

EXECUTION
RISK

All the strategies discussed in previous chapters rely on two vital features for success. The first is a carefully defined stop loss condition to protect capital, and later a precise exit condition designed to capture the, sometimes slim, profit from the trade. The second feature is an excellent, no-nonsense, reliable straight-through processing of orders delivered either by a mouse click at the right time, or managed automatically and electronically. We examine some of the options in the next chapter.

The application of stop loss techniques in a way consistent with the 2% rule designed to protect capital has been well covered in *Trading Tactics* and *Better Trading*. We do not intend to repeat those discussions here. We assume you are familiar with the concepts, so our focus is on the differences in the way stop loss and protect profit techniques are applied in these shorter timeframes. Previous chapters have shown the vital importance of entry and exit points. The small change approach shoots for profits of $300 so a slip of just $0.01, or fraction of a cent, has a significant impact on the trade. Stop loss techniques are modified in planning the trade, and orders are carefully managed in the order line to achieve the best entry possible.

Order management starts with pre-trade planning to ensure the size of the trade – the number of shares purchased – is consistent with the volume, depth and liquidity of trading. Depth is indicated by the number of orders in the order line waiting to be filled. The order screens should show at least three levels, or types of orders.

The first component of these figures – Level 1 data – tells the trader the number of buyers at the highest current bid, and the number of sellers at the current ask. The second component of these figures – Level 2 data – is usually shown on a different screen and shows the consolidated volume each buyer and seller is offering at each price level. When the term 'undisclosed' or 'u/c' is added to the order line it normally means a very large order. These are consolidated summary figures. The third – Level 3 data – screen shows a summary of the number of buyers and sellers at each price level below and above the current market price. It also shows the detailed volume of orders at each level. This is used to confirm chart support levels. This full depth-of-market, or Level 3, data is the most useful for traders.

A stock with an order for 50,000 shares at $1.00 is not an attractive trade if the next buy order is for 1,000 shares at $0.60. This order line has no depth. Once the first order is filled there are no other buy orders near the same price. The market could fall dramatically to the next active buy order at $0.60.

Liquidity has two slightly different meanings. The first considers the number of potential buyers and sellers – the 'free float' in American terms. The more tightly a stock is held, the less shares are likely to be available for trading. A company where 20% of the shareholders have 95% of the shares means, most times, only around 5% of shares are available for active trading. This makes for large price moves as bidders cannot rely on mass psychology to move the market. The downside is when one of the large holders decides to sell. The market is overwhelmed and prices fall dramatically.

This is similar to the 'free float' methodology used by Morgan Stanley in deciding which stocks are included in the Australian component of the MSCI index. The percentage held by the top 20 is available from company reports. Setting a high level of liquidity, or free float, as a precondition for day or short-term trading can be misleading. There are other opportunities to take advantage of short-term bursts of trading liquidity which run counter to the size of the free float.

The second meaning of liquidity is related to the velocity or speed of trading. A stock with a high number of trades for the day has a higher velocity or liquidity than a stock with a low number of trades. This low liquidity makes some high-percentage gainers essentially untradable because there is only a handful of trades. A stock with high velocity is traded heavily and consistently during the day. Liquidity is very useful when the number of trades today is about the same as yesterday and the same, on average, as the preceding week or more. The velocity or liquidity of trading should not be confused with the volume of trading. Volume tells us total number of shares traded, but not the number of trades. So 100,000 shares might be traded as a single trade, or as ten smaller trades of 10,000 shares each. The difference tells us a great deal about the nature of trading in this stock. The velocity of trading is a key factor in the success of any short-term day-trading, or intra-day trading strategies.

SLIPPAGE

A third term, slippage, applies to short-term trading in particular. This describes the difference between the price you would like to buy the shares at, and the actual price you end up paying. You might intend to pay $1.00, but end up paying $1.02 because the market is moving very quickly. Slippage also occurs on the other end of the trade, where profit is reduced because you cannot get out at your preferred price. Slippage applies to a stop loss exit and this is the area traders seem most concerned about. When a stop loss exit slips they like to blame their broker for poor trade execution. Others dismiss stop loss planning because the exit cannot be guaranteed. Such reactions are good examples of traders refusing to accept responsibility for their actions.

No entry or exit price is guaranteed. Our planning reflects the prices at which we would like to do business. The movement of price may prevent us from executing an order at those levels. The fault, if any, lies in the difference between our planning and market reality. The order execution system we use, broker or electronic, is not to blame. We must accept that slippage plays a part in our trading results. The objective is not to eliminate it, but to keep it within acceptable limits.

When we analyse our exits we must expect to get out of some trades very close to the top, while we sacrifice a greater proportion of open profit with others. It is important to stand back from the individual trade result and assess the effectiveness of the exit strategies across a range of similar trades. If, on average, the exit is acceptable then we must accept others will be very good and some will be relatively poor.

The schematic diagram in Figure 25.1 shows the preferred outcome. Only a few trades exit at the very high of the trend move. In position trading, the majority of trades should cluster around 10% below the high in planned trend trades. Short-term traders aim for an exit within 3% to 5% of the top. A few of these trades suffer a significant profit loss due to unexpected events, such as sudden profit downgrades. Note how these trades can fall below the lower line. While there is a cap on how good our exit is compared with the absolute high of the trend move, there is no limit on how bad our exit could be. When evaluating exits, put them within the context of a scatter diagram as shown. It tells us if a poor exit is unusual, and therefore acceptable, within the context of our normal exits, or if the poor exit is depressingly normal for our trading style.

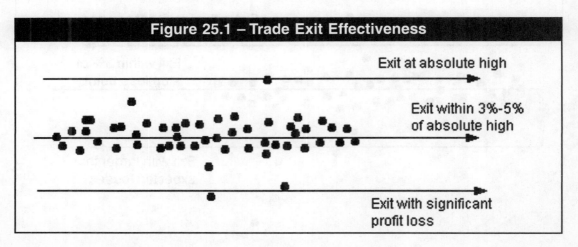

Figure 25.1 – Trade Exit Effectiveness

Exit at absolute high

Exit within 3%-5% of absolute high

Exit with significant profit loss

Some traders use this type of diagram to lift their exit performance to an average of 3% of the absolute high. This type of measure is designed to assess the efficiency of the trading system and is more fully discussed in some of Chuck Le Beau's work.

The diagram in Figure 25.2 shows how the same type of analysis is applied to entry techniques. Generally we aim for a consistent approach to get us within 3% to 5% of the planned entry point. Many entries have a lower absolute limit defined by the pivot point low of the downtrend prior to the breakout.

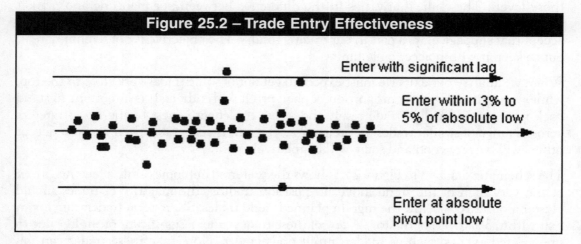

Figure 25.2 – Trade Entry Effectiveness

Enter with significant lag

Enter within 3% to 5% of absolute low

Enter at absolute pivot point low

The stop loss slippage picture is different, as shown in Figure 25.3. There are no upper and lower limits. It is possible to do much better than we expect when the stop loss price is triggered.

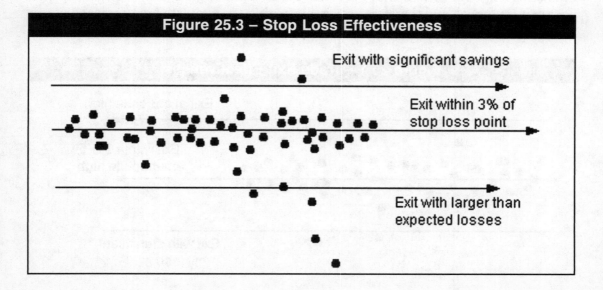

Figure 25.3 – Stop Loss Effectiveness

Exit with significant savings

Exit within 3% of stop loss point

Exit with larger than expected losses

The downside is more dangerous. Prices tend to fall more rapidly than they rise. This means there are more stop loss failures where the exit price is significantly lower than the planned exit price. More dangerously, there are some stop loss exits which are substantially below the planned exit point. We cannot prevent these. An adverse earnings report may cause a gap down on the open, dropping price way below our stop loss. Then we reach for the gap open techniques explored by Oliver Velez. The objective with stop loss execution is to cluster most of the exits close to our planned points. On average, we expect to stay with the 2% rule which limits the loss of capital on any one trade to no more than 2% of our total trading capital.

APPLYING STOP LOSS

The search to find the perfect stop loss method is a waste of time. Our search is better directed towards finding the most appropriate stop loss for the trade. Some methods, like those discussed in the small change and bullish flag strategies, have clear, independently calculated stop loss conditions. Others rely on a variety of different methods. We prefer the count back line approach and this is often compared with the two times Average True Range method – 2xATR. We find both methods effective in short-term trades.

Setting the best profit stop loss, or trailing stop loss, is a perennial problem. In stocks showing a slow moving and steady uptrend the issue is not difficult to solve. Any of a variety of stop loss techniques work equally well. The differences are minor.

In trades showing faster rally behaviour, or fast breakouts, managing the trailing stop loss is more important because it has a significant impact on the total profit from the trade. This is particularly so where prices show large range days followed by pullbacks. The range of price is the distance between the low for the day and the high for the day. This is also a measure of volatility. When volatility increases, the volatility-based stop loss conditions may lag too far behind the current price action. When a new exit signal comes, the trader may end up surrendering a significant amount of the potential profit.

Setting a protect-capital stop loss uses well-known techniques to match position size, price, risk and trading capital. Protecting profits does not yield as easily to the same formula based approach. In trades based on volatility and momentum we apply two stop profit loss techniques to lock in better returns. These are the count back line and the 2xATR stop loss methods. Each has its weaknesses, and each has its strengths. By combining the two, the trader more tightly manages the trade to trap profits.

The count back line uses the cumulative range value of three higher days to set the stop loss conditions. In the diagram in Figure 25.4 the count back line calculation includes five days of price activity. The calculation starts at $1.15. The top of the calculated range is at $1.35. This gives a range of $0.20. This calculation ignores the 'inside' days, or days of equal highs. As a method of confirming breakouts, the count back line increases the probability of success considerably. When applied as a trailing stop loss to protect profit this cumulative range strategy may lag too far behind the current high point used in the calculation.

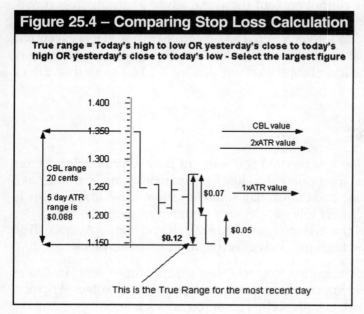

Figure 25.4 – Comparing Stop Loss Calculation

True range = Today's high to low OR yesterday's close to today's high OR yesterday's close to today's low - Select the largest figure

This is the True Range for the most recent day

The Average True Range calculation compares the price range for today with the highs and lows of the previous day. The highest of these values – the largest range – is selected as the true average range for the period. This figure is calculated each day. In most Average True Range applications this value is averaged over five or ten days. In this example the five-day average true range is $0.088. Many Average True Range applications multiply the Average True Range value by 1.5 or 2. Our preference is to use 2xATR, and this gives a five-day 2xATR value of $0.176.

This means the 2xATR is more sensitive than the count back line in this example. A close above the 2xATR value signals the end of the downtrend. A close above the CBL value also verifies the end of the downtrend. Sometimes the values agree but most times they are slightly different. This difference is used when applying both these tools as an exit management approach.

When applying the 2xATR we prefer to use a dotted display as shown in Figure 25.5. Each dot represents the current 2xATR value. When we use the 2xATR as a stop loss we use only the highest value so the points circled are ignored. Once price has broken out above the downtrend line we apply 2xATR as a stop loss. The first, second and third stop loss points follow the rising price. As prices pull back, the 2xATR value falls. These lesser values shown in the circled areas are ignored. The most recent highest value is retained as the stop loss trigger point. When a new, and higher, 2xATR value is plotted as the fourth stop, then the stop loss point is lifted again to follow the rising trend.

STOP LOSS APPLICATION

When the count back line is used as a protect-profit stop loss, the danger is the cumulative range may trail too far behind the current price activity. On the GTM example in Figure 25.6, the first count back line calculation is made from the high at $0.058. This sets the protect-profit stop loss at $0.044. This is a long distance below the high point. As price action continues the range of price narrows. Ideally we want to lift the trailing stop loss to higher values. If price collapses from around $0.053 we want to capture a good profit.

The count back line protect-profit stop loss does not shift upwards again until a new high is made at $0.059. This lifts the trailing stop to $0.054, as shown in Figure 25.6. The problem is our profit remains at risk until a new high is made and the count back line calculation lifts the stop loss level. In fast-moving stocks with large price ranges, the cumulative range is very large. It takes 18 days before a new, and tight, stop loss is created for GTM.

By combining the count back line and 2xATR approaches we establish an alternative way to fine-tune the exit in these fast-moving stocks. The exit trigger is based on the highest stop loss value set by either method. Once the count back line stop loss is set, the 2xATR values set new stop losses as shown by points 1 to 8 in Figure 25.7. These values

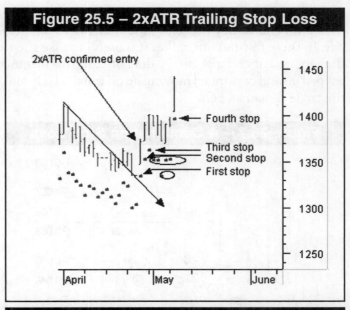

Figure 25.5 – 2xATR Trailing Stop Loss

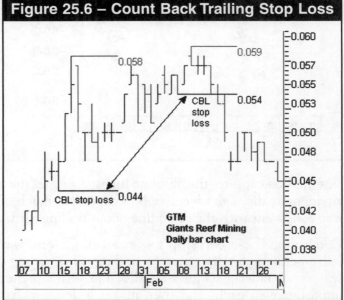

Figure 25.6 – Count Back Trailing Stop Loss

better reflect the decline in ranging activity and volatility with GTM. If prices should collapse before a new count back line calculation high is set, the 2xATR triggers an earlier exit and protects more of the open profit. The 2xATR values circled are ignored. They are all lower than the highest ATR value at the time.

The first exit signal comes when GTM prices close below the 2xATR value marked 2. This is an end-of-day trigger, so the trader does not act upon it until the open of the next day. In these fast-moving rallies it is useful to take the time to watch the open of prices, as the rebound or collapse can be dramatic. In this instance the 2xATR signal is false. Prices gapped up and continued moving up on the next day and, on the basis of this price strength, the trade remains open.

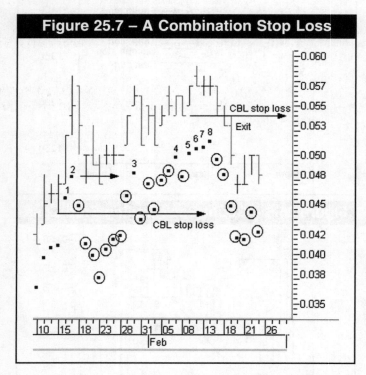

Figure 25.7 – A Combination Stop Loss

For the next 17 days, prices remain above the 2xATR values. The first exit signal is triggered by a close below the new count back line value at $0.054. This is an end-of-day signal, and the open of trade the next day confirms price weakness. Price recovers a little, but then falls. The trader acts on this and exits on this day.

The danger with using two different, but related, stop loss techniques is in deciding which signal to act upon. We overcome this by using the higher value but watching the open of trade the next day for verification. The break is confirmed by subsequent price action.

No exit method is perfect. No exit method captures the absolute highs. At times the trader is stopped out of a trend on a temporary dip. Our objective is to capture as much of the rally or trend as possible in a way consistent with the discipline of our trading plan.

Combining these two stop loss strategies is one way to achieve this but it calls for judgement and for discretionary trading. This trading style puts the trader in the driving seat. The trader assembles a collection of his preferred indicators, assigns a level of importance to each, and then makes a decision based on his understanding of the indicator readings and trading signals. This inevitably involves some subjective judgement, and this creates room for error.

Mechanical trading seeks to remove human intervention – and hence subjective behaviour – as much as possible from the trading equation. Typically such systems rely purely on mathematical relationships, although in establishing many systems there is subjective human input to determine the most desirable outcomes. Trade management requires discipline and a great deal of faith in the system. The temptation is to second-guess the trading signals.

Intuitive trading develops from experience and should not be confused with the gut feelings used by the novice. Experienced traders are subconsciously aware of certain patterns and market set-ups. When they see them they act intuitively drawing on many years of trading experience. This requires a high level of confidence and skill so trades are managed with certainty. These trading processes are difficult to explain. *The Intuitive Trader* by Robert Koppel examines these issues in detail. Good short-term and day traders start with discretionary trading approaches and eventually combine them with an intuitive feel for their chosen market.

Setting stop loss points in stocks is not the same as setting stops with derivative trades. Liquidity and depth play a significant role in our ability to execute buy and sell orders in this market so techniques are modified slightly. We examine these in the next chapter.

≡TRIGGER FINGER NOTES

➜ Use real-time, Level 3 depth-of-market screens.

➜ Understand the differences between depth, liquidity, volume and velocity.

➜ Plan for slippage.

➜ Aim to cluster entry and exit points near the preferred prices in most trades.

➜ Use a combination of the count-back line and 2xATR methods to manage protect-profit stops.

➜ Watch order flow to verify exit signals.

➜ Short-term trading is discretionary trading.

Chapter 26

CRASH
AND BURN

Every pilot has a secret fear. I discovered this while flying regularly in light aircraft as my work, at that time, took me to remote communities on Cape York Peninsula, and the tiny islands scattered in the Torres Strait. After several emergency landings, aborted take-offs and mid-air incidents I decided the flying risk associated with the job was too high. Pilots I flew with had been killed and aircraft I travelled in had been destroyed. On some island airstrips we landed over the carcasses of abandoned aeroplanes that had crashed on take-off in the crocodile-infested waters just off New Guinea.

In these difficult flying conditions pilots always worry about the prospect of a crash but the potential to crash and burn really terrified them. On one memorable occasion I watched as a twin-engined light aeroplane burst into flames shortly after landing on a remote airstrip. The pilot escaped unharmed. The next concern was the $50,000 cash payroll in an old ammunition box that was part of the onboard cargo.

In just a few minutes the aircraft was reduced to a scattering of aluminium foil and two engine lumps. When the remains of the airframe cooled we retrieved the strong box and found neat piles of charred notes which were eventually replaced in full by the Reserve Bank.

Every trade has the potential to crash but when we trade derivatives like warrants and options, there is a real possibility of a crash and burn. When it happens we need to make sure that our capital survives like the cash in the payroll strong box.

Unexpected trading errors are a fact of life no matter how experienced we are as traders. Trading is about managing risk, and when we move into markets and instruments where it is more difficult to manage risk, there is an increased risk to our portfolio. Derivatives like warrants and options are often promoted on the grounds they provide a way for traders to limit risk because the risk is ultimately limited to the actual amount used in the trade. It is not a good trading tactic to hold onto the derivative until it expires. Better trading takes the trader out of the trade at some higher level to preserve most of the capital used in the trade.

DERIVATIVE COUNTER MEASURES

Derivative trading calls for experience, skill and careful monitoring. It is not an area for inexperienced traders with a small amount of capital. When derivative trades work, the leverage offered provides an excellent way to quickly grow profits. When they fail, they are a fast way to destroy trading capital, again because of leverage, but also because of volume problems.

There are three main approaches to managing the risk in a derivative trade. They are:

1.   Limit position size to the maximum allowable portfolio risk – the absolute disaster exit.

2.   Reduce the derivative's position size, based on the entry and estimated stop loss exit conditions using delta to anticipate pricing.

3.   Accept a larger loss, letting it grow to the equivalent of two ordinary size positions by planning for a 4% loss of trading capital.

The worst-case scenario is when the trader still holds the warrant when it expires so the loss is total – the absolute disaster exit-point. Limiting position size to the maximum allowable portfolio risk is the most effective way of managing derivative trades from this risk perspective. Using a $100,000 portfolio size, this means any derivative trade is limited to a maximum position size of $2,000. The approach assumes the trade is not closed before warrant expiry, so the maximum amount lost is $2,000. This is the absolute disaster exit-point. The diagram in Figure 26.1 shows an entry at $0.20 and an exit at $0.00. The position size, shown by the width of the box, is equal to $2,000.

The disadvantage of this approach is the small position size making even a 50% return

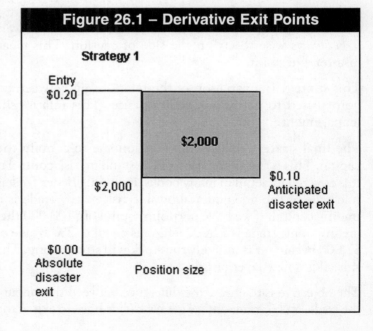

Figure 26.1 – Derivative Exit Points

Strategy 1

Entry
$0.20

$2,000

$2,000

$0.10
Anticipated
disaster exit

$0.00
Absolute
disaster
exit

Position size

239

small in dollar terms. Many traders feel the dollar return is not adequate compensation for the risk involved. For inexperienced traders this type of approach is very useful when first learning to trade derivatives because it overcomes the extreme risk derivative trades pose to smaller portfolios.

Our preference is to use price leverage with ordinary shares to achieve the same effect. Then, if the trade crashes, the trader is left with listed shares. This provides a wider range of recovery options. The primary difference with derivatives is the way they stop trading after a specified period so the inexperienced trader has no prospect of recovering any of his trading capital if he fails to act before the expiry date.

Limiting position size to the maximum allowable risk is a viable strategy for traders with large accounts where the risk may translate into $10,000 to $20,000 position sizes. A variation on this approach estimates the maximum reasonable potential price fall and uses this figure to calculate the position size. In exploring these issues we concentrate on warrants, but similar conclusions apply to other derivatives.

The anticipated disaster approach assumes the trader exits after a substantial fall in the warrant price – more than 50%. This is shown by the shaded box in Figure 26.1. With an entry at $0.20 we assume an exit at $0.10, or lower. This is a broad-brush approach to warrant price performance. It recognises there may be difficulties in getting out, and it assumes substantial price falls can take place. The success of the strategy rests on the accurate estimation of the exit point.

Some warrants move slowly to these near-disaster points. Others move much more rapidly, with lots of gapping activity. There are no hard-and-fast rules available for setting this anticipated disaster point. The performance of related warrants may provide a guide, but it is always wise to err on the side of caution. This means setting a lower anticipated disaster exit point.

This strategy is a variation of the relationship between portfolio capital, entry and exit points used to determine position size. This relationship lies at the core of all risk management.

The final strategy reduces the position size to contain the loss to within 2% of trading capital. This is the application of the standard risk control methods used in equity trading. It is covered in detail in many books, including *Better Trading*. The 2% money management rule tells us the maximum allowable risk in any trade is no more than 2% of our total trading capital. If we have portfolio capital of $100,000 then the maximum allowable risk on any single trade is $2,000 which is equal to 2%. Trade or position size is not limited to $2,000 because it is unlikely the stock will stop trading. This is not true with warrants and this adds a new layer of risk.

The objective is to ensure the difference between the amount we spend at our entry price in the trade, and the amount we get back if we have to exit at the stop loss price, is no more than

2% of our total trading capital. With a $100,000 portfolio this is a $2,000 loss on the trade. The dollar size of any loss is calculated by using the proposed entry point and the proposed exit-point to contain a loss. This relationship sets the maximum allowable position size.

The key to success in this approach matches the proposed stop loss exit price with a logical chart-based support level. This is designed to prevent whipsaws and false exits triggered by a temporary weakness in the trend. The application of this calculation to ordinary stocks is straightforward. The application to derivatives is more complex.

The behaviour of the warrant price is dependent upon the behaviour of the price of the parent share. Warrant price behaviour is leveraged, so a small move in the parent stock results in a larger percentage move in the warrant, or derivative. This is what makes them so attractive as a trading opportunity.

The challenge is to manage this leverage. There are two approaches.

➜   Use the activity of the parent stock to trigger an exit in the derivative.

➜   Use the price activity of the derivative to trigger an exit.

The trader's selection of one of these approaches has a significant impact on his position size in the warrant trade. Select the first option and the trader applies standard equity analysis to the parent stock. This sets both the proposed entry price and the proposed exit price, based on a stop loss condition and chart analysis. The trader follows the exact analysis steps used in selecting any stock trading opportunity.

Rather than buying the stock to trade the opportunity, the trader turns to the warrant, buying it instead. The entry is signalled by the parent stock's price action, but the trade is implemented by the purchase of the warrant. When the parent stock delivers an exit signal, the warrant trade is closed.

Here leverage works against the trader. What is an acceptable dollar risk in the parent stock quickly turns into an unacceptable risk in the warrant. In the diagram in Figure 26.2, the risk in the parent stock is defined by an entry at $1.00 and an exit at $0.98. The loss is $2,000 or 2% of a total trading capital of $100,000. This is acceptable if we are trading the stock, but we are trading the warrant, so the relationship changes.

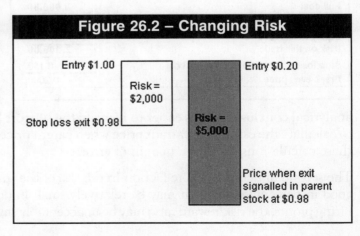

Figure 26.2 – Changing Risk

Entry $1.00

Risk = $2,000

Stop loss exit $0.98

Entry $0.20

Risk = $5,000

Price when exit signalled in parent stock at $0.98

We choose a warrant because its price action is a leveraged

multiple of the price action in the parent stock. This is excellent when prices increase in a long side trade. When prices fall in the parent the same leveraged relationship works against us as shown in the shaded area. Using the trigger points in the parent stock as a signal for an entry and exit in the warrant delivers a $5,000 loss in this example.

The exact size of the loss depends on the delta. The delta calculation defines how sensitive a financial derivative is to movements in the price of the underlying stock. It is used to assess the size of the percentage move in option and warrant prices when compared to a given move in the stock. Use the delta calculation to adjust warrant trading size so any exit price trigger generated by the parent stock is matched with an estimated warrant price. Use the estimated price as the calculation figure for determining the warrant position size under the 2% rule requirements.

In plain terms with the example in Figure 26.2, when the parent price hits $0.98, what is the price we expect the warrant to be trading at? The answer provides the exit figure for the warrant trade. The shaded area sets the warrant exit at $0.15.

The solution for risk control applies the same calculation as an equity trade, but uses the warrant entry and exit price instead of the stock price. The calculations are shown in Figure 26.3 with an entry at $0.20 and planned stop loss exit at $0.15. Applying standard risk and position calculations we find the maximum position size is $8,000. When warrant prices fall to $0.15 an exit limits the loss to $2,000.

Figure 26.3 – Matching Position Size

EQUITY DETAILS	Theoretical warrant
Equity name	
Maximum # of shares	40,000.0
Purchase price	0.200
Net cost	8,000.00
Av Brokerage	0.00
Full cost	8,000.00
RISK PARAMETERS	
Equity risk @ 2%	2,000.00
Risk on this trade	2,000.00
Stop loss exit price based on full cost	0.150
Break even price (2x brokerage)	0.2000

Reducing the position size to take into account the volatility of the warrant is the most obvious solution to the management of risk in derivative trades. This approach has two drawbacks.

The first is the difficulty in making an accurate estimate of the exit price. Delta calculations are difficult and should be treated as well-informed guesses rather than as sound analytical conclusions. It is easier to identify the support level with the parent stock than to calculate the estimated warrant price when parent prices hit the support level. Applying these calculations calls for a margin of error.

The second difficulty is the reduction in the size of the trade. Although the return may be good in percentage terms, it may be relatively small in dollar terms. Despite the leverage lifting profits, the risk/reward ratio may be unacceptably small. If we reduce the dollar return we run the danger of negating the very benefits we want from trading derivatives. We trade them because of their potential to add significant leveraged returns to our portfolio.

The safest way to apply derivative trading strategies is to limit absolute disaster risk to 2% of total trading capital. The next safest way reduces the position size based on the entry and estimated stop loss exit conditions using delta to anticipate warrant pricing.

The third strategy, shown in Figure 26.4, accepts the risk of a larger loss, letting it grow to twice the normal position size. Here the trader plans for a 4% loss of trading capital. The success of this strategy rests on excellent analysis of the parent stock to increase the probability of success. Traders who find their success rate is less than 60% cannot effectively apply this strategy because the risk is doubled by a single error. The impact of letting risk grow beyond 2% is discussed in more detail in *Better Trading*. Risk control is a more important factor than trading skill in determining long-term trading success. This strategy calls for a success rate of 70% or higher, and even then, the risk in this approach is not substantially reduced. The trade may still crash and burn.

The objective in this application is to trade at a position size optimising the returns in both dollar and percentage terms from the trade. This is the least effective strategy for controlling derivative risk because a single trade has the same impact as two losing trades managed within the 2% rules. Two trades are likely to be independently correlated. When one trade fails it does not automatically signal the failure

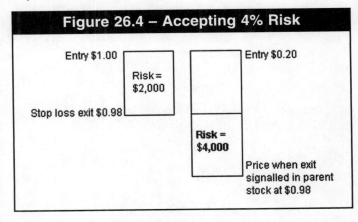

of the second trade. This diversity of risk helps to control the actual risk across multiple trades. Unless all the trades are in the same, small sub-index, there is a low probability of them all hitting their stop loss points at the same time.

The theoretical risk of two open trades may be a cumulative 4% but the practical risk is more likely to be 2%. By doubling the size of the risk in a single derivative trade we make the potential risk equal the practical risk. With a potential 4% capital loss in every trade, we can afford few mistakes before our trading capital is reduced substantially.

Despite the limitation on returns, our preference is to keep derivative risk within the confines of the standard application of the 2% rule. This does not prevent a crash but it reduces the chances of a crash and burn. Planning is the first step towards success but sloppy trade execution is the major threat to short-term and day trading. The mechanics of better trade execution are explored in the next chapter.

≡SHARPSHOOTER'S NOTES

➡ If you plan to ride the trade to zero then position size must match the maximum dollar risk calculated with the 2% rule.

➡ Plan for a significant fall in derivative prices and set position size using the 2% rule based on these assumptions.

➡ Set derivative exits based on delta calculations to contain loss to 2% in the derivative trade based on parent price exit triggers.

➡ Expanding risk to 4% is suitable only for skilled traders with consistent success rates above 70%.

Chapter 27

MECHANICS
OF EXECUTION

The difference between tools and toys is clear to every craftsman. Trading the market is a skill and a craft in every timeframe. Day trading and short-term trading take those skills to a faster and more polished level, where the control and speed of order execution is vital. Applying these trading techniques with brokerage services which do not offer stop loss facilities is an invitation to witness the execution of your trading capital. It is the difference between playing with toys and working with tools.

All trading comes down to buying and selling within a centralised continuous auction. We generally do not have to try to guess the intentions a professional market maker. This is why so many imported day trading books make little sense in our order driven market. Instead we go head to head with the person on the other side of the trade. They may be a professional, or a beginner making their first trade. There are no L-plates in the market.

Although we talk of the market as an auction, it is not the best description of the trading process. The auctions we are familiar with involve continuously rising prices. Bid for a house, leftover furniture from the Ansett airline collapse, or equipment at a farm-clearing sale and prices move only in one direction – up.

The stockmarket is closer to haggling in the markets of Indonesia, Malaysia and Shanghai. There is a price on every item but it is negotiable. The stall-holder wants the maximum price possible. The tourist wants to pay the lowest price achievable. The starting spread is usually very wide but somewhere between these two extremes lies a point of agreement. It is not necessarily in the middle, nor is it constant. How much you pay depends on your skill and when haggling in these markets you are pitched against professionals.

Each of these transactions has a price maker and a price taker. Knowing when to act appropriately as a taker rather than a price maker is a matter of experience and dignity. Long-term success depends on knowing the difference, both in the Tung Choi street market in Hong Kong and in our ASX market.

MAKE OR TAKE?

Who 'makes' prices and who 'takes' prices? Successful short-term trades depend heavily on getting the price we want. Most of us have had the experience of making the high for the day when we buy a stock, or 'printing' the low of the day when we sell. While we put this down to experience in individual trades, the distinction is more important when dealing with low-priced stock where a price change of a cent or two makes a difference to the success or failure of our trade.

We 'make' the price when we outbid all others in the order line. We play an aggressive part in the traded price. We 'take' a price when we match the buy or sell order already in the line. We do not add any new order. We simply accept the price on offer.

There are times when we want to be a price maker. At other times it is more appropriate to be a price taker. Understanding the difference improves our trading. The CHF five-minute tick chart spread over two days in Figure 27.1 show examples of both approaches. On the first day, Monday, CHF started a fast moving rally, driving prices from $0.76 to $0.98. Price takers had ample opportunity to participate in the rally.

The next day many people expected the rally to continue, particularly as the DOW had staged a good recovery. The price makers wanted to get ahead of their competitors so they outbid each other in the order line. The opening of trade was driven by price makers – and they failed. After the initial burst of buying, prices dropped for the remainder of the day. The price makers missed out on much better entry prices enjoyed by the price takers who collected 18% for the day – low to close.

The price maker sets the opening price. If the opening price is near the closing price of the previous day, this is not a disadvantage. The traders who bought the first traded shares on Monday were price makers. Their buying drove the price up, but it was supported by solid buying from other traders interested in CHF. The result was a steady rise during the day.

The price maker set the opening price on Tuesday. This gap up price is created when buyers outbid each other in an attempt to get the market open. The price maker accepts the risk of setting the opening price rather than taking what is offered once trading starts.

With CHF this was not a good strategy. Once the opening price was made at $1.04, aggressive buying pushed the price higher on small trades and low volume. In this case, being a price maker was a bad strategy as CHF was available at much lower prices during the day.

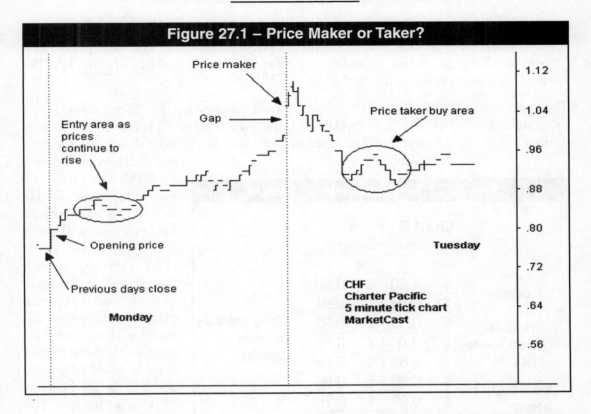

Figure 27.1 – Price Maker or Taker?

Price maker

Gap →

Price taker buy area

Entry area as prices continue to rise

Opening price

Previous days close

Monday

Tuesday

CHF
Charter Pacific
5 minute tick chart
MarketCast

1.12
1.04
.96
.88
.80
.72
.64
.56

The behaviour of the market as it opens is a good guide to which is the best strategy to follow. The order line, as shown in the extract in Figure 27.2, shows when it is useful to be a price maker. The top buying bid at $1.00 is higher than the previous close at $0.90. The sellers have also lifted their prices above the previous close. In this example the first sell offer is at $0.99. The sell line has low volume, and is uneven. It moves steadily above $0.99. We need access to the full order line to make this judgement. A display limited to the top 10 or 20 orders in the line is not good enough.

Here we see strong buying pressure and weak selling pressure. These sellers want to hold onto their stock. Typically only one or two trades may be available at each price level.

Figure 27.2 – Sample Order Line

Price maker OK

Chart A	
buy order line	sell order line
$ 1.00	$ 0.99
$ 0.99	$ 1.00
$ 0.98	$ 1.01
$ 0.95	$ 1.02
$ 0.90	$ 1.03
$ 0.89	$ 1.04
$ 0.88	$ 1.05
$ 0.86	$ 1.06
$ 0.85	$ 1.07

Previous close price →

This order line prevailed on Monday on the CHF chart in Figure 27.1. When we see this relationship there is an increased probability of prices continuing to rise so it pays to be a price maker. We place our buying order, perhaps at $1.01 to get to the head of the line. We 'make' the opening price by lifting the bid.

The order line extract in Figure 27.3 shows a situation to avoid. We do not want to be a price maker here. The first clue of weakness is the lowest sell price. It is at the same level as the close of the previous day. The best buy order is at $1.00. Why does a seller leave a sell order in the market for $0.90 when he sees a buy order at $1.00? He sells at this level because he knows he will get a higher price due to the ASX opening match procedures. He effectively gets the market open price and believes this may be about the best price available during the day. He could be wrong, and if he is, the buyer at $1.00 gets a bargain. The order line suggests the seller is probably correct.

Figure 27.3 – Price Maker's Risk

Chart B	buy order line	sell order line	
Few buyers	$ 1.00	$ 0.90	
	$ 0.99	$ 0.91	
Previous	$ 0.98	$ 0.92	Many sellers
close →	$ 0.90	$ 0.93	at lower
price	$ 0.89	$ 0.94	prices
Most buyers	$ 0.88	$ 0.95	
below	$ 0.86	$ 0.96	
yesterdays	$ 0.85	$ 0.97	
close	$ 0.84	$ 0.98	

This order line is tight knit. It goes up from $0.90 to $0.91, $0.92 in consistent $0.01 increments. Plenty of other shareholders have the same feelings as the seller at $0.90. They believe the rally is close to finishing and their selling helps confirm this. It is more than a matter of sellers overwhelming buyers. The way they have lined up to take reverse advantage of the ASX matching process to get the best exit price on the open reveals their intentions.

When trading starts on this order line we see the same result as shown on the right-hand chart in Figure 27.1. The sellers just keep coming, and they sell at progressively lower prices to lock in profits. In this environment we do not want to be a price maker.

A price taker does not attempt to bully or lead the market. The trader waits for prices to fall back to levels consistent with his trading plan, and then he enters, accepting the current bid or offer. This is a more passive approach to the market and it does not involve a rush to start trading in the first minutes of the day.

The XAO chart in Figure 27.4 shows a rapid rise in the first 15 minutes of trading, driven by a crowd reaction to higher overnight closes in the US. Once the initial buying, driven by the price makers, has finished, the market is dominated by the price takers. The result is a slow decline, and a prolonged sideways drift finishing with a slight upwards bias.

Price making traders acted in the first 15 minutes of trading, buying at or near the highs for the day. Price taking traders who

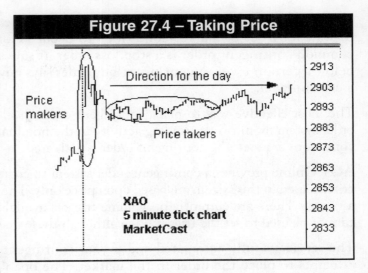

Figure 27.4 – Taking Price

Direction for the day

Price makers

Price takers

XAO
5 minute tick chart
MarketCast

2913
2903
2893
2883
2873
2863
2853
2843
2833

turned to their screens after the first 30 minutes of trading obtained better buy prices.

TOOLS, NOT TOYS

Trading without a stop loss is like driving a fast car with your eyes closed. You may travel some distance but eventually you will crash.

Brokers who do not offer stop loss services are like used car salesmen who sell cheap, but very fast and expensive motor cars. They are cheap because they have no seat belts, no airbags, and no brakes. When the customer drives the car at any speed down the road he has few effective means of stopping. Drive at high speed and the crash, and capital burn, is inevitable.

I believe one of the most important safety features that ought to be introduced to the Australian brokerage industry is the compulsory availability of stop loss facilities for clients. Very few brokerages offer stop loss facilities. The effort to help save their clients and capital is apparently too much for them.

The effective use and execution of stop loss orders for day traders and short-term traders is one of the most significant factors in success. We use AOT Online – www.aotonline.com.au – to place electronic stop loss and other contingent orders. They use the Web Iress platform which is used by a number of other brokerages. Some of these have chosen not to activate the stop loss and contingent order facilities. In the section below we look at how the AOT order screens are structured. Use these facilities as a benchmark to judge the performance of your current brokerage arrangements. It may be time to trade up to real tools.

A stop loss is a contingent order. This order structure is used when the trader wants to wait for a set of market conditions to occur before he takes action. The most common contingent order is a stop loss order. It says sell this stock if the price falls below a certain level. A contingent buy order says buy this stock if prices rise above a certain level.

The most effective way to place contingent orders is electronically. The computerised order system monitors the trading activity in the nominated stock. When the buy or sell conditions are met, the contingent order is activated.

AOT Online provides a contingent order system to create stop loss and buy orders. The criteria used in this system are based upon price only. The last bid or ask prices are used as a trigger. There are currently no volume triggers available and a percentage movement cannot be used to set the trigger price although these may be added in the future.

The service is fully automated and if your contingent order is triggered, the system attempts to place the order in the market. The opening phase of the market often shows increased volatility. To avoid having the stop loss order triggered unnecessarily, traders either drop the stop loss trigger one tick below the planned stop loss, or wait until the opening phase is completed before activating the stop loss order. Using a time delay is a more effective method. In Figure 27.5 the stop loss order does not become active until after 10:20 a.m.

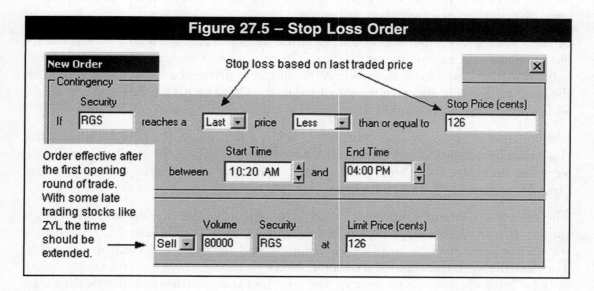

Figure 27.5 – Stop Loss Order

Traders selecting bid or offer as the stop loss trigger should be aware the order may be triggered during the opening or closing market match phase. Stops may be triggered purely by changes in the bid and ask order lines rather than actual traded prices. By extending the time limit to 5:00 p.m. and using the last traded price the trader has an opportunity to exit in the closing settlement period after 4:00 p.m. There are times when this is an advantage.

CONTINGENT BUY ORDERS

A further advantage of the electronic contingent order system is the ability to place contingent buy orders. This is most useful when traders are waiting for a particular price move. This might be a breakout from an up-sloping triangle. In the example shown in Figure 27.6 a price move to $1.26 signals a triangle breakout. The trader buys as soon as this price trigger appears. He does not have to monitor the price during the day and he no longer has to wait to download end-of-day data before acting on the day after the breakout.

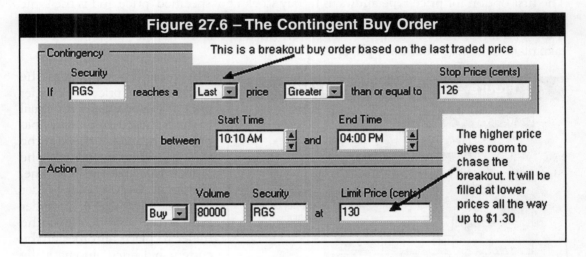

Figure 27.6 – The Contingent Buy Order

Contingent buy orders are most effectively executed by placing the buy limit price higher than the trigger price – in this example it is lifted to $1.30. Once the breakout occurs there is a good chance of prices moving rapidly. A buy order with a limit set on, or just above, the breakout trigger might not be filled. By setting a higher limit, the system enters a buy at this higher price and immediately takes out all lower offers up to the selected limit price. This enhances the probability of the buy order being filled and effectively completes the trade by meeting the lower 'at-market' asking price.

The real advantage of contingent orders is the flexibility they give traders. Instead of watching a screen all day, we can do something else, go to our day job, or relax. The automatic electronic execution of the order makes trading easier and more efficient.

The simplest buy order instructs the broker to purchase a set number of shares at a particular price. This is the order option provided by many online brokers. However, some electronic brokers provide a broader range of buy order options. This gives the trader an opportunity to set an exact buy order suitable for a variety of conditions.

There are three options in the advanced order screen used by AOT Online. They are:

1.   Price type

2.   Order type

3.   Expiry date.

Each includes a variety of choices. This is intelligent use of electronic ordering. It allows you to duplicate the service of the very best and most expensive full-service brokers. And even then, only a few full-service brokers provide a stop loss service for anyone but their most valued clients.

The first option for price type allows us to buy stock at a 'specified' price and is the same as the basic buy order screen shown in Figure 27.7. The order is only executed when ANZ trades at $18.18. If the order is not completely filled it remains in place until more trades take place at $18.18 or a lower price.

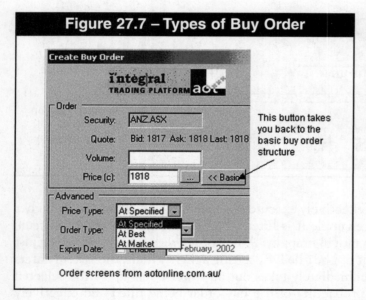

Order screens from aotonline.com.au/

The second option buys the stock 'at best' price. The order price is automatically set equal to the highest current buy or bid price in the market depth at the time the order is created. The order is placed in the order line, but not at the head of the order line. The advantage of this order type is the way it allows the trader to place an order at the current bid price automatically in a fast-moving market.

The final price type option is an 'at-market' order. Here the order price is equal to the lowest sell or ask price in the market depth lines, at the time the order is created. This order matches the asking price so the order is filled as soon as it is sent to market. At-market orders always meet the asking price so do not use them if you want to join the current highest bidding line.

These orders carry an unexpected twist. If the order is not completely filled at the specified price level then the order does not automatically adjust upwards to chase rising prices. If we want 10,000 shares, but only get 8,000, the unfilled portion of the order remains in the market. The order price must be amended for it to trade at the next price level.

We make a true at-market order where the order is filled at progressively higher prices by selecting other order options. This includes using a set price order placed well above the current highest ask. It is filled at lower prices all the way up to your specified price if necessary.

These at-market orders are executed immediately when the market is trading. When these types of orders are placed outside of market hours, such as prior to the open, there are some important modifications.

Specifying an at-market order in these pre-open periods does not mean the order price is automatically amended as the market price changes. Once an order has been generated before the market opens, the price is only changed manually. This also applies when a stock has been suspended from trading prior to a news announcement. These interactive orders only operate with an actively traded market. When an order is generated outside market trading times there is always the possibility the market depth may be further amended by other traders so your order is no longer at the market price when trading resumes.

This order instruction is used in rally and momentum trades to capture the current traded price. Chasing the market price in this situation carries some additional risks as the market often overreacts in the initial 20 minutes of trading. Market orders are used with caution in this environment and there are advantages in delaying the start time for the order.

ADVANCED ORDER OPTIONS

The order type screen gives the trader total control over the way the order is executed. The first menu choice is a two-part instruction as shown in Figure 27.8. The 'default lifetime' choice means the order remains in the market for a maximum of nine weeks. If the order falls too far outside the market range set by the ASX, the order is withdrawn at the end of the day.

The second choice makes the order good for the day only. Unfilled, or partially filled orders at the end of the day are deleted from the order lines. The third choice is an 'all or none' order. If we use this and place a buy order for 10,000 ANZ at $18.18 then the order is filled only if it is possible to buy the 10,000 shares in a single

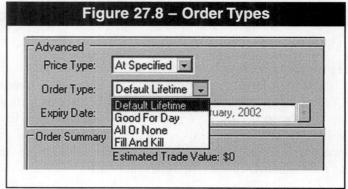

Figure 27.8 – Order Types

purchase. The order trades only if the full volume at the specified price is available. There are no partial fills. This order structure is used with caution as an order may be filled in several tranches over the course of the day as prices move above and below our preferred order price. A set price order is filled in this situation, but the 'all or none' order may remain unfilled. This order structure is used when position size is critical to the success of the trade, or where the trader wants to ensure minimum liquidity requirements are met.

The final choice is 'fill and kill'. This order trades immediately at the specified price. Any remaining volume of the order which was not filled is withdrawn – killed. If no order exists on the opposite side of the market when the order is created, the order fails. This order is used in fast-moving markets where you want to pay a specific price for the stock. You are not interested in the trade if you cannot get stock at the price you specify. The danger is missing out completely, or collecting only a handful of shares. This may mean the trade is useless if your trade plan was based on 10,000 shares and you end up with just 100.

These order instructions are applied in slightly different ways in futures markets. L-Quay Futures uses the Iress system for SFE trading. In futures trading you should note the following changes.

Good Until Cancelled

This order does not have an expiry date and remains in the market until fully traded.

Market Limit Order

The order is filled at the price specified. The bid price may be over the current sell price, and the sell price may be under the current bid price. This is the opposite of the limit order.

Limit Order

If the bid order is placed above the current sell price it fails. If a sell order is placed below the current buy price, it fails.

Fill and Kill

The order is active for 20 seconds. Any untraded volume at the end of this time is killed.

The final order choice is to set the expiry date. This tells the system how long the order is valid.

This order structure is used with some trades based on chart patterns which have definite completion dates. A triangle pattern may show a completion date of 20 February 2002. Like many traders, we want to catch this price as it moves back towards the value of the up-sloping trend line. We place our buy order at this level, but it remains valid only for a few days. The screen shot in Figure 27.9 sets an end date for this order. The electronic order system makes it easier for the trader to use these time-based orders without the need to remember to cancel the order manually.

Electronic order systems offer many potential advantages in fine-tuning the exact execution of our buy and sell orders. Unfortunately, only a few brokerages currently permit clients to make full use of these advantages. Most times we use the basic order screen because it meets our needs. We simply enter the price we wish to pay for the stock, check the calculated value of the trade and place the order. When we want to use a specialist order to trade a specific opportunity effectively there are advantages in using the advanced buy screen.

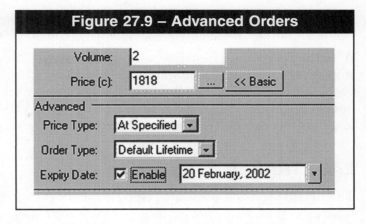

Figure 27.9 – Advanced Orders

HYBRID STOPS

Traders have a choice of a fully-automated, computer-driven system or a manually executed system where action is triggered by computer alerts. DataTech – www.datatech.net.au – uses a hybrid stop loss system. It works in conjunction with E*TRADE and has developed a fully-managed, online 'Stop Loss/Start Gain' system. Clients of DataTech place their buy and sell orders directly through E*TRADE.

DataTech uses an electronic monitoring system to detect when the client's price and volume order conditions have been met. Once met, the order is manually executed within seconds by DataTech staff.

One of the problems with an automatic stop loss system is that stock may be dumped or sold, well below market prices when prices gap down. The electronically triggered manual stop loss execution requires human intervention. Many traders feel this is an advantage.

This is stop loss execution by a third party acting on your electronic instructions. The trader purchases 5,000 TLS at $5.50 through E*TRADE and immediately places a stop loss order at $5.10 through DataTech's website, as shown on the order screen in

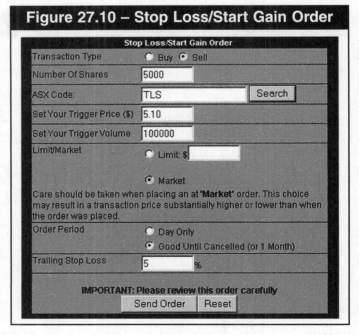

Figure 27.10 – Stop Loss/Start Gain Order

Figure 27.10. Traders have the option of placing a Trigger Volume with their order which helps prevent being 'spiked out' on negligible turnover.

'At-market' orders are also accepted and if a Trigger Volume is included, all turnover traded below the client's Trigger Price is calculated and when exceeded, the order is executed.

A 'trailing percentage stop loss' order is also available as a means of protecting profits. The stop loss order is amended upwards to follow a strengthening share price. The trigger price of these Good Until Cancelled orders follow a share price higher. The amended trigger price is calculated from the closing sale price each day the order is outstanding. This stop loss and order management service offered by DataTech is an intelligent use of technology.

LAST TRADES

The hybrid approach offers interesting possibilities and the example below details actual trade execution. This is not *our* fishing story. It comes from one of our newsletter readers and shows how this hybrid stop loss approach is applied to a stop loss exit. Two brokers were used in this trade and it provides an ideal case study of the difference between tools and toys.

On 27 March the support level shown in Figure 27.11 was broken as 2.6 million shares were dumped on the market. On Thursday morning 28 March a full-service broker was instructed to sell 9,000 shares if the company traded $0.01 below the previous day's low of $1.27. A second stop loss order was placed with DataTech at $1.27.

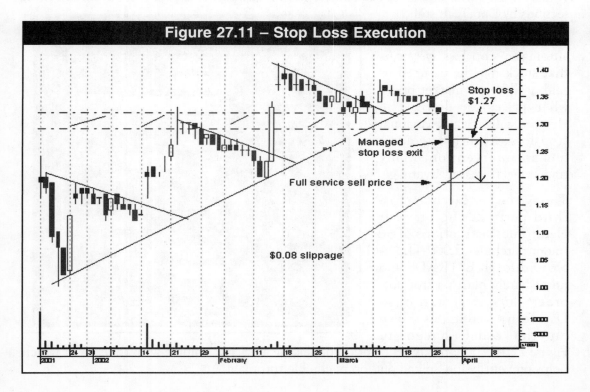

Figure 27.11 – Stop Loss Execution

Just after 2 p.m. the trader was advised by his full-service broker that the company CEO had resigned. Unfortunately the broker had been out to lunch when the news was announced. The price fell on the news and he had executed the stop at $1.19 when he returned from lunch.

Compare this with the hybrid stop loss approach. DataTech sold at the stop loss price of $1.27 in the hour before the announcement. The manual implementation of the electronically monitored stop loss order delivered a better result.

The course of sales data in Figure 27.12 shows the way the two sell orders were handled.

As we noted in earlier chapters, the market leaks like a sieve so news is rarely totally unexpected. In the hour before the official announcement it was possible to exit this trade at the specified stop loss price.

Figure 27.12 – Course of Sales Extract

Time	Price
10:00	$1.30 (open)
10:09	$1.29
11:10	$1.28
12:28	$1.27 **(stop loss triggered and sold by Datatech)**
12:28-13:44	$1.27- $1.28
13:34	$1.27 (Announcement to market)
13:57	$1.15 Low for the day
14:02	$1.19 **(Full service broker returned from lunch and sold parcel on the rebound)**

The DataTech system is structured so no order is left unattended. If an operator leaves his desk, the alert comes up on another operator's desk if triggered. In this case the full-service broker had lunch – at the trader's expense.

Successful trading calls for careful planning and intelligent choices. Traders aiming for short-term or day trading success limit their ability to succeed if they play with delayed so-called real time data, slow order execution, and without stop loss facilities. The choice of tools or toys is not really in your hands. The market soon destroys those who take on trading in these timeframes with toys.

Survival in this area is not a tourist's snapshot that captures a single moment of success and happiness. Survival comes from consistent trading with the level of lethal accuracy demanded of the finest sharp shooters. These are the cavalry tactics of trading, so plan screen raids with care and execute with precision.

≡CAVALRY NOTES

→ Understand who makes and takes price.

→ Use the order line to decide the best strategy to make or take price.

→ Always use stops.

→ Electronic contingent orders offer significant advantages.

→ Understand electronic order instructions to ensure the best execution.

→ Hybrid electronic and manual stops offer alternative execution strategies.

→ Volume trigger and percentage trailing stops are available.

Chapter 28

SCREEN
RAIDERS

D ay trading is screen-based trading and there is no escape from this reality. Each trade requires our full attention. Some trades demand we stay in front of a live data-feed screen for the duration of the entire trade. Day trading is done most effectively in short bursts to avoid burn out. Traders walk away from the screens, taking a break to go fishing, to travel or just relax. They return refreshed and are more effective traders.

Most traders use short-term and day trading tactics as one part of their wider approach to the market. In nervous markets, where an uptrend is threatening to fall, it makes sense to shift to short-term trading strategies. They reduce the risk in each trade because the timeframe is limited. Good short-term opportunities exist in a bull market, but most traders follow the easy-to-trade trend opportunities. Contrary to the impression given by popular press coverage, day trading is most effective and more widely applied in nervous markets. There is not the same bull market surge in numbers of those who claim to be day traders. Instead, a smaller number of skilled traders consistently apply a number of successful day trading strategies.

The core of practical application of these market approaches relies on the screens available to any private trader at a reasonable cost. They are not free. Trading with free, but delayed, or non-dynamic data, is trading with toys. This is a tough market so you cannot afford to trade with anything other than real-time data. Despite some fancy advertising, real-time data means data delivered in a fraction of a second after the trade takes place on the SEATS system. Forget the ingenuous distinctions between dynamic, and dynamically-updated data. Data is either a real-time data flow or it is not.

The screen shots in this chapter illustrate the components of real-time data feeds, real-time charting and order execution screens. They follow the combination I use. The exact combination you use may be different. Treat these screen shots as an example of what is currently available. Shop around to assemble the pieces you want. The best combination is unlikely to come from a single supplier. These are the screens and we are the raiders.

MAPPING MARKET TERRAIN

We start with an overview of the general market. The screen shot in Figure 28.1 comes from the MarketCast broadcast data service – www.marketcast.com.au. This is a data signal delivered alongside the SBS television signal, or by satellite. The company provides a decoder to plug into your desktop computer. An extension cable runs from your television aerial to the decoder which extracts the data signal. This is not a teletext signal so the data is displayed as shown in the screen shot.

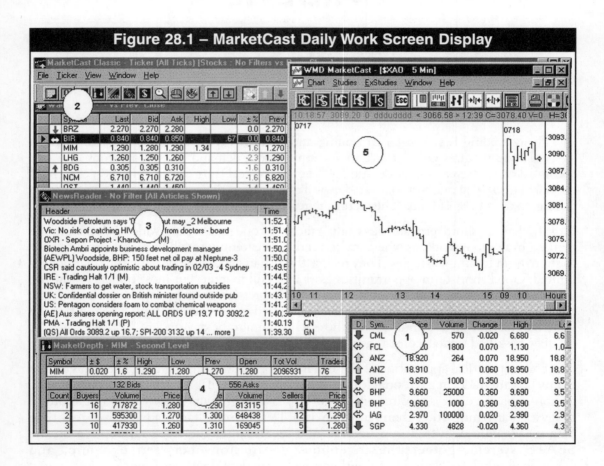

Figure 28.1 – MarketCast Daily Work Screen Display

This data service has several advantages. The most important are its speed and reliability. This data is as close to real-time as possible without having a direct feed from the ASX SEATS computers. Additionally, the broadcast delivery frees up the internet connection for other uses. Traders do not need to be online all day, and nor do they need a dedicated internet connection.

We run this display all day on a separate computer. The alert function sounds an audible alarm when buy or sell conditions are met. In slow moving trades this gives us time to log onto the net and execute our orders. The screen is a necessary requirement for short-term and intra-day trading but it is also useful for monitoring longer-term position trades. The screen has five main elements.

The first, in Figure 28.2, is the trade ticker. This shows every trade as it takes place. The arrows show where prices have increased, decreased, or remained unchanged since the last trade in the stock. On an active trading day this live screen moves too quickly to follow. It is a useful indicator of the speed or velocity of trading. It helps to gauge the level of excitement or panic.

The watch screen in Figure 28.3 is the first main working screen. It includes all open positions and all stocks which we are potentially interested in trading. The price increase and percentage gain for the day are interesting, but the most important feature is the price alert columns.

These are used to set trigger points for each trade. The BIR trade includes a high price figure to alert us when a breakout has occurred. This is a pattern-based trade, so the first trade at $0.86 tells us price has broken above the pattern. This is used with the Tony Oz approach, and when the alert is triggered we turn to the internet screen for order verification and execution. The lower price, $0.80, is the stop loss level.

Figure 28.2 – Real Time Ticker

Ticker (All Ticks) [Stocks : No Filters vs Prev. Clo...

D.	Sym...	Price	Volume	Change	High	Low	Ti
⟷	BHP	9.660	3935	0.360	9.690	9.500	
⇧	ASX	12.990	1123	0.040	12.990	12.870	
⬇	AMC	8.060	167	0.050	8.100	8.050	
⇧	SRP	5.190	1500	-0.010	5.230	5.180	
⟷	NCP	10.130	1127	0.050	10.180	10.100	
⇧	NCP	10.130	374	0.050	10.180	10.100	
⟷	NCP	10.110	16900	0.030	10.180	10.100	
⟷	WOW	11.930	417	-0.100	12.100	11.800	
⟷	WOW	11.930	130	-0.100	12.100	11.800	
⬇	WOW	11.930	700	-0.100	12.100	11.800	
⟷	WSF	14.350	385	0.100	14.350	14.250	
⟷	CRG	8.250	500	0.000	8.250	8.250	
⟷	BHP	9.660	1065	0.360	9.690	9.500	
⟷	BHP	9.660	75	0.360	9.690	9.500	

Figure 28.3 – Watch Screens and Alerts

WatchPage - - vs Prev. Close

	Symbol	Last	Bid	Ask	High	Low	± %	Prev	Open	Last	± $	High	Low	Tot Vol
▶	BRZ	2.270	2.270	2.280			0.0	2.270	2.270	215	0.000	2.280	2.270	14327
↑	BIR	0.850	0.840	0.850	.86	.80	1.2	0.840	0.850	2000	0.010	0.850	0.840	79764
	MIM	1.290	1.280	1.290	1.50	1.27	1.6	1.270	1.280	20000	0.020	1.290	1.280	2663189
	LHG	1.260	1.260	1.270			-2.3	1.290	1.280	700	-0.030	1.280	1.260	572085
↑	BDG	0.305	0.305	0.310	Buy and sell		-1.6	0.310	0.305	4200	-0.005	0.305	0.300	165000
	NCM	6.710	6.700	6.710	alerts are		-1.6	6.820	6.820	5198	-0.110	6.820	6.690	397233
	OST	1.440	1.440	1.450	set here		-1.4	1.460	1.440	950	-0.020	1.450	1.430	345319
	SEN	0.135	0.135	0.140			0.0	0.135	0.135	12858	0.000	0.135	0.135	62858

The MIM trade is an open position. Our stop loss is set at $1.26 and the screen is structured so we get an audible alarm when MIM trades at $1.27. Our electronic stop loss is already in place but we use this screen to alert us to impending doom. The sell alert at $1.50 is well above market. If this alert sounds we turn to the depth of market screens to fine-tune our exit.

Some trades rely on news events, including earnings and dividend announcements. We have suggested that most times these announcements are carefully leaked to the media beforehand. The screen display in Figure 28.4 is where they show up before they appear on the television news or in the financial press. This news feed comes from AAP and the Australian Stock Exchange. The full details of each headline are viewed in the sidebar, or enlarged to a full screen with a mouse click.

Figure 28.4 – Live News and Exchange Announcements

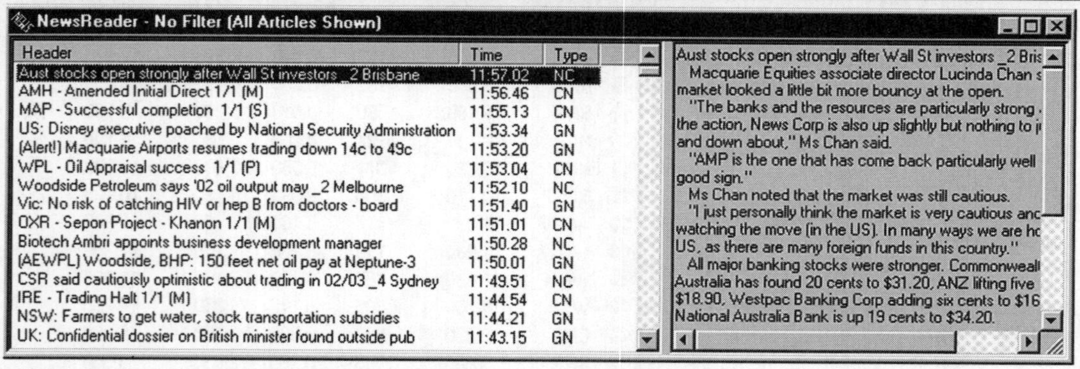

This type of news feed is vital to success for strategies which rely on trading surprise news and other unexpected events. We supplement this service with the news and market feed from CNBC-Asia to provide a broader coverage of world markets and activity.

The real working screen in this display is the depth-of-market and course-of-trades display shown in Figure 28.5. We use this to verify trading orders and to decide the best way to ensure our order is executed. This information is also available from the broker's screens but we find there is an advantage in making the initial assessment with the MarketCast screen. When we log onto the net we are less likely to be frustrated by slow internet connections. We already know the market situation so orders are placed quickly.

The course of trades is the stock-specific equivalent of the real-time tick data screen. It tells us how trading is developing with this stock. This gives us a tactical advantage in setting the buy or sell order and this edge is sometimes significant in intra-day or fast moving rally trades. This screen layout provides the detail of the market terrain where our trades are placed.

Figure 28.5 – Depth of Market, Order Lines and Course of Trades

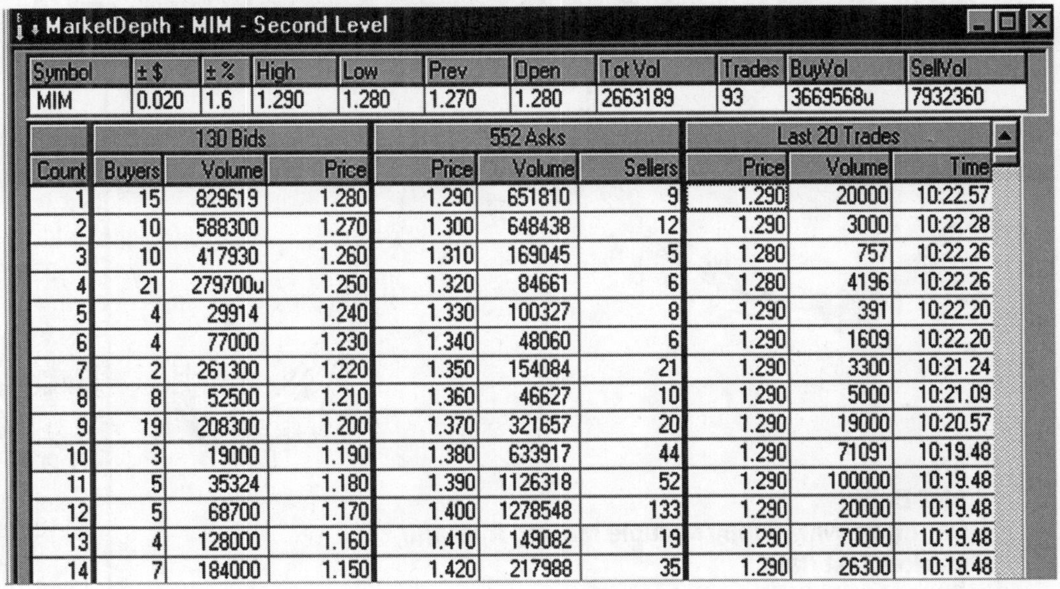

MarketDepth - MIM - Second Level

Symbol	± $	± %	High	Low	Prev	Open	Tot Vol	Trades	BuyVol	SellVol
MIM	0.020	1.6	1.290	1.280	1.270	1.280	2663189	93	3669568u	7932360

130 Bids				552 Asks			Last 20 Trades		
Count	Buyers	Volume	Price	Price	Volume	Sellers	Price	Volume	Time
1	15	829619	1.280	1.290	651810	9	1.290	20000	10:22.57
2	10	588300	1.270	1.300	648438	12	1.290	3000	10:22.28
3	10	417930	1.260	1.310	169045	5	1.280	757	10:22.26
4	21	279700u	1.250	1.320	84661	6	1.280	4196	10:22.26
5	4	29914	1.240	1.330	100327	8	1.290	391	10:22.20
6	4	77000	1.230	1.340	48060	6	1.290	1609	10:22.20
7	2	261300	1.220	1.350	154084	21	1.290	3300	10:21.24
8	8	52500	1.210	1.360	46627	10	1.290	5000	10:21.09
9	19	208300	1.200	1.370	321657	20	1.290	19000	10:20.57
10	3	19000	1.190	1.380	633917	44	1.290	71091	10:19.48
11	5	35324	1.180	1.390	1126318	52	1.290	100000	10:19.48
12	5	68700	1.170	1.400	1278548	133	1.290	20000	10:19.48
13	4	128000	1.160	1.410	149082	19	1.290	70000	10:19.48
14	7	184000	1.150	1.420	217988	35	1.290	26300	10:19.48

CHARTING ACTIVITY

Intra-day and short-term trades are usually planned on end-of-day charts. We use the GuppyTraders Essentials package and MetaStock for this analysis. During the day we use intra-day tick, and five-minute charts to monitor short-term trades. The standard charting package supplied with the MarketCast data feed is shown in Figure 28.1 on page 260. It is a more than adequate intra-day charting package.

We combine the real-time version of the GuppyTraders Essentials package to chart intra-day prices as shown in Figure 28.6. This allows us to apply the Guppy Multiple Moving Average and count back line calculations easily to intra-day charts. This charting package is compatible with MarketCast, MarketSource, Orange Data and a growing number of other real-time data suppliers.

Many internet providers including AOT Online, Sanford, Hubb data, E*TRADE, ComSec and others provide internet-based charting. These are useful as a last minute backup but they do not always offer a good range of indicators. They are also sometimes excruciatingly slow to load – usually just when you need them most. They are best suited to traders who occasionally use short-term trading techniques.

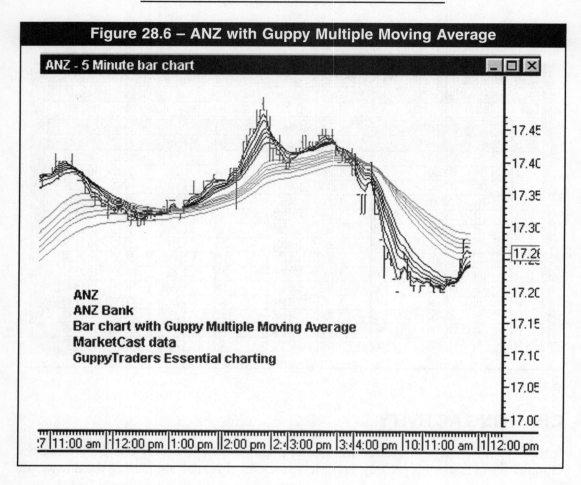

Figure 28.6 – ANZ with Guppy Multiple Moving Average

ANZ - 5 Minute bar chart

ANZ
ANZ Bank
Bar chart with Guppy Multiple Moving Average
MarketCast data
GuppyTraders Essential charting

THE LAY OF THE TRADE

Internet screens provide three types of services. They include the ability to track news and trading action in the same ways as the broadcast service from MarketCast. They provide an order execution facility, and finally a research facility.

It is always useful to delve into the background of the company prior to making a trade. If our trade is based on an earnings announcement then this research facility tells us when the last announcement was made. Armed with this date we turn to the end-of-day chart and evaluate how price behaved at the time. It provides valuable clues as to how it might behave this time round. Internet providers like Hubb Data – www.hubb.com.au – are very useful in this search to establish the lay of the trade. As a service backed by Dow Jones Telerate, it also provides access to data from markets throughout the world as shown in Figure 28.7. Many brokerage services also provide this facility for Australian markets.

Figure 28.7 – Hubb Data Screen

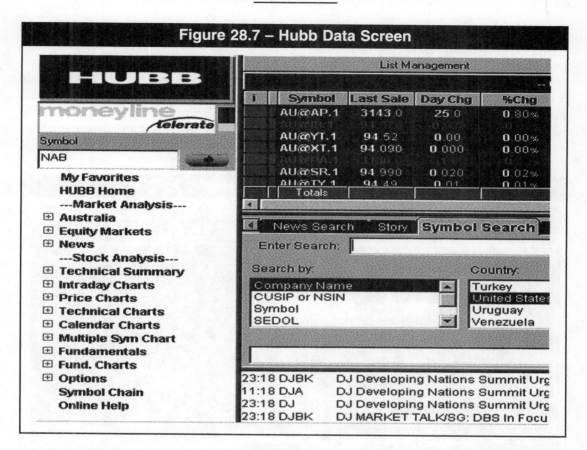

Figure 28.8 – Dividend Information

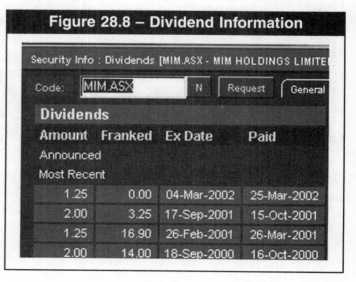

The internet shines when it comes to research. The details of past dividend dates shown in Figure 28.8 make it easier to anticipate the times when smarter traders are beginning to build positions in anticipation of good dividend announcements. This is an edge in assessing the most appropriate warrants for trading strategies based on dividend releases. The data provider, JustData – www.justdata.com.au – provides a rolling list of last year's dividend announcement dates.

Other research and non-chart based analytical tools include the market map available from AOT Online – www.aotonline.com.au. This is designed to show how each sector is performing on a real-time basis. Sectors are displayed on a graduated colour and area scale. All the stocks in each sector are contained in a separate box. The 'Materials' sector is outlined in white in Figure 28.9. Within each sector the performance of individual stocks is displayed and details are brought to the front with a mouse click as shown. This type of display provides traders with an alternative way of identifying real-time market strength and strong sectors.

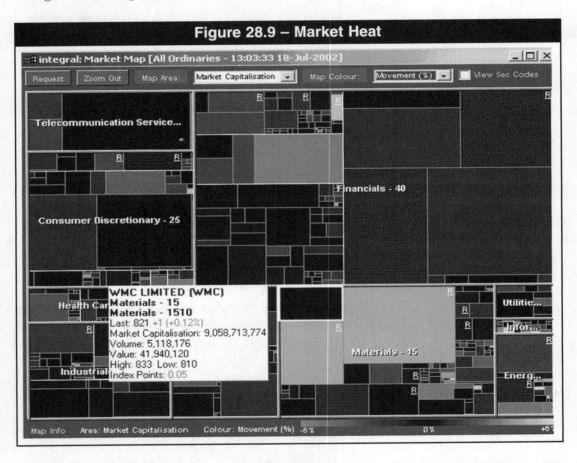

Figure 28.9 – Market Heat

With any live data feed we expect to run basic price analysis scans to identify stocks with gap activity, percentage gains and other features. These scanning tools are a feature of Hubb Data, AOT Online and other internet suppliers. We use the scanning module in MarketCast as shown in Figure 28.10. This real scan includes 16 options. These analysis results help in the final selection of the day's best trading candidate based on volume, leverage and trading velocity.

Figure 28.10 – Market Scan

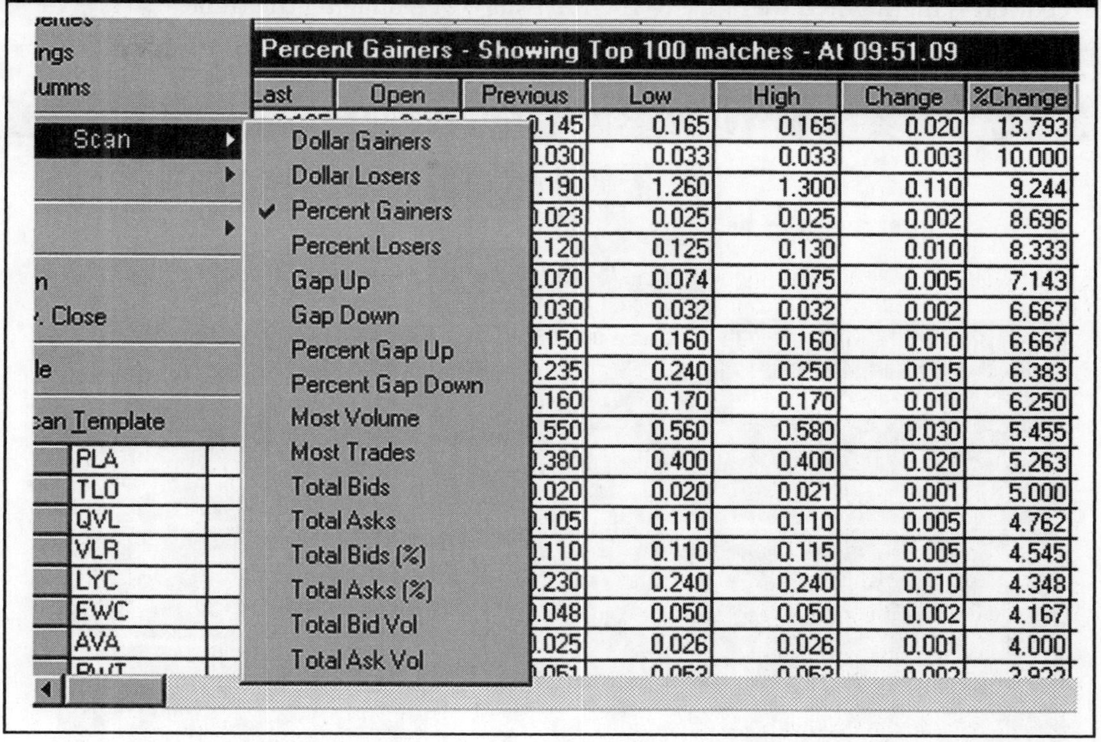

		Percent Gainers - Showing Top 100 matches - At 09:51.09					
Last	Open	Previous	Low	High	Change	%Change
		0.145	0.165	0.165	0.020	13.793
		0.030	0.033	0.033	0.003	10.000
		1.190	1.260	1.300	0.110	9.244
		0.023	0.025	0.025	0.002	8.696
		0.120	0.125	0.130	0.010	8.333
		0.070	0.074	0.075	0.005	7.143
		0.030	0.032	0.032	0.002	6.667
		0.150	0.160	0.160	0.010	6.667
		0.235	0.240	0.250	0.015	6.383
		0.160	0.170	0.170	0.010	6.250
		0.550	0.560	0.580	0.030	5.455
		0.380	0.400	0.400	0.020	5.263
		0.020	0.020	0.021	0.001	5.000
		0.105	0.110	0.110	0.005	4.762
		0.110	0.110	0.115	0.005	4.545
		0.230	0.240	0.240	0.010	4.348
		0.048	0.050	0.050	0.002	4.167
		0.025	0.026	0.026	0.001	4.000
		0.051	0.053	0.053	0.002	3.922

Menu items (left panel):

- Scan ▶
- Dollar Gainers
- Dollar Losers
- ✓ Percent Gainers
- Percent Losers
- Gap Up
- Gap Down
- Percent Gap Up
- Percent Gap Down
- Most Volume
- Most Trades
- Total Bids
- Total Asks
- Total Bids (%)
- Total Asks (%)
- Total Bid Vol
- Total Ask Vol

Left column: Close, Scan Template

Symbols: PLA, TLO, QVL, VLR, LYC, EWC, AVA, PWT

EXECUTION SCREENS

The success of every trade finally rests on execution and this demands a straight through processing facility. When our order meets the posted bid price we expect to see the order executed almost as quickly as we press the mouse button. This is not an unreasonable request given the advances in modern technology. We use AOT Online broking and we find the speed of execution flawless. Every trader adjusts the screens to suit his personal requirements. We use this combination because when we turn to the internet to execute an order we have already gathered additional information from the MarketCast data feed and display.

Our first stop is the Level 3 order line shown in Figure 28.11 and taken from the AOT Online Iress system. It confirms any last changes in price moves and shows the most recent 'prints', or course of trades. This is used when it's time to pull the trigger and we do this using the standard buy or sell order screen. When the order details are completed, a mouse click sends the order to market for execution. When any part of the order is filled it is highlighted in the course-of-trades screen. This valuable feature means we do not have to guess which is our order and our trade. As soon as the order execution is highlighted we move to the next stage of managing the trade.

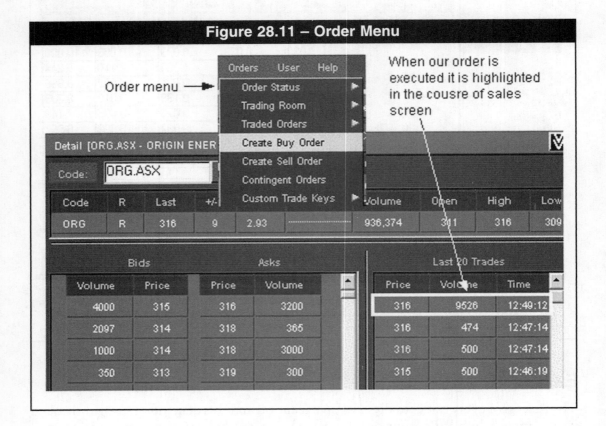

Figure 28.11 – Order Menu

This includes creating stop loss and contingent orders as discussed in the previous chapter. The trigger prices are also entered on the MarketCast watch screen. The alert from the broadcast screen is a signal to log back onto the internet and manage the exit.

Using this combination of broadcast and internet screens my total time on the internet is limited to a few minutes while each trade is executed. This combination suits my trading style and the disadvantages imposed by geographic isolation. I must make some allowances for living and trading from the far north of the Northern Territory.

These are the screens I raid. As new types of information and analysis become available, these combinations will change. The screens and layouts you choose may be different, reflecting your personal preferences and choice of data suppliers. The differences are superficial because we use the information from the screens in the same way.

SCREEN RAIDER NOTES

→   Screen layout should show watch lists, news, order lines and charting at a glance.

→   Broadcast data systems free up telephone lines.

→   Confirm order lines and course of trades using a broker's internet screen.

→   Use the internet for research.

→   Intra-day charting works best with two or three indicators.

→   Live data suppliers should include basic price scanning facilities.

→   Technology changes so be prepared to explore new research and analytical tools.

Chapter 29

SKILL TRIGGERS

SUCCESS

Why do I give away trading secrets? This is one of the more polite variations of a question I am often asked. It implies that any information given to the general public has limited value simply because others know about it. The questioner assumes his greed is a normal human condition so he cannot understand how we all benefit from an exchange of knowledge rather than money. This line of thinking comes directly from those who believe market success is guaranteed by access to inside, or secret, information. It ignores the capacity for human beings to thwart even the most comprehensive written instructions.

We have covered a selection of short-term trading tactics in this book. We included precise detail to enable readers to duplicate and test these approaches so they can decide which, if any, are appropriate for their trading. Are these secrets and is the effectiveness of the methods diminished simply because many others have read the book?

These are not secrets. Trading success depends on many other factors. Understanding the correct application of a trading method is just the first step in a lengthy process that leaves plenty of room for human error. Although we start from the same analysis point, use the same end-of-day data and may use the same database explorations, when it comes to implementing the trade we all take different approaches.

In Homer's epic poem *The Odyssey*, the future is determined by the gods. The gods reveal the secrets of the future to some men, but many of them are determined to go their own way, even if it means failure. When they fail, they blame the gods and not themselves. Zeus complains about:

> "...the way these mortals blame the gods.
> From us alone, they say, come all their miseries, yes,
> but they themselves, with their own reckless ways,
> compound their pains beyond their proper share."

Some traders have a similar approach. They blame the trading system or method for their lack of success. They take a known outcome, a defined process, and then distort it when they apply it in practice. In their own reckless ways, these traders fail because they compound the strategy beyond the clear plan in the original outline. Some of these modifications enhance the strategy for particular traders and lead to better applications and new techniques.

When people talk of trading secrets it tells me a lot about the way people think about the market. They believe success comes from knowing something others do not know. They believe a trading edge comes from early access to information. There is an important trading edge related to information, but as we have shown, it depends on analysis rather than timeliness. Getting early information – getting a secret method that reveals the future – is not an advantage unless we know what to do with it, and this depends on how we understand and analyse the news. The edge comes from the analysis of information and not from its early delivery.

When information is widely spread it is effectively used by many other players in the market to make profitable trades. To verify this we recently completed some research with the co-operation of our weekly internet newsletter readers. We started with a single entry opportunity shown on a chart. Each week we followed the development of the trade and asked readers to tell us if they thought we should exit. We collated their replies which confirmed the exit decision depends more on the trader than on chart indicators and information.

We provided readers with exactly the same data and three indicators – a count back line, 10- and 30-day moving averages, and the Guppy Multiple Moving Average. Readers all received the information at exactly the same time. There was no inside trading opportunity as the selected stock chart was deliberately anonymous.

The results displayed in Figure 29.1 show the exit decision has a great deal more to do with trader psychology, greed, fear and the level of our trading skill and discipline than it does with the technical indicators we use or the information we have. A group of people can start from exactly the same point, follow exactly the same data, use exactly the same group of indicators and end up with very different profits from a trade.

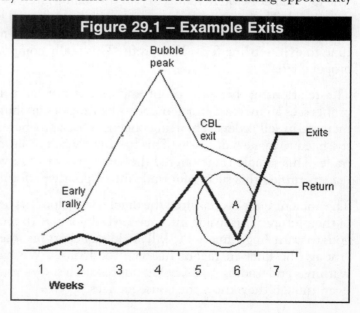

Figure 29.1 – Example Exits

Trading success depends upon the way tools are applied and not on the tools used. Our trading edge comes from what we do with what we have. Our edge is not created by having information that others do not have, be it data, news, or secret indicators. It comes from making better use of the information that is available to everyone.

In this trade the bubble peak, with a profit of around 68%, attracted a surge in sellers. Their reasons for exiting the trade were sound, but they were generally not consistent with the trading plan or the indicators used for analysis. This was a judgement call. It turned out to be a correct call, and allowed them to lock in profits. It is difficult to distinguish the reasons for this exit from those used by traders who jumped ship near the top of the first rally.

We used the count back line to set the exit and this signal saw a surge in email exits. The exit did not lock in the best profits available, with a 40% return, but the discipline of the exit serves the trader well. In the next trade the same discipline may get him out very close to the top. When a trade starts we cannot determine in advance the exact nature of the trade. We may lock onto a trade that is perfectly suited to the count back line approach and capture an excellent trade. In others the result may be closer to that shown in the example.

A particularly interesting relationship occurs after the count back line exit signal is generated in area A. The trade was down to 30% profit. This is the area of greatest hope. As price action developed it became clear there was little hope of a rebound. The sensible strategy was to act on the count back line signal. Instead most traders held on. They wanted confirmation of the worst scenario.

The rational decision here was to join the selling after the close below the count back line exit signal. The emotional decision was to hold on and hope. This is what many traders did. Finally, when the trade was performing really badly, many more traders decided it was time to exit, settling for a 25% profit. This really compounded their "pains beyond their proper share"!

The relationship between profit and exit is not quite inverse. The time of maximum profits sees an increase in sell orders. The time of maximum or confirmed loss, also sees an increase in sell orders. The real concern is area A where many traders seem paralysed by the need to make a decision. This has the capacity to turn a reasonable trade into a poor trade. This sample trade offered the same prizes to everyone but a substantial number of readers turned this successful trade into a poorly performing trade.

The ancient Greeks consulted the oracles at Delphi to glean information about the secrets of their future. This inside information did not give them an edge. Hermes was sent by the gods to warn Aegisthus not to kill Atrides or court his wife. Aegisthus ignored this warning "though he knew it meant his own total ruin". We have provided you with stop loss warnings and trading plans, but as our research shows, many traders ignore these warnings even though they know the consequences.

You now have a better idea of the risks and the rewards associated with these short-term trading techniques. Your success depends on how you choose to apply your knowledge and skill. Despite the best information available, it is still possible that your actions will sabotage the effectiveness of the trading methods examined in this book.

There is only one advantage or trading edge and it is not a secret. It comes from the way you apply this information to your own trading to improve your trading skill. The information in this book will help you to find intra-day and short-term opportunities but your skill is the trigger for success in these snapshot trades.

INDEX

Index

DISCOUNT COUPON – TRADING WORKSHOPS

10% off the regular seminar fee – single and group rates. (These workshops are held in Australia Asia, the USA and the UK.)

Trading looks easy, but it takes skill. How best to approach your market and survive is a skill that can be learned, and improved. Trading success means knowing how to GET IN by identifying a trade. It means knowing how to manage the trade so you GET OUT with an overall profit.

You can become a better trader by attending a half-day or full-day workshop because Daryl Guppy will teach you how to understand the market from a private trader's perspective, how to use your advantages, and how to manage a trade to lock in capital profits.

All traders – those considering entering the market and those who want to improve their trading – benefit from these workshops.

Nobody can give you the ultimate trading secret, but Daryl Guppy will show you, using local examples selected by the audience on the day, how a private trader identifies and manages a trade. You will enter the market better informed than your competitors.

Daryl Guppy holds regular trading workshops. Dates and details are posted on www.guppytraders.com eight weeks before each workshop.

How to claim your workshop discount

When you book your seminar mention that you own *Snapshot Trading* and get 10% off the advertised fee. Bring this book with you to confirm your discount. It can be autographed for you if you wish.

Some comments from workshop participants

"The workshop, like your book, was practical and informative. I enjoyed it, and more importantly, I learned from it. For me it brought a lot of the theory into perspective." – Private equity trader

"The workshop covered all the essential building blocks of the trade better and more effectively than any book that I have come across." – Hong Kong equity analyst

"In my seven years attending continuing education programs I have never found a session as useful and interesting as the one which you have conducted." – Remisier, Singapore

"On the subject of the seminar, I must say that it was an inspiring night. Daryl was energetic, spontaneous and his comments were thought provoking. Additionally, he was very generous with his time, staying back after the official closing time to discuss specific issues with us. I've not been to a trading seminar before where the examples used during the evening were drawn from the audience (not pre-planned)."

– Private equity and derivatives trader